D1093824
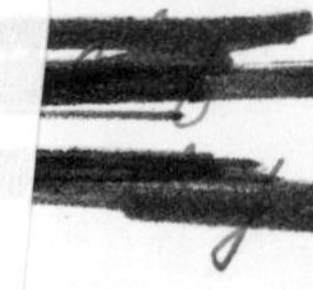

Everyday Life in Ancient Times

HIGHLIGHTS OF THE BEGINNINGS OF WESTERN CIVILIZATION IN MESOPOTAMIA, EGYPT, GREECE, AND ROME

By RHYS CARPENTER, EDITH HAMILTON, WILLIAM C. HAYES,

E. A. SPEISER, RICHARD STILLWELL

GILBERT GROSVENOR, LL.D., Litt.D., D.Sc., Editor in Chief

With 215 illustrations; 120 paintings by H. M. Herget

NATIONAL GEOGRAPHIC SOCIETY
WASHINGTON, D. C.

Contents

First through fourth printing: 90,000 copies
Fifth printing, 1961: 50,000 copies

Library of Congress Catalog Card No. 61-10035

Originally printed in NATIONAL GEOGRAPHIC MAGAZINE issues of October, 1941; March, 1944; November, 1946; and January, 1951

Manufactured in the United States of America

Everyday Life in Ancient Times

By Gilbert Grosvenor

President, National Geographic Society, 1920-1954

IF ONE could go back in time and space to the first humble origins of Western civilization, he would find himself in Mesopotamia in about 4500 B. C. From here he could advance with the years to Egypt, then on to Greece and Rome.

These four ancient countries put in more time on the progress of mankind than did any other country or people up to modern times.

Mesopotamia gave us writing, metallurgy, law, and such basic inventions as the wheel and the true arch. From it also came such familiar things as the razor, the frying pan, and the 60-minute hour.

Egypt developed great technical skill in art and construction.

Greece, a laboratory of democracy, contributed philosophy, sculpture, architecture, and, what has survived most strongly, the love of freedom.

Rome, which preserved and carried on Greek science and learning, offered numerical symbols, language, and politics.

This 356-page volume presents highlights from these four ancient civilizations. It re-creates the everyday life of these peoples who played such a big role in the beginning and early development of Western culture from 4500 B. C. until the fall of the Roman Empire.

The book is richly illustrated in both color and black and white. It contains 120 full-color reproductions of outstanding paintings made exclusively for the NATIONAL GEOGRAPHIC MAGAZINE by the late H. M. Herget, 90 photographs, and five maps. Here also are fascinating, authoritative accounts of ancient peoples, their daily life, and their accomplishments. Thus the book's compact format gives the reader a clear, over-all picture in paintings, photographs, and words.

In preparing his paintings, Mr. Herget worked hand in hand with four topnotch archeologists. Each of these specialists has personally directed excavations in the country he writes about. They assembled all available documentary source material and authentic objects from archeological "digs," such as recorded costumes, jewelry, weapons, furniture, eating utensils, pottery, and tools.

The artist and archeologists then decided how these relics could best be tied in with descriptions of customs and life to picture a phase of early times. The result of such close collaboration not only produced virtual photographic accuracy but instilled living, breathing life into each painting. Some of them record historical incidents. Others present scenes reconstructed by the scholars.

This painstaking attention to detail enables the reader to visualize the everyday life of the ancient Mesopotamians, Egyptians, Greeks, and Romans. The scholars chosen to present the peoples are:

DR. E. A. SPEISER, chairman of the Department of Oriental Studies at the University of Pennsylvania, who prepared the material on Mesopotamia.

DR. WILLIAM C. HAYES, of the Department of Egyptian Art, Metropolitan Museum of Art, New York, who wrote the section on Egypt.

DR. RICHARD STILLWELL, professor of Archeological Studies at Princeton University, who furnished the information on Greece.

DR. RHYS CARPENTER, professor of Classical Archeology at Bryn Mawr College, who wrote the chapter on Rome.

The introductory articles on Greece and Rome by the brilliant writer Edith Hamilton are taken from her books, *The Great Age of Greek Literature* and *The Roman Way,* by special permission of her publisher, W. W. Norton & Company, Inc.

To give the Herget paintings a genuine flavor of early times, actual quotations from contemporary literature have been used for title lines. The scholars culled them from ancient papyri, from inscriptions in tombs and temples, from epic stories and legends, and from the works of famed Greek and Roman writers.

All the articles in this book are taken from the NATIONAL GEOGRAPHIC MAGAZINE. This volume brings them together under one heading for the first time. From its pages, four outstanding peoples and their civilizations spring vividly to life.

Mesopotamia: Light That Did Not Fail

By E. A. Speiser

Formerly Director of the American School of Oriental Research in Baghdad; Chairman of the Department of Oriental Studies, University of Pennsylvania

MESOPOTAMIA, the historic land between the Tigris and the Euphrates, has meant many different things (map, page 9).

For readers of the Bible, the name—or any one of its synonyms or near synonyms—may conjure up a picture of the Garden of Eden, the Tower of Babel, or the Great Flood; or it may call to mind the story of the patriarchs, of Daniel and Nebuchadnezzar, of the handwriting on the wall.

To some the name has associations with the Code of Hammurabi (page 49), the death of Alexander the Great, the exploits of Harun al-Rashid. Others will think of Chaldean astrology, the Royal Tombs of Ur, or the fabulous oil deposits of the Middle East.

Mesopotamia gives tremendous perspective to our modern civilization. In common with the rest of the ancient Near East—Egypt, Palestine, Syria, and Iran—Mesopotamia had put in more time on the progress of mankind, before the rise of Greece and Rome, than has elapsed between the Homeric age and our own times. When Rome, founded, according to tradition, in the 8th century B. C., was less than a hundred years old, Nineveh in Assyria had ended a 4,000-year career.

Yet what Mesopotamia achieved during several millenniums of steady progress did not come to an abrupt close when the Greeks took over. Through one channel or another, the fruits of that accumulated experience had already spread to Europe, to enrich the classical world and to be passed along eventually to our own culture as a living and tangible force.

Stored-up Evidence

Civilization is basically the sum of man's answers at any given stage to the problems of society and the universe. Until man had begun to live in settled communities, little could be done about such questions.

Ancient urban centers, however, leave remains that may be reconstructed into a meaningful record long after the cities themselves ceased to exist.

The Near East was the place where the first urban centers emerged. To retrace our present civilization to its roots and see it as a growing organism, we must go back to the Near East, the cradle of Western civilization.

Over much of its total course to date, the story of mankind was but the story of cultural progress along the Nile, the Tigris, the Euphrates, and the immediately adjoining areas (pages 15 and 22). Each of these ancient lands thus has something significant to relate.

If the testimony of Mesopotamia has fewer blurred passages than that of its sisterlands, its clarity is due chiefly to two factors: one, the vast amount and the astounding variety of written records that have come down to us from that country, a full and eloquent commentary on more than 2,000 years of preclassical history; the other, the number and nature of the ancient Mesopotamian sites.

These sites contribute their share to the material illustration of historic times, but are especially valuable as witnesses of cultural progress in the prehistoric age. In other words, the ancient mounds of Mesopotamia have proved to be buried treasures in more ways than one.

How Mounds Grew

Ancient mounds, to be sure, are not restricted to the watersheds of the Tigris and the Euphrates. Mesopotamia, however, exceeds the neighboring lands in the number of artificial hills that go back to the early stages of settled occupation. Since Egypt did not encourage to the same extent the building of cities in successive levels, that country is less well suited than Mesopotamia to take us down, rung by rung, through the centuries that precede written history.

Let us take as an example the site of Tepe Gawra, which is situated 15 miles northeast of modern Mosul and ancient Nineveh (pages

24-27). I use this instance for two reasons. For one, as the discoverer and first excavator of Tepe Gawra I am necessarily better acquainted with it than with any other ancient mound; for another, there probably is not in any case a single illustration that could be used to greater advantage as an index of mankind's gradual emergence from the obscurity of prehistoric times.

As recently as the mid-1920's very little was known about the prehistory of Mesopotamia. Inscriptions and monuments had told us a great deal about the Assyrians of the first millennium B. C., the Babylonians of the second millennium, and the Sumerians of the third millennium. When we had worked back, however, to about 4,500 years ago, reliable information all but ceased.

Yet it was perfectly clear that even that remote stage was far from the beginnings of settled occupation. The only trustworthy guide to the farther and deeper past would be a site consisting of many successive prehistoric levels, to disclose in orderly sequence the gradual progress of man since the beginning of agriculture. Such a site might do for science infinitely more than could thousands of documents and roomfuls of objects from periods already known.

In 1926 I had the good fortune to obtain a Guggenheim Fellowship for study in Mesopotamia, coupled with the post of Annual Professor of the American School of Oriental Research in Baghdad. A small grant from the Dropsie College of Philadelphia left me free to examine hitherto unexplored regions without the usual pressure to bring back something spectacular. With that combined support I devoted six months to an archeological survey of northern Iraq, concentrating chiefly on prehistoric sites.

First Sight of the Great Mound

In April, 1927, when I was covering the area to the north of Mosul, my eye was attracted from a distance by a tall mound which rose some 75 feet above the surrounding plain.

My first thought was that the mound would prove to be an example of Assyrian occupation, if not of later date. But a preliminary examination of the surface remains—broken sherds and fragments of stone implements—promptly disclosed that this was no routine site. Only its upper third bore signs of historic occupation, while the remaining two-thirds appeared to date from prehistoric times.

In other words, unless surface appearances were wholly misleading, we had here a long and hitherto missing record of virtually unknown times, a record piled up at least 50 feet high. The near-by villagers called the place Tepe Gawra, or "The Great Mound," because of its height. But if actual digging should bear out the surface estimate, the world of science would have a much more valid reason for applying that name to the mound.

Systematic excavations were begun in 1927 and carried on through eight separate campaigns, four of which I had the opportunity to direct in person. The final results exceeded our greatest expectations. Tepe Gawra proved to contain 26 individual occupation levels, yet only the upper six of these fell within the historic age (page 14).

Light on Prehistory

The long period prior to the introduction of writing, reaching back to the fourth millennium B. C. and beyond, was no longer obscure; for it was now illuminated by a full score of successive settlements, one on top of the other. The continuous account of early man could be pushed back by perhaps 20 centuries.

The unfolding picture yielded a pattern of steady advance in pottery and in architecture, in religion (page 24) and society, in work and in play. Other sites of comparable age have since been uncovered, each adding something that the others lacked, each helping to place some new detail in sharper relief.

Why did the ancient Near Easterners in general, and Mesopotamians in particular, continue to build on man-made hills when space —excepting in Egypt only—was certainly not at a premium? The reasons are simple. The first settlers would choose a site which had a good water supply, and whose location was convenient for agricultural and commercial needs. The initial advantages of environment remained attractive after the first town had been destroyed—by fire, floods, or war.

To level a place built of sun-baked bricks was not a great problem; the upper sections of walls still standing might have to be torn down and some dirt might need to be added to fill the openings that the fallen debris had not covered up. In this process a few feet of the old occupation were sealed up and the next settlement was that much higher above ground level.

But the main reason for continuing on the old site was not alone the ease with which this could be done. More important was the desire to follow, wherever possible, the outlines of the old buildings, particularly temples, in order to earn the protection of the gods and spirits that the previous town had propitiated (page 11).

Here is tradition at work from the ground, so to speak. As occupation followed upon occupation, the site grew not only in height

7

The Oriental Institute

Sargon II's Colossal Winged Bulls Shed the Assyrian Dust of Centuries

Assyrian Kings of the first millennium B. C. erected monstrous human-headed figures as gateway guardians of their temples and palaces. The Oriental Institute uncovered these mythological twins at Khorsabad (Dur Sharrukin), Sargon's capital (page 62). (For Sennacherib's colossus, see page 65).

but also in prestige and defensibility. With this growth there came also a proportionate rise in the influence of tradition upon each successive occupant.

Small wonder, therefore, that a storied site like Tepe Gawra was not finally abandoned—to the oblivion of time and the eventual ministrations of archeology—until its summit had become too small and inaccessible for all practical purposes.

Nearly 5,000 Years of Pioneer Work

The time covered by the history of Mesopotamia is more than twice the length of the present era—some 2,000 years of prehistory and more than two and a half millenniums of historic progress. The scene shifts constantly and there is a bewildering variety of actors who speak many tongues and represent various peoples, some of whom will be described later, a Tower of Babel transposed from parable to fact.

It is indeed this varied background as much as anything else that helped to make the resulting civilization a cosmopolitan and lasting factor, in contrast to provincial achievements of brief duration. But because progress can be traced only against the framework of time, a rough chronological outline must be provided and the principal characters identified.

A few of the many pertinent details are given in the brief historical introductions that accompany the descriptions of each painting in this series. Inasmuch as the paintings have been arranged in chronological order, the descriptions add up to a short but comprehensive account of cultural progress as seen in a definite time sequence.

The initial stage lasts roughly until about 3000 B. C. Specific dates for that period are not available because absolute dating requires written records, whereas the period in question was preliterate.

This was the last prehistoric phase in the evolution of mankind, starting with the end of the Stone Age and continuing through the many centuries in which copper was used sparingly with stone, but real metallurgy had not as yet been introduced.

In other words, the first phase in the career of Mesopotamia takes in the last Neolithic settlements and the whole of the Chalcolithic, or Copper-Stone, period.

That this was not, however, a primitive phase is clear from numerous facts. We find here several distinctive and individual cultures, each of which has perfected its own special type of painted pottery and maintains lively relations with the neighboring cultures, the combined territory involving a considerable portion of western Asia.

The advance is recorded plainly, in material remains if not in actual words, in the successive occupations which the mounds of Mesopotamia have preserved, layer upon layer, for our own age to decode.

The number of such prehistoric levels varies from site to site. In each instance there may be a time lag of varying duration between two given strata. Nevertheless, we have seen that some sites may contain as many as a score of successive prehistoric settlements. The total length of this phase cannot have been less than 2,000 years.

The Third Millennium

The historic age is ushered in by the two revolutionary factors of metallurgy and writing. The first of these, which had begun well back in prehistoric times, brought a profound change in the old concept of space; it stimulated geographic exploration by forcing man to look for new and ever more distant sources of the precious metal (page 28). The other, and this time specifically Mesopotamian development, revolutionized the existing idea of time by forging indestructible links between the past and the present and between the present and the future (page 30). History can now embrace faraway lands and ages.

The principal actors now come to be known by name as well as by deed. In Lower Mesopotamia, the region at the head of the Persian Gulf—which at that time reached much farther up the valley than it does now—the dominant ethnic group used the Sumerian language and called its land Sumer (Biblical Shinar; Genesis 10:10).

Although this language has disclosed the secrets of its structure to the patient efforts of modern scholarship, no relative of it, either ancient or modern, has yet been discovered. Its users were evidently a people apart, in an ethnic no less than in a linguistic sense; we shall see presently that they were also highly distinctive in culture.

The most plausible way to explain this situation and account for the absence of kindred elements is by assuming that the Sumerians had come a considerable distance, having left their immediate relatives somewhere in farther Asia. Be that as it may, the particular gifts and abilities of the Sumerians blended so well with the other cultures of Mesopotamia that the resulting product was to have a decisive bearing on the evolution of civilization in general.

The eastern neighbor of Sumer was the Iranian land of Elam. To the north dwelt numerous mountain peoples who appear to have been akin to the Elamites (Genesis 10:22). Adjoining Sumer in a westerly semicircle were the Semites; their contacts with the Sumerians were to become ever more close and intimate.

The earliest representatives of the Semitic family of peoples are known in Mesopotamia collectively as the Akkadians (Genesis 10:10). Later on they come to be distinguished in the south as the Babylonians, in the northwest as the Assyrians, and in the west as the Amorites.

The greater part of the third millennium was under the political and cultural domination of the Sumerians. It constituted the brilliant Early Dynastic period. This phase is featured by written and material illustrations from Ur (of the Chaldees),* Lagash, Uruk (Biblical Erech; Genesis 10:10), Khafaje (the ancient name of this site is in doubt), and Eshnunna, among others (pages 32, 34 and 36).

Following this long phase of Sumerian ascendancy came the first period of established Semitic supremacy, under the vigorous dynasty founded by Sargon of Akkad. Sumerian and Semite might contend interminably with each other for political leadership in the land, but the prevailing culture was very much of a joint effort.

Toward the end of the millennium there was a brief resurgence of Sumerian dominance, under Gudea of Lagash (page 42) and the founders of the Third Dynasty of Ur.

This last assertion of Sumerian political power is known as the Neo-Sumerian period. The people responsible for it soon disappeared as a distinctive ethnic element.

The Second Millennium

The culture of which the Sumerians had been the prime catalysts spread, however, to more and more distant reaches. Their lan-

* See "New Light on Ancient Ur," by M. E. L. Mallowan, NATIONAL GEOGRAPHIC MAGAZINE, January, 1930.

Drawn by Harry S. Oliver and Irvin E. Alleman

Mesopotamia: the Birthplace of Writing, the Cradle of Civilization

The area includes the Garden of Eden; ancient Sumer and Babylon; Jarmo, earliest known village in the world; and Tepe Gawra, the 3,000-year-old mound that was the site of 26 settlements, each built upon the ruins of its predecessor.

guage lived on, as the tool of religion and science, just as did the Latin of the Middle Ages—some three millenniums later.

Under the increasingly powerful impact of written and oral tradition, the civilization of Mesopotamia expanded; but it separated into two individual channels. In the south its guardians and beneficiaries at this time were the Babylonians, whose peak of power and glory was reached in the 18th and the early 17th century B. C., under the First Dynasty of Babylon, and more especially under that dynasty's best-known ruler, the far-famed Hammurabi (page 49).*

In the north, the city of Ashur gradually rose to prominence (page 54). The state which that city founded—Assyria—was to grow in the course of the succeeding centuries, not unlike the Roman state of a much later age, into a great world empire.

To carry the parallelism still further, Ashur's relations with Babylon followed the same pattern that was to become so typical of Rome's relations with Greece: The political and military superior in each case became deeply indebted to its rival culturally, and

* See, in the NATIONAL GEOGRAPHIC MAGAZINE: "Cradle of Civilization," by James Baikie; and "Pushing Back History's Horizon," by Albert T. Clay, both February, 1916.

A Forgotten Race Built a Village Citadel on This Hilltop Some 8,000 Years Ago

Archeologists in recent years have noted that, no matter how deep they have dug into civilization's cradlelands, the beginnings of settled life still seem some distance away.

Tepe Gawra's lowest level, for example, was already a few rungs up the ladder of mankind's progress in settled communities (page 6). The bottom layer at Hassuna, south of Mosul, pushed prehistory back a little further.

But the absolute beginnings of settled occupation, which mark man's divorce from nomadic existence, are believed to have been found only in 1948 with the discovery of this primitive site in Iraqi Kurdistan.

Expedition members of the Oriental Institute of the University of Chicago here stand at the top of Jarmo, civilization's oldest known village.

Dr. Robert J. Braidwood, head of the expedition, has reason for dating the settlement between 5000 and 6000 B. C. Its ruins stand 30 miles east of Kirkuk, the Iraqi oil center.

Wide World

"Jonah's" Tomb at Nineveh Swallows Older Assyrian Remains Beneath

Nineveh's sprawling ruins lie just across the Tigris River from Mosul. Excavations in the ancient city have given us a rich picture of Assyria's life, religion, history, and literature (page 64).

But all of this eloquent evidence has come from the site's main mound, which bears the modern name of Kouyunjik. It is to this section that we owe the remains of Assyrian temples and palaces, with their impressive yield of sculptured monuments and written documents. Here, too, deep below the Assyrian levels, five layers of prehistoric Nineveh have been found.

A short distance south of Kouyunjik another tall mound rises. Though attached to the original city compound, it has remained intact. This history-rich mound cannot be disturbed because it bears the mosque of Nebi Yunus, which, according to Moslem tradition, contains the tomb of Jonah, who foretold Nineveh's doom (Jonah 3:4).

Dorien Leigh Ltd.

E. A. Speiser

Ceremonial Wrestlers, Jars on Heads, Struggle in Bronze

Wrestling and boxing, both of religious significance in ancient Mesopotamia, were depicted on monuments dating from the first half of the third millennium B. C. Battles between heroes and demons were often portrayed. One wrestling bout involved the great Gilgamesh and his one-time opponent, Enkidu, who later became the hero's inseparable companion. This bronze cast came from an Early Dynastic level at Khafaje, east of Baghdad. Archeologists do not know why jugs were balanced on heads unless they constituted an extra hazard (page 33).

remained just as resentful for psychological reasons. Before the second millennium was half over, however, both Babylon and Ashur were to be subjected for long stretches of time to foreign rule.

In each instance the conquerors were outsiders; they had no family connections either with the Sumerians or the Semites. Their cases were similar, however, in two respects. Both conquering groups were attracted by the civilization that had evolved and matured in the fertile valley; and both descended from the same long chain of mountains which form the northerly boundaries of Mesopotamia.

Babylon was conquered by the Kassites (page 51), a people whose home lay in the Iranian highlands. Their victory had been all but assured by an earlier crushing raid at the hands of the Hittites (Genesis 15: 20), a people of Indo-European stock, settled in Asia Minor.

The paralyzing effect of these twin blows did not wear off fully until some 400 years later, in the 12th century B. C., when Babylonia was at last restored to native rule. Ashur, on the other hand, found itself under the influence of the Hurrians—the Horites of the Old Testament (Genesis 14:6)—a people from the region of Armenia (page 53).

By the middle of the second millennium this exceptionally active group had made its presence felt all the way from the borders of Egypt to the foothills of Iran, leaving substantial traces of its influence, in the form of cultural elements, in Palestine, Syria, Asia Minor, Assyria, and the districts to the north of Babylonia. Much of what they contributed was merely a new version of old traditions, which the Hurrians had acquired from the Sumerians and Akkadians in the third millennium. Thus Mesopotamian civilization was now active on a broad front, in the manner of a chain reaction, propagated by collateral as well as by lineal descendants.

The Concluding Phase

But the political power of the Hurrians was not equal to their culture. Assyria, at all events, managed to emancipate itself as early as the 14th century. Thereafter, this vigorous state based on the middle Tigris experienced a long period of steady growth and expansion, which was not checked for nearly 800 years.

The first millennium B. C. sees first one and then the other branch of the Mesopotamian family attaining a height of power never hitherto equaled, only to be followed in rapid order by a decisive and permanent decline.

Assyria enjoyed its greatest expansion in the middle of the 7th century B. C., when its kings established themselves in Egypt, the cultural rival of Mesopotamia since remote prehistoric times.* It was, however, a case of fatal overexpansion. Before the century ended, the capital at Nineveh succumbed to the combined assault of the Medes and the Babylonians, in 612 B.C. (Zephaniah 2:13).

The last king of Assyria was able to maintain himself in a western province a bare half dozen years longer. In 606 B. C. the might that had been Ashur was extinguished for all time.

Albert T. Clay

The Heroic Epic of Gilgamesh Is Written in Clay

The world became acquainted with the Gilgamesh Epic through a version discovered in the Library of Ashurbanipal (668-626 B. C.) at Nineveh. This Babylonian fragment, now in the Yale Collection, is at least 1,000 years older. The Nineveh relic's Eleventh Tablet tells the story of the Great Flood (page 40).

Babylon continued for a few decades on borrowed time. Under Nebuchadnezzar II, the city displayed all the outward signs of the world's leading center, which indeed it was (page 69). The golden age of Hammurabi appeared to have returned—with modern improvements. But just as that age had been only decades away from alien domination, so was the reign of Nebuchadnezzar the last but one under a native ruler of Babylon.

Once again the rude awakening stemmed from Iran. This time, however, the victors were neither Kassites nor Medes. The conqueror, in 539 B. C., was the great Cyrus at the head of the upsurging Persians.

Ironically enough, the strength of the Persians, like that of the Medes and the Kassites before them, flowed in large measure from the pervasive cultural influence that Mesopotamia had been exerting on its neighbors ever since the third millennium.

The Persian conquest did not in itself bring an end to the cultural career of Mesopotamia. Two centuries later, Alexander the Great was to make Babylon his own and the world's capital—a telling tribute to the country's prestige throughout the civilized world.

* See "Daily Life in Ancient Egypt," by William C. Hayes, with 32 color reproductions of paintings by H. M. Herget, pages 71 to 167; from NATIONAL GEOGRAPHIC MAGAZINE, October, 1941.

E. A. Speiser

Excavators Reach a Point More than Halfway down Tepe Gawra's 3,000 Years

Discovered by the author in 1927, Iraq's "Great Mound" has been explored in eight digs, four of them under his direction (pages 6 and 25). Each of its 26 levels represents a century or more. Counted from the top, this is Gawra XVI. Ten levels exist beneath it. Olive groves stand in the background.

MATS, Official

Southern Mesopotamia, as in Antiquity, Is an Immense Network of Irrigation Canals Fed by the Euphrates River

In the days of the Sumerians and Babylonians the river's low banks made irrigation easy (page 23). Rain was scarce; but the alluvial soil, when watered by artificial means, proved enormously fertile. Floods and Mongol invaders destroyed the ancient water systems; Iraq now tries to restore them.

The Oriental Institute

A Lowly Dog Left His Signature Beside That of a Powerful Assyrian Emperor

Sargon (II) was the first Mesopotamian emperor to enjoy the fruits of the conquest of Israel. Khorsabad, his capital, has yielded many impressive sculptures and wall paintings (pages 7 and 62). It also contained many small inscriptions. One of these has an added, unscheduled touch. Before the clay was dried and baked some 2,670 years ago, a stray dog trod upon it, leaving his paw prints.

The death of Alexander the Great in Babylon wrote an end, at long last, not only to that city's hopes and ambitions but also to the individual existence of the country and to its age-old independent culture. Mesopotamia, as such, ceased to be.

Its inner vitality, however, was far from spent. Sundry elements of the civilization that had grown up in Mesopotamia continued to live on and blend with other notable achievements of mankind, under Hellenism and its successors. And thus they survive to our own day, in common with other Mesopotamian contributions that had found their way in the meantime to Palestine and Asia Minor, and thence had entered the main stream of western civilization.

A Way of Life Endures

What then are the enduring cultural values that make of Mesopotamian civilization a light that did not fail with the collapse of the political structure? A full list would take us too far afield. Nor is an exhaustive tally needed. For nearly all of the region's achievements that time has been unable to obliterate are grouped into a harmonious pattern which adds up to the Mesopotamian way of life. Once that pattern has been outlined, the main details will fall readily into place.

If civilization is largely a way of fixing man's place in Nature and society, how did the ancient Mesopotamians make these all-important adjustments? Very briefly, Nature was to the thoughtful inhabitant of the Tigris-Euphrates Valley a combination of capricious and violent forces, each personified by one or more gods.

The gods' actions were unpredictable; hence life on earth was ever restless and uncertain. Man must be everlastingly at pains to please and appease the gods, so as to influence his own fate for the better.

This requirement applied to the mightiest king no less than to his lowliest subject. The king was no supernatural being, as in Egypt, but a mortal, abject in his submission to the powers of Nature. To this extent, at least, all men were equal.

The place of society in Nature becomes ultimately a matter of the rights and responsibilities of the individual—any individual. Here we have the essentials on which democracy is founded.

Yale University News Bureau

Lettered Clay Sheaths Ensured the Safety of Important Clay Documents

Mesopotamia sometimes inscribed legal matters on so-called case tablets (page 30). The inside tablet carried the text. The outer envelope, protecting and identifying the enclosure, usually was limited to an excerpt.

The fact that a rudimentary form of democracy was the keynote of the Mesopotamian way of life is abundantly clear from countless details involving government, religion, law, literature, and art. Since the king was just as fallible as the next mortal, he must maintain constant vigilance to avoid upsetting the precarious balance between Nature and society.

A person in authority could best guard against a fatal misstep in a major undertaking by seeking the advice and approval of other heads than his own. The necessary powers came to be lodged in a constituted assembly. They formed an effective check against authoritarianism.

Assembly approval came to be regarded as an integral part of the Mesopotamian way of life, so much so that even the gods were subject to it in their celestial setup (page 38). And government by assembly means parliamentary democracy.

Equality of individuals before the laws of gods and men implies, furthermore, a measure of personal dignity and security. This encourages in turn a sense of personal property. In Egypt, where the Pharoah was god and absolute master of all he surveyed, the individual technically could call nothing his own. In Mesopotamia it was the natural thing for a ruler to pay the current price for anything he wished to acquire.

All things considered, the Egyptian way led to a sense of resignation; in Mesopotamia, anxiety pointed a way to hope.

How well the Mesopotamian system worked can best be judged by its broad appeal to various ages and to widely differing peoples. It was viewed as the essence of civilized life. Because it was effective, it was an influence for general progress in fields of human endeavor not directly connected with government and society; particularly so in literature and the natural sciences.

The Key Position of Writing

The common denominator in all these incidental advances was writing. The local philosophy of life had led to the discovery of writing in the first place. Writing promoted progress on a broad front, making life fuller and richer and causing the whole system to be widely copied by others. The borrowers, for their part, were often able to make further contributions of their own.

The earliest inhabitants of Mesopotamia in times approaching the historical period are known as the Sumerians.

Sumerian culture, itself a composite product, gradually developed into a cooperative civilization embracing the whole of Mesopotamia. The basic social, intellectual, and material attainments of that broader civilization appear eventually as the common property of the larger section of western Asia known as the Fertile Crescent.

They spread also to other adjoining areas, and in course of time crossed over to Europe. Like bread cast upon the waters, they proved amply rewarding, in that Mesopotamian civilization lived on after the mother country had fallen under foreign domination. By then the foreign conquerors had become in many ways the disciples and the zealous guardians of the Mesopotamian way of life.

It remains only to show how the separate cultural elements relate to one another as parts of a harmonious and living pattern. If the entire system got its start from the local concept of the individual in relation to society and of society in relation to Nature, it was writing that emerged first as that system's most notable by-product, and later as its very nerve center.

The strongly developed sense of private property which characterized the Sumerians led them to identify their possessions—notably those that were presented to the gods as offerings—by means of personal markers engraved on their cylinder seals. The seals were rolled out on soft clay and the impressions could then be attached to the given object as labels (page 30).

Similar identifying markers were used for temples and cities. As such, they were more than just pictures to be seen; they were at the same time names to be pronounced. From proper names the notations extended to objects of importance to contemporary economy, finally to words in general.

At the same time, means were devised to express not only entire words but also component syllables, the development proceeding from the concrete to the abstract. It was a decisive step forward; for it marked a genuine liberation from mere word painting, a step, incidentally, made possible largely by the peculiar characteristics of the Sumerian language. Thus we soon have a flexible medium for recording speech and thought.

It is tempting, but vain, to speculate on how much longer man might have taken to discover writing without the favorable background of the Sumerian social system and of the Sumerian language. The fact is that the earliest Sumerian written records are also the oldest forms of actual writing from anywhere. Moreover, the complicated process, from concrete symbol to abstract syllable, takes place, step by step, before our very eyes, as it were.

The possibility that the entire procedure was repeated independently elsewhere is extremely remote. It is true that Egypt constitutes the other great cultural center whose antiquity is comparable to that of Mesopotamia. We know, however, that Egyptian writing appears after the Sumerians had perfected their medium, and that it is full-grown virtually from the moment of its appearance. The preliminary experimental stage is lacking.

Since Egypt and Mesopotamia are known to have maintained close cultural contacts with each other in the centuries prior to the advent of writing, particularly so after the coming of copper, the means were there for the idea of writing to be readily communicated from one to the other. For all these reasons many scholars are now agreed that Egypt took over the basic idea from Mesopotamia, but employed its own specific symbols to put that idea into effect.

Achievements of this magnitude are difficult and rare. Even though the basic problems had been overcome, it required more than 1,000 years before the next great stride was taken—this time from syllabic to alphabetic writing.

That secondary discovery, which was to prove of inestimable value to all mankind, was likewise the contribution of the Near East, worked out somewhere along the eastern shores of the Mediterranean.* This achievement would not have been possible, however, without the underlying labors of the early Mesopotamians.

Mesopotamian Words Still in Use

Writing by means of separate signs for words or syllables is a complex procedure. It calls for a key if it is to be used with speed and precision. Since the symbols are based on models found in daily life, the key takes the form of lists of things and beings systematically catalogued.

Even the earlier Sumerian documents contain lists of birds, fishes, domestic animals, plants, implements, and the like—all intended as aids to writing and reading. Such groupings imply careful observation and organization. They are in fact the first steps in a scientific approach to zoology, botany, mineralogy, and so on.

* See, in the NATIONAL GEOGRAPHIC MAGAZINE: "Secrets from Syrian Hills," July, 1933; and "New Alphabet of the Ancients Is Unearthed," October, 1930, both by Claude F. A. Schaeffer.

It should not surprise one, therefore, to learn that we still use botanical terms which first appeared in cuneiform records—that is, in the wedgelike script into which Mesopotamian writing developed (pages 16 and 17). Words like cassia, chicory, cumin, crocus, hyssop, myrrh, nard, and saffron are all borrowed from Mesopotamia.*

Among the other fields of culture which writing helped to promote or stimulate are linguistics, mathematics and astronomy, law, and literature (page 13).

The study of language was a subject of immediate practical importance to Mesopotamian society because the cultured stratum of that society had to be bilingual. Together with the vernacular Akkadian one had to be versed in the totally dissimilar Sumerian.

To meet this need, local scholars had produced by the end of the third millennium such seemingly modern manuals as grammars, lexicons, and commentaries; they compiled numerous bilingual texts, occasionally with interlinear translations.

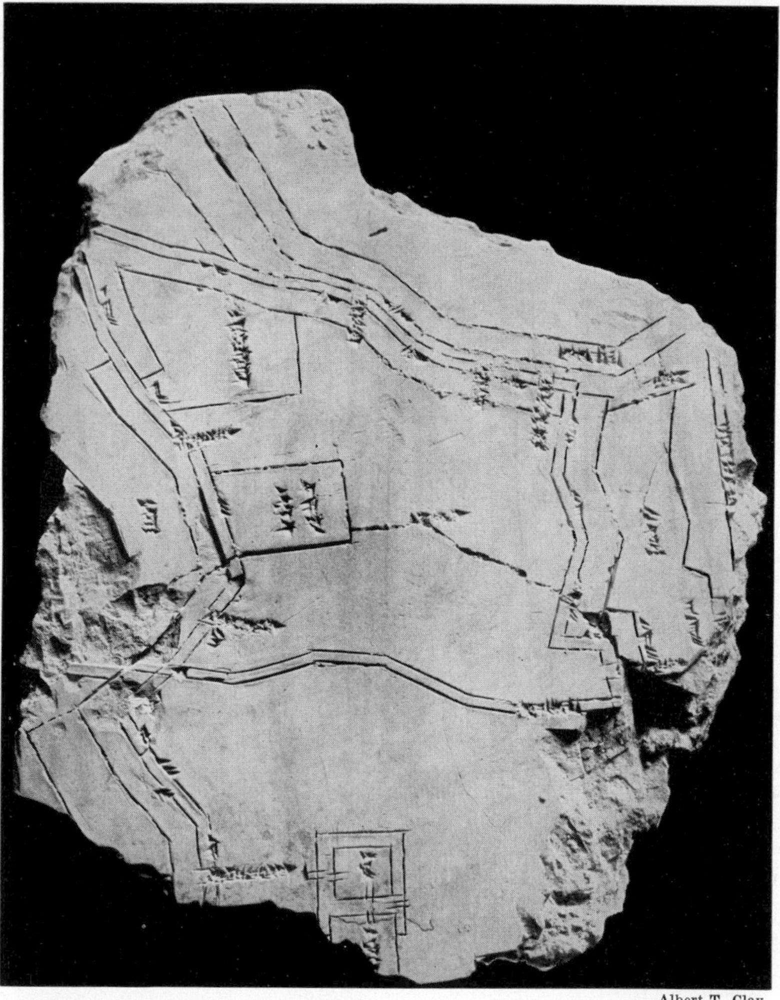

Albert T. Clay

Builders of Ancient Nippur Had a Clay Blueprint to Guide Them

Nippur was the religious and scientific center of ancient Babylonia. From its libraries, which were uncovered by the Museum of the University of Pennsylvania half a century ago, have come collections of religious, literary, and historical masterpieces, as well as elaborate grammars and dictionaries. Small wonder, therefore, that building, too, proceeded according to careful plans. This city map was first published by H. V. Hilprecht in 1904.

Mesopotamian mathematics made many contributions which it takes an expert to appreciate. But all of us have had ample proof of the vitality of its sexagesimal system—in the division of the circle into 360 degrees and the division of the hour into 60 minutes and 3,600 seconds.

The allied discipline of metrology was so proficient that Babylonian weights and measures spread to neighboring centers, and beyond these to the Hebrews and the Greeks. Progress in mathematics encouraged advances in astronomy, a field of many applications, some practical, as in the case of agriculture and fiscal organization (page 49), others quite abstruse. The astrological lore of the Chaldeans, a late name for the inhabitants of Babylonia, has remained proverbial to this day.

Law and Literature

Law was accorded a place of special honor and prominence in the cultural structure of Mesopotamia (page 42). It was indeed in many ways the keystone in that structure. The legal code was the charter and the con-

* See "The World's Words," by William H. Nicholas, National Geographic Magazine, December, 1943.

 National Geographic Photographer Maynard Owen Williams

Boat and Donkey Have Complemented Each Other since Prehistoric Times

Modern Iraq has had railroads for more than 30 years, and its oil deposits help run the world's communications, but the ever-present donkey remains unimpressed; he is just as important as ever. These river boats, tied up near a Baghdad bridge, are successors to the primitive, round *gufas* of the past (page 28).

stitution that guided the ruler and safeguarded the subjects—a charter of human rights.

Even though the king became the head of a vast empire, he was still the servant, not the source, of the law and was responsible to the gods for its enactment. Such divinely guaranteed protection of the individual's vital rights probably meant more to the average citizen than any other boon. This helps to explain the countless thousands of legal documents which have been dug up from the mounds of ancient Mesopotamia; it accounts also for the series of law codes from that area.

The framework and the practice spread to the Elamites and the Hurrians, the Syrians and the Hittites, each of whom employed the given local language or dialect for the purpose, but retained the Babylonian cuneiform and the Babylonian clay tablet.

The huge stele on which the Code of Hammurabi was inscribed (page 48) was not recovered from its home site in Babylon but from the Elamite capital at Susa. Obviously a priceless war trophy, it was deemed worth all the effort that its transportation must have entailed. And well it might be, for this code was not only a general charter of human rights but also a precise book of instructions concerning the family, the society, and the government, as well as commerce, the arts and crafts, and the professions.

For similar reasons, the cuneiform script and the Akkadian language were studied in the second millennium throughout the western civilized world. Some of the finest epics of Mesopotamia are known to us today not in Mesopotamian copies but in cuneiform transcripts made in Egypt for the training of that country's scholars and diplomats.

Various forms of Mesopotamian literature were taken over, either directly or in some adaptation, by other peoples near and far. Ritual and omen texts (page 51) became an important feature of the Hittite archives in central Asia Minor. The epic literature in particular enjoyed great popularity abroad.

The immortal tale of Gilgamesh (pages 13 and 41) appears by the middle of the second millennium in as many as four different languages—Hittite and Hurrian, in addition to Akkadian and Sumerian.

It has been pointed out frequently that the Odyssey has various points of contact with this great literary achievement of Mesopotamia. And even though Homer stood in no need of outside assistance, the literary form which he employed was originated in Sumer. The legend of Uranus and Cronus is traceable, through Hurrian channels, to a Babylonian source.

The influence of Mesopotamia on the Old Testament cannot be indicated within the limits of a brief article. It was inevitable, for the simple reason that the patriarchs came originally from the Euphrates Valley and were thus automatically ambassadors of Mesopotamian civilization. Viewed in this light, the supreme place of the law in the Bible assumes added significance.

When the Bible uses the incident of Egyptian bondage as a recurring refrain, it would seem to allude to much more than the relatively brief period of Egyptian oppression. Rather it appears to stress the fact that the Egyptian way was abhorrent, incompatible with its own way and hence also with that of Mesopotamia.

The ideals that have sustained mankind to this day are in many ways the same ideals that were tested and refined in the magnificent laboratory which Mesopotamia maintained during the thousands of years of its historic progress. In a final survey, therefore, it will not be the sundry survivals of that civilization which call for our close attention.

Not the wheel and the true arch, the razors and cosmetic sets and frying pans; neither will it be shepherd's pipes or the princely harps, nor yet the dials on our clocks, or the astrological charts that constitute our greatest debt to Mesopotamia.

What are really vital are law and writing, and beyond these the abiding sense of the rights and obligations of the individual in a changing and dramatic world—pointing a way to hope in man's struggle for civilization. We are only beginning to appreciate the role of Mesopotamia in this epic struggle.*

How the Herget Paintings Were Composed

IN efforts to present, in collaboration with the artist, the basic features of a great civilization of antiquity, the archeologist dealing with Mesopotamia is less favored by circumstances than were his colleagues representing Egypt, Greece, and Rome.

We know that the artists and artisans of Mesopotamia were no less accomplished than their contemporaries in the Nile Valley. Climate and soil, however, combined to preserve the products of the one center and to destroy those of the other. In Mesopotamia woodwork and textiles simply disintegrated and wall paintings did not fare much better.

Fortunately, the cylinder seals from Mesopotamia are a source of information that is practically inexhaustible. Sculptures in the round, and more especially the vast number of reliefs in stone and bronze (pages 7 and 12), contribute their share of vivid and vigorous representations.

Within the years since 1930 chance and the refinements of archeological methods have preserved for us several important examples of local frescoes—at Til Barsib and Mari, Khorsabad and Nuzi, Dur Kurigalzu, and 'Oqair on the Arabian coast of the Persian Gulf—so that we are no longer reduced to guesswork when it comes to the question of color on anything other than pottery.

In the following paintings by H. M. Herget the facts about a complex civilization that lasted several thousand years, including nearly three millenniums of historic progress, have been compressed into 24 subjects, arranged in chronological sequence from remote prehistoric times down to the middle of the first millennium B. C.

Each picture stands for a whole age, or for a significant phase of the given age. The episodes, based on fact or on imagination, may be descriptive of a moment in history or of a whole era.

The archeologist has invented an incident if the texts did not furnish him with something better and stranger than fiction; but he has sought to be true to the spirit of the time. Details rest on a solid foundation.

This need for highlighting a composite and dynamic civilization by instilling life into each individual painting, imposed an added strain on the artist. Mr. Herget's experience and interest proved to be a unique combination. He faced the problem, delighting in its challenge. It is a source of deep regret that he did not live to see his last major project published.

* For additional articles on Mesopotamia, see the National Geographic Magazine Cumulative Index in two volumes, 1899 to 1946, and 1947 to date.

© National Geographic Society

Painting by H. M. Herget

Fourth Millennium B. C. "He Created the Grass, the Growth of the Marshes, the Reeds, and the Forest . . . A Swamp He Made into Dry Land"—Eridu Creation Story

Man Helps Build Southern Mesopotamia

"No shrub of the field was yet in the earth, and no herb of the field had yet sprung up" (Genesis 2:5).

This sentence might well apply to southern Mesopotamia—the traditional region of the Garden of Eden—at a time when the surrounding lands had already been long established. The land here had to be built up slowly, by the silt brought down from the mountains of Armenia by tireless rivers. And man had to do his share in making the ground firm.

Northern Mesopotamia is hilly and old; the south is flat and relatively recent. Lower Mesopotamia owes its very ground to the unceasing activity of the Tigris and the Euphrates. Their silt is constantly adding to the land surface and cutting down the water area at the head of the Persian Gulf.

What had been seaports even in comparatively late prehistoric times are now modern towns or ancient sites lying hundreds of miles inland.

The first settlers arrived in Lower Mesopotamia from neighboring and long-established lands.

They were real pioneers, working with the reeds that grew from the marsh bottom and matting them into a cover over the slime. The land which they helped to form with their own hands was new, but their civilization was old and mature. What they achieved in the course of the first few centuries was a blend of the old and the new, a blend of discoveries and experience imported from neighboring centers but adjusted to the new surroundings and materials.

It was on this truly flimsy foundation that a new civilization was to emerge in course of time, one which was to develop into a dynamic force crossing barriers of language, race, and political boundaries, and becoming in many important respects the cradle of modern civilization.

While Lower Mesopotamia was gradually drying out, there developed in the highlands to the north and northeast three distinctive cultures, each of which was typified by a particular kind of painted pottery. The latest of these three painted pottery cultures is often called El Obeid (page 27), after a small site near Ur.

All three phases were well acquainted with animal husbandry and enjoyed well-developed forms of agriculture, architecture, and religion. Their pottery served primarily a variety of domestic uses, but the best pieces were reserved for ceremonial and religious purposes.

The pottery soon develops local characteristics and acquires the features which are sampled on this plate. The same is true of the architecture. Alongside the temples which are known to us from the north there develops also a special local style which features the reed as the basic building material.

A bundle of reeds tied near the top yields the graceful curves which come to be associated with the mother goddess, since art, architecture, and religion are already in intimate association.

The plate seeks to compress several centuries of development into a single scene. The men in the painting are stamping down the ground and laying mats over the slowly drying marsh. A patch previously wrested from the marshes already bears the cult hut whose goddess will be implored to protect man and beast as she receives offerings from the treasured pottery vessels assembled for the purpose.

Painting by H. M. Herget

Fourth Millennium B. C. "That City Was Ancient, and So Were the Gods Within It"—Epic of Gilgamesh

This Northern Acropolis Was Buried Under 12 Settlements

WHILE MOST of the south of Mesopotamia was still a steaming marsh, the north had been climbing steadily up the ladder of prehistoric progress—a fact about which even the specialists were vague as recently as 30 years ago. Since then, however, excavations in the area of ancient Nineveh—modern Mosul—have helped to fill huge gaps in our knowledge of the past.

Perhaps the single site which has told us more about these lost ages than any other mound has been Tepe Gawra, 15 miles northeast of Mosul, discovered and first excavated by the author in 1927. Subsequent excavations, largely under the author's personal supervision, have not only confirmed but exceeded his original estimates of the promise of the mound.

By 1936 Tepe Gawra had become a landmark in Mesopotamian archeology, duly marked on the National Geographic Society's Map of Bible Lands. This plate and the next are based on the work at Tepe Gawra.

Of the 26 levels uncovered at Tepe Gawra the first 20 deal with prehistory, that stage in the progress of man which extends from the end of the Stone Age to the beginning of the Copper Age proper.

This period in which copper was used sparingly together with stone, lasted perhaps 2,000 years, down to about 3000 B. C. It saw great improvements in pottery techniques and decoration, steady growth of architecture, the invention of the wheel, and the introduction of the stamp, or button, seal as a magic link between the individual and the powers of Nature.

All of this stage was experienced in the north of Mesopotamia, whereas the south was in a position to enjoy the fruits of this progress only toward the end of the period. The dominant theme of the Stone-Copper Age was religion. The principal buildings in most of the levels of Tepe Gawra were the temples.

Because venerated religious centers found eager builders after each destruction, whatever the cause, the mound witnessed many successive occupations, layer upon layer. With each new stratum the area at the top became more and more restricted, until at last it would no longer support any kind of structure worthy of the site's tradition.

By 1500 B. C. the place had to be abandoned, and within a century or two it was worn down to a tall, cone-shaped hill.

The three temples illustrated on this plate were built by the people of Gawra XIII, after the site had already gone through 13 earlier occupations.

The shrine to the left retained the natural coloring of its light-brown, sun-baked bricks. The central shrine was decorated with white plaster, and the building on the right bore traces of vermilion decoration. Each shrine used bricks of a special and exclusive size, but all three employed piers and pilasters which yielded niches and gave the whole a sophisticated appeal.

At the time of its discovery (1937) the Gawra acropolis was the oldest example of monumental architecture in the world. It still remains an eloquent witness to the great strides which prehistoric man had made since his emergence from the obscurity of the Stone Age.

Painting by H. M. Herget

Fifth-Fourth Millenniums B. C. "The Labor of Them Brought Sighs to Every Craftsman"—Building Inscription of Sennacherib

Prehistoric Man Had Much to Occupy Him

This plate seeks to highlight several of the most interesting achievements of Mesopotamian prehistory. It is a composite picture in more ways than one. The features here illustrated could not be found together in any single level, but each is authentic for a particular occupation; and all date from an age prior to the beginning of history, that is, from before 3000 B. C.

At Tepe Gawra, however, the prehistoric period is represented by as many as 20 individual levels, and a similar time span is required by the evidence from other sites.

With so much ground to be covered, it was necessary to compress into a single composition here, and in the two preceding plates, the story of several centuries. Some of the pottery, for instance, belongs to Gawra XX (counting from the top) and below; the arched doorway, on the other hand, is a product of Gawra VIII, or very close to the beginning of history proper.

The painted pottery of prehistoric Gawra falls into two main groups; the earlier of these bears the name of Halaf, and the later of El Obeid, a relative of the earliest pottery from the Elamite capital at Susa. The Halaf pottery is celebrated for its high firing, its glossy polish, and especially for its extraordinarily intricate decoration in more than one color. The El Obeid pottery from Gawra is often decorated with naturalistic designs—plants, birds, animals, and even landscape composition.

The potter by then had discovered the closed kiln, which enabled him to control his temperatures. The painter ground his materials on stone palettes and used them with infinite skill and patience. The stonecutter, too, left us fine examples of his work, ranging from weapons to engraved stamp seals.

None of his masterpieces, however, can match his best efforts in translucent obsidian, such as the spouted bowl depicted here beside the pottery. When it is borne in mind that this volcanic glass cracks rather easily under pressure, that the whole bowl had to be ground, spout and all, out of a single core, and that many a piece must have been nursed along to the last stage only to collapse under the finishing touches, the work of these nameless artists of some 5,000 years ago will stand out as incredible.

The barber used straight razor handles made of slate and furnished with obsidian blades which were attached to the holder with bitumen. The author can testify from experience that these razors were efficient and convenient to handle.

The playing pipes were made of bone. They occur as early as Gawra XII. One of the best preserved specimens was found in the grave of a young boy, the right hand still clutching the instrument.

Gawra VIII produced the first known example of a true arch, made of sun-baked bricks. This level contained another acropolis different in details and general design from that of Gawra XIII (page 24), but no less impressive.

The new architectural features are sufficiently distinctive to suggest that a change in population had taken place after Gawra XIII. But who these newcomers were, and who their predecessors may have been, will probably never be known. It is true of the prehistoric peoples more than of any other, that only by their works shall they be known.

Painting by H. M. Herget

End of Fourth Millennium B. C. "The Steadfast House the Pickax Builds . . . the Steadfast House It Causes to Prosper"—Sumerian Myth about the Creation of the Pickax

The Introduction of Copper Ushers In a New Era

THROUGHOUT the Chalcolithic, or Stone-Copper, period the metal was used sparingly and, what is far more important, was treated in much the same way as stone.

The real age of copper could not set in until the discovery of the basic principle of metallurgy: that by smelting the ore one could make the metal pliable and cast it into any desired shape. Only then could the flexibility of the material be fully utilized and a variety of shapes achieved that could never be forced out of the resistant stone.

Once discovered and perfected, metallurgy became responsible for a revolution in the life of the ancients that remained without parallel until the advent of the Steam Age. In industry and in warfare, the users of stone could not compete with the handlers of copper. Acquisition of the new technique became literally a matter of life and death.

Since the known sources of supply were limited and widely scattered, control of the supply routes gained an importance never hitherto experienced, and peaceful commercial intercourse became an international concern. The tempo of life had been vastly accelerated.

Level VII of Tepe Gawra, which represents the last Chalcolithic occupation, and which yielded a few hammered copper objects, had the rich brown color of the earth in which these objects were embedded. But Gawra VI, the first witness of the Copper Age on the mound, only a few feet above Level VII, was literally green with the patina of copper.

In the south of Mesopotamia the coming of copper was accompanied by a number of other drastic changes. Some of these suggest strongly that a new element had been added to the population. In the early historic period the resulting new features—in dress, physical type, the substitution of the cylinder for the stamp seal, and the like—come to be associated with a people whom we know as the Sumerians.

It is reasonable, therefore, to assume that the Sumerians arrived in the country in the latter part of the prehistoric period, after painted pottery had given way to undecorated wares. If this assumption should prove right, it would not be out of order to go a step further and identify the Sumerians with the group that introduced metallurgy into Mesopotamia.

In this they might be compared to the Biblical Philistines whose familiarity with iron was to give them a monopoly in Palestine nearly 2,000 years later (I Samuel 13:19-20).

This composition reflects the view that the Sumerians brought the new technique to the country. A group of them have arrived on boats, landing near one of the settlements which were to become inland towns later on. Their larger vessels are tied up alongside the circular local *gufa*.

The newcomers are a squat type, compared with the slender-waisted natives, and they wear flounced skirts which contrast with the shorter tunics of the local inhabitants. The copper wares the outsiders offer are spread on the ground.

The headman of the village examines an ax, while his wife divides her admiration between a cosmetic set and a frying pan. Behind them stand other villagers, including a mother with a child on her shoulders. A boy looks wistfully at the shining objects on the ground, whose excellence is brought into relief by the few stone pieces behind him. The Sumerian boy holds ancestors of our modern dice.

How Seal Engraving Led to the Invention of Writing

Of the many contributions of Mesopotamia to the progress of mankind, no other can compare in importance with the achievement which was to result in the introduction of writing to the world. It was a discovery that literally made history, for no true history is possible without the help of written records.

Today many scholars consider it certain that the idea of writing was first developed in southern Mesopotamia, among the Sumerians of the late prehistoric period.

Other peoples, near and far, soon came to appreciate and put to use the fruits of this discovery; and systematic progress in various sciences, particularly in language and in the natural sciences, received a powerful stimulus.

The mainspring in this development was the strong sense of private property, which was particularly characteristic of the Sumerians, and with it their use of the cylinder seal to identify such property for temple and private economy.

The cylinder seal was to the Sumerians what the stamp seal had been to their predecessors. The gradual spread of Sumerian cultural influence, as far as Egypt and the Aegean, can, in fact, be gauged by the appearance of the cylinder in other countries.

Significantly enough, when the cultural heirs of the Sumerians—the Assyrians and the Babylonians—succumbed at length to conquerors from the east, in the first millenium B. C., the stamp seal came back with the invaders. By that time, however, writing had long been established, not only in Mesopotamian cuneiform and in Egyptian heiroglyphs but also in the form of several alphabets developed in Syria and Palestine, the forerunners of our own alphabetic writing.

Some time before 3000 B. C. the Sumerians made the discovery that the same symbols which could be used to identify persons, cities, or gods when engraved on cylinders, could also serve the same purpose when impressed on clay tablets. Once that transition had been made, the rest was largely a matter of time. When the scribes had progressed from the expression of names to the expression of words and sentences, full-fledged writing appeared.

This plate seeks to emphasize the close connection between the cylinder seal and the beginnings of writing. The scene is laid in a temple yard of ancient Uruk (Biblical Erech), inasmuch as it is this site that has provided us with the earliest known forms of actual writing. The time is that of Uruk IV—that is, four main occupation levels before the first historic stratum on that site.

An old seal cutter is completing his newest piece, while a young apprentice has been rolling out on clay some of the seals already finished. To point up the details, the seals have been made slightly larger than natural size.

Near by is seated another seal cutter, working with a stylus on clay. The stylus he is using is designated for the writing of numbers. To judge from later illustrations of the Assyrian period, the stylus was not held between the fingers but under the thumb in an otherwise closed fist.

In the background are seen several attendants who look after various commodities that have been brought to the temple. One is pouring water into a fish bowl, and the scribe is listing the fishes just delivered.

Painting by H. M. Herget

End of Fourth Millennium B. C. "The Art of Writing Is the Mother of Orators and the Father of Artists"—Sumerian Proverb

The Temple Courtyard Was the Scene of Varied Pursuits

THE DISCOVERY of writing came toward the end of the prehistoric age in Mesopotamia. It did not require many generations to perfect this amazing new tool and make it available for the use of the individual, the temple, and the state. Side by side with this development came an increasing mastery over metals.

By the beginning of the third millennium B. C. the land emerges into the full glare of history. No longer are we faced with a series of cultures that are impressive but nonetheless inarticulate.

The principal actors on the stage are now plainly identified. We are confronted with specific languages and peoples, cities, and city-states. We know by name many of their individual kings and some members of their families; we are able to follow their successes and their setbacks, their problems, achievements, and occasionally even their dreams.

The first historic phase is a long one, extending down into the second half of the third millennium. In the south, which by now calls itself Sumer, there arise from anonymity several prominent cities, such as Ur and Uruk, Lagash and Umma, Kish and Eshnunna.

Methodical and painstaking excavations have given us a fairly clear picture of peacetime life in those days. The sum of the many scattered reports emphasizes that the economic and social life of the period centered about the temple.

The Early Dynastic period reveals itself to us in more than one type of temple. The one chosen for illustration here has been recovered from the oblivion of nearly 5,000 years by the excavations of the Oriental Institute of the University of Chicago conducted at Khafaje, some 10 miles to the east of Baghdad.

The general arrangement of the enclosure is that of a temple oval, and we have chosen to compress several features of the everyday life of the times on the upper platform of the oval, which was crowned by the temple itself.

The economy was essentially rural and agricultural, with sheep breeding and dairy farming playing important roles. The cows were milked from behind. The attendants are often portrayed wearing a curious feathered headdress not otherwise in common use, the normal type being a cloth turban.

The typical male garment was the flounced skirt, which varied in length according to the owner's prosperity and station in life. The upper part of the body was often left bare. Women's skirts appear to be less elaborate in cut but more varied in color than those of the men.

Except for the days given over to stated major festivals, which were numerous and solemn, the temple courtyard could be the scene of considerable gaiety and social pastimes. The visitors might be entertained by an occasional musician strumming on a lyre.

Wrestling and boxing were recognized forms of skill, but they were obviously associated also with the religious and mythical lore of the age. This pair of wrestlers, copied from a contemporary bronze composition which was discovered in a dig under the author's direction, portray the match of semidivine beings, such as the combat between the hero Gilgamesh and his rival Enkidu, which is celebrated in one of the great epics of Mesopotamia (page 40).

© National Geographic Society

Painting by H. M. Herget

Early Third Millennium B. C. "Cow and Calf He Caused to Multiply, Much Fat and Milk He Caused to Be Produced"—
From a Sumerian Myth about the Farmer-God

"Modernized Warfare" Was Known 45 Centuries Ago

One of the best known centers of Early Dynastic Sumer (third millennium B. C.) is the city of Lagash, modern Telloh. Excavated by the French in the course of 20 archeological campaigns, Lagash has revealed itself brilliantly to our own age, thanks to the artistic merit of its remains as well as the eloquence of the written accounts left us by its rulers.

Some of these so-called priest-kings—older books refer to them as *patesis,* but the correct title is *ensi*—managed at times to overthrow powerful cities like Ur, and even to make their own might felt outside Mesopotamia, in the country of Elam to the east.

Our illustration has drawn upon the combined evidence of written and material remains and has utilized not only the monuments and smaller objects from Lagash itself but also the existing finds from Ur.

The scene depicts a battle between Lagash and its traditional rival, the neighboring city-state of Umma. The victorious leader of the charge is Eannatum, one of the early rulers of Lagash, who in his celebrated Stele of the Vultures left us a record that is significant for both its historical and its artistic content.

The king's chariot and equipment are based partly on the so-called War Standard from Ur and partly on the finds from the Royal Tombs at that site. The city emblem of Lagash was a lion-headed eagle sinking his claws into the bodies of two animals, usually lions standing back to back.

A beautiful example of this emblem has been preserved on the famous silver vase of Entemena, nephew of Eannatum. This symbol may never have been used to identify chariots, as has been done here, but the slight liberty taken by archeologist and artist in making the illustration serves a good purpose.

The animals which are drawing the chariots are not horses but onagers, or wild asses. For the sake of contrast, the chariots of Umma have been copied from the smaller of the two known types of that period.

It should be added, to supplement the illustration, that at this particular time stout collars kept the steeds hitched to the pole. Some 2,000 years later, in Assyrian times, three straps passing under the forepart of the animal's belly hitched harness and pole together.

The foot soldiers include lancers and archers. The headgear consists of a helmet, of leather or metal, depending on the soldier's rank. The heavy cloaks are joined only at the neck to allow greater freedom of movement. The members of the massive phalanx, which anticipates the classical phalanx by 2,000 years, are protected by curved shields.

Victory was usually celebrated by a sumptuous banquet, such as is depicted on the Peace Standard from Ur. The festivities were followed by more constructive occupations: repair of the damage caused by the war, the building of temples, and the extension of irrigation works.

The desert must forever be kept from encroaching on the sown land, and constant attention to irrigation was thus the most effective guarantee of prosperity. Modern Iraq has a long way to go to match the industry and the perseverance of its inhabitants of 45 centuries ago.

© National Geographic Society

Painting by H. M. Herget

Middle Third Millennium B. C. "I, Eannatum, in Umma Wrought Destruction Like the Whirlwind"—Eannatum, Stele of the Vultures

The Royal Tombs of Ur Hide a Grim Secret

EVER SINCE the discovery of the great death pits at Ur by C. Leonard Woolley, who excavated the site on behalf of the British Museum and the University Museum of the University of Pennsylvania, the meaning of these mass burials has posed an acute problem. The best preserved of the tombs are specially built chambers with human victims in each, sometimes 70 or more.

The wealth of the funerary furnishings and the title "King" which is inscribed in connection with one of the principals entombed in this unusual fashion have caused the excavator to regard these particular interments as Royal Tombs.

That is why the names of King Meskalamdug and Queen Shubad have become familiar terms to all those who have had the opportunity to view the many beautiful objects that have been recovered with these burials—in museums of Baghdad, Philadelphia, and London, or in the marvelous publication of the finds. The mass deaths of the attendants have been explained as more or less voluntary acts on the part of the faithful followers of the royal dead.

This theory is attractive but not entirely free from doubt. A king by the name of Meskalamdug is not known in the official lists. Neither is there anything in Sumerian literature or religion to account for such a frightful aftermath of the normal death of a ruler. Others have tried, therefore, to explain the practice as a barbarous survival from more primitive times when the all-important rites aimed at ensuring fertility may have required large-scale human sacrifice.

Still others would look for an explanation to the Mesopotamian custom of setting up substitute kings at the time of the great drama celebrated annually in connection with the New Year, or at times of some overwhelming national calamity (page 44). Such ritual kings might eventually be put to death. In the Early Dynastic period the practice may well have entailed the death of many attendants.

Not to decide among the theories, but to direct attention, however, to the existence of such a practice and to some of its details, we have introduced a picture of a procession on the way to a death pit.

Some of the victims may already have "gone to their fate"; or the death scene may yet have to take place, so that only the rich furnishings are being transported slowly in the melancholy procession. The lances of the warriors point down as a symbol of ill fortune.

These attendants may be among the designated victims, or they may merely reflect their genuine dejection at the calamity that has already overtaken their peers.

The same would apply to the young girl in the foreground, who is pictured as wearing decorations recovered from the burial of Shubad and now displayed in the University Museum in Philadelphia. She might be Shubad herself, or she might be a mourner close to the dead lady.

One thing is certain. The dramatic conception of the universe to which the Sumerians and their cultural successors subscribed did not in later times exact a toll on such a heroic scale. The Early Dynastic age boasts many notable achievements in more than one field of human endeavor. The periods that follow may not match this one in sheer exuberance of effort, but they reflect steady gains toward a more humanized view of life.

Painting by H. M. Herget

Middle Third Millennium B. C. "The Anunnaki, the Great Gods, Foregather. Death and Life They Determine; but of Death, Its Days They Do Not Reveal"—Epic of Gilgamesh

Even the Gods Were Guided by Democracy

THE ANCIENT Mesopotamian made his gods much in his own image. He portrayed them as subject to all the ordinary human emotions—love and hatred, good will and ill, moderation and excess. Life among the gods was merely an idealized reflection of life among men.

The basic feature of Mesopotamian society was a profound regard for the rights of the individual. The king was no supernatural being, no god like the Egyptian Pharaoh. Because he lacked autocratic powers, he was dependent in matters of consequence upon the favor of his gods and the consent of his Council of Elders.

This emphasis on consultation and council approval is met with throughout Mesopotamian history. And it is this same essential democratic feature that gave Mesopotamian civilization its dynamic drive and carried its benefits to many lands and peoples.

Since the gods of Mesopotamia were little more than idealized mortals, we expect the ideal of rudimentary democracy to be evident among them. That such was indeed the case is shown with rare simplicity and charm by the main religious work of Mesopotamia, the Creation Epic.

This epic concerns itself largely with the battle which the benign gods wage against the powers of chaos, who are led by the destructive goddess Tiamat. None of the opposing gods had the courage to face her.

In desperation, shrewd Ea designated young Marduk as the leader most likely to succeed. Marduk was resolute, but his price was staggering. If he was to champion the fight, he must be rewarded with the permanent chieftaincy of the gods.

There was no alternative but to accept Marduk's terms. Yet no act of such importance could be valid unless approved by the full Assembly of the Gods.

Foreseeing objections from the old guard, Ea first entertained the parliament at a banquet. When at length he broached his plan, his guests were too far gone in their cups to demur. The motion was carried unanimously.

Armed with his new authority, Marduk vanquished Tiamat and remained supreme forever after.

The scene before us is the divine banquet of the epic. All the attendants have been transferred from reliefs of the Early Dynastic period: the men carrying the heavy jars of beverages; the pottery stands for the jars; the servants bearing mounds of pancakes on their heads; the musicians; and the boy with the sheep.

The divine guests are distinguished chiefly by their horned miters, four horns for the leading deities and two for the minor gods in the background. The drinking is done through tubes, as frequently shown on cylinder seals.

The older of the two standing gods is Ea, explaining his plan. He is identified by his favorite symbol of the vase with the flowing waters, which we have taken the liberty of depicting as embroidered on his waistband.

The youthful god behind him is Marduk. He holds the ring-and-rod symbol, and his saw-toothed dagger is in his belt. His robe is decorated with starlike rosettes, a feature of Marduk in Assyrian times.

The significant thing about this scene is, of course, not how consent was obtained, but the fact that consent was necessary even among the gods. Representative authority, not autocracy, was the foundation of Mesopotamian society.

© National Geographic Society

Painting by H. M. Herget

Third Millennium Background. "As They Drank the Strong Drink, Their Bodies Expanded; They Became Languid as Their Spirits Rose"—the Creation Epic

The Mesopotamian Noah Paints an Appalling Picture of the Great Flood

THE EPIC tale of Gilgamesh is one of the great creations of world literature.

In his struggle against the fate of all mortals the hero seeks out at long last the survivor of the Great Flood, in order to learn from him the secret of immortality. The quest proves unsuccessful, but the end finds Gilgamesh at peace with himself and his surroundings.

The impact of the epic may be gauged by the fact that as early as the second millennium B. C. it was known in at least four languages. Its influence on art and thought spread to many lands and cultures.

Because of its close Biblical associations, the episode chosen for illustration has been taken from the epic's account of the Flood. After a long and fateful journey, Gilgamesh is at last in the presence of Utnapishtim, Mesopotamia's counterpart of Noah. Utnapishtim has just reached that point in his tale which finds the Ark come to rest on Mount Nisir, while the slowly receding floodwaters present a picture of bleakest desolation.

To be sure, the distance between Mount Nisir—an 8,489-foot peak near modern Sulaimaniya, 175 miles northeast of Baghdad—and the place of Utnapishtim's permanent retreat "in the faraway" was imagined to be far too great for compression into a single picture. But so vivid is the tale which is being unfolded to Gilgamesh that the reader should have no more difficulty than did Gilgamesh himself in seeing the distant outlines of the Ark with his mind's eye.

The Ark is described as a perfect cube consisting of seven stories, each divided into nine compartments. Since the description in the epic is quite specific, our modern notions as to what is seaworthy had to be discarded. Nothing is said, however, about the appearance of Utnapishtim, and the artist re-created him according to his own inspiration.

As for the figure of Gilgamesh, no Mesopotamian monument is definitely known to depict him. We have chosen as a prototype the supernaturally conceived figure of Naram-Sin, one of the kings of the dynasty of Akkad, as portrayed on that ruler's celebrated Stele of Victory.

The dynasty of Akkad, founded by the great Sargon of Akkad, flourished toward the end of the third millennium B.C. It marks the end of the Early Dynastic period and the beginning of a new era in Mesopotamia.

The Akkadian age accomplishes the gradual integration of the new elements, which are predominantly Semitic, with the inherited culture as developed by the Sumerians. It is a period of rapid political and geographic expansion, tremendous vigor, and bold adventure.

Naram-Sin pictures himself on his great stele as a warrior clad in sandals and knee-length garment, and armed with bow and quiver, a battle-ax, and a mace. But it is no ordinary warrior that he affects to be, nor even just a regal hero. His horned crown marks him as a divine being.

If we look for a worthy superhuman model that this king would be likely to copy as his counterpart, we could scarcely suggest a better one than the epic hero Gilgamesh, "two-thirds of whom was god and one-third man." It was he "who scaled the mountains and crossed the seas" in search of the life that he was not to find.

Painting by H. M. Herget

Late Third Millennium Background. "I Looked at the Weather; Stillness Had Set In, and All of Mankind Had Returned to Clay"—
From the Flood Tablet, Epic of Gilgamesh

The Law Protects Zealously the Institution of Marriage

THROUGHOUT the 3,000 years of its historic progress Mesopotamian society was noted for the supreme position which it assigned to law. The law guided the ruler and safeguarded his subjects. It penetrated every walk and phase of life: the family and the state, commerce and industry, science and religion.

In the last analysis, it was interest in the law that had led to the introduction of writing. Because of the confidence and sense of dignity that it inspired in the individual and in society, Mesopotamian law became the model for similar institutions among other peoples who at one time or another came within the orbit of the civilization of Mesopotamia. Among them were the Elamites and the Hurrians, the Hittites and the Hebrews.

Until recently, the distinction of having been the first to assemble the existing laws into a systematic code was generally ascribed to Hammurabi (page 49), the greatest king of the First Dynasty of Babylon, who is now dated to the end of the 18th and the beginning of the 17th century B. C. Within the last two years, however, two new codes of law have been discovered, each older than the Code of Hammurabi.

One of these turned up at the University Museum of the University of Pennsylvania. Its text is Sumerian and it has been published by Dr. Francis R. Steele. The other contains the laws of the city of Eshnunna, in an Akkadian formulation published by Dr. Albrecht Goetze.

Even these two pre-Hammurabi collections are not likely to have been the first codes used in Mesopotamia. The inscriptions of Urukagina, the last of the early rulers of Lagash, at the end of the Early Dynastic period, already imply the existence of established legal norms.

It is therefore a reasonably safe assumption that by the turn of the third millennium—that is, in the so-called Neo-Sumerian period which followed the dynasty of Akkad—the land enjoyed the security of broad legal protection. It is in that period that the accompanying scene is laid.

The scene depicts the sealing of a marriage contract in Lagash, at the time of Gudea. The father, having received the stipulated bride price, indicates his readiness to give away his daughter by affixing his personal seal to the required document, as the betrothed couple respectfully watch.

The impression is larger than normal size, since otherwise the detail would be impossible to follow. Dress and furniture are based on monuments from the time of Gudea, whose statue occupies a place of honor on the right. The bride's mother is modeled after the famous representation of a "spinning woman."

For the sake of directing attention to another important feature in the life of Mesopotamia, we have chosen to make the bride's father a physician to the king. The inscription on the seal, copied from a real cylinder, says so explicitly.

The design, however, has not been found with this inscription. It was taken from a carving on a contemporary vase because of its significance to the medical profession. The motif is that of entwined serpents. It was to become known as the caduceus, a symbol of medicine and, in modern times, a mark also of the barber profession, whose incidental association with the art of healing, however, still is remembered.

Painting by H. M. Herget

Twentieth Century B. C. "If a Man Takes to Wife a Man's Daughter Without Asking Her Father and Her Mother and Without Executing a Sealed Marriage Contract . . ."—Laws of Eshnunna

Painting by H. M. Herget

Early 18th Century B. C. "That the Dynasty Might Not Come to an End, King Erra-Imitti Placed the Gardener Enlil-Bani as a Substitute Figure upon His Throne"—Chronicle of an Old Babylonian King

A Mock King-for-a-Day Stays On to Rule for a Lifetime

In describing an earlier plate (page 36), we mentioned that one possible explanation of the so-called Royal Tombs at Ur was that those mass burials were due to awesome rites connected with the death of a substitute king.

At any rate, there is no doubt that Babylonia and Assyria, the twin heirs to the Mesopotamian civilization of the third millennium B. C., knew the institution of a substitute ruler. The practice was designed to weather particularly acute periods of crisis. And since each New Year was regarded as a fateful period, the crowning of such a king-for-a-day appears to have been also an annual occasion.

The Mesopotamian New Year, which was normally celebrated in the spring, was a highly dramatic festival reflecting man's constant dependence upon unpredictable Nature. Anxiety over the disposition of the gods gave way at long last to uninhibited joy (page 68).

The substitute king seems to have been a feature of the concluding celebration. The person selected for the unwanted privilege of appeasing the gods while amusing the uproarious populace, by paying with his life for his brief occupancy of the throne, may have been a prisoner, political or otherwise, who had already run afoul of the laws.

A Babylonian chronicle states laconically that King Erra-Imitti of Issin, member of an early second millennium royal family which followed the Third Dynasty of Ur but preceded the First Dynasty of Babylon, set up the gardener Enlil-Bani as substitute ruler.

Things did not go off at all according to plan, however. The all too brief statement goes on to say that, after the crown of royalty had been placed on the substitute's head, "Erra-Imitti died in his palace while sipping a hot brew. Enlil-Bani, he who was on the throne, did not arise [from it] but was himself installed as king."

In other words, the victim who had been set up as a mocking stock seized upon a rare prank of fate and went on to rule, very capably, as we know from independent sources, for no less than 24 years.

The scene takes place in front of the royal palace. A ziggurat, or stage tower, modeled after the nearly contemporary structure of the Third Dynasty of Ur, is seen in the background.

The victim, decked in royal garb, is seated upon a throne which has been placed in the center of the square. An official bows before him in mock adoration, while others in the riotous gathering give vent in various ways to their long-pent-up emotions.

Dancing and singing girls—note the two with hand on throat to obtain the desired effect—dressed in colors preserved on an Egyptian painting which depicts contemporary Asiatics, do their best to follow the music; and a pair of boxers has attracted a masculine group of spectators to another section of the square.

Enlil-Bani has just removed the mask which was given him for the occasion, to glance anxiously at the noose that an attendant is fastening to the top of the palace wall. At that moment a servant bursts out of the palace with the startling and sobering news that the legitimate king has died. Enlil-Bani's resolve will not be found wanting at this juncture.

Painting by H. M. Herget

Eighteenth Century B. C. "Obtain for Me a Fine Slave Girl, One Who Has Attracted Thine Eye"—Old Babylonian Letter

A Prosperous Babylonian Matron Shops for a Slave Girl

BABYLONIAN LAW, as represented by the famous Code of Hammurabi, recognizes slaves as the third class in contemporary society, together with the two upper groups who correspond to the patricians and plebeians of the Romans.

Always an economic asset under that system, slaves were the victims of capture in war or of hopeless indebtedness in their own community. They could also be acquired through purchase in the open market.

Especially sought after for servitude were the men and women from the mountains to the north and northeast of Babylonia, the region of ancient Subartu and Lullu. Numerous letters and business documents of the second millennium make special mention of Subarian and Lullu slaves, a tribute to the sturdiness and other desirable qualities of these mountaineers, though one hardly enjoyed by the victims.

So widespread was their reputation that the cuneiform symbol for "male slave" is made up of the signs for "male" and "eastern mountains," while the symbol for "female slave" is similarly composed of the signs for "woman" and "eastern mountains." Clearly, then, this situation is as old as cuneiform writing itself.

Interestingly enough, the highly competent porters of modern Baghdad are members of a special ethnic group, not Arabs or Kurds, but Lurs, from the Iranian district of Luristan—an area adjacent to that which provided the favorite slaves of the third and second millenniums B. C. Possibly the Lurs are descendants of the ancient Lullu.

The cost of slaves was subject to variation from place to place and from period to period. Prevailing political and economic conditions also had their effect on the slave market. The average price was between 30 and 40 shekels of silver, or as much as the cost of three or four ordinary bulls.

The Code of Hammurabi allows surgeons for a serious operation, successfully performed, 10 shekels from a patrician, five from a plebeian, but only two from a slave.

In Hammurabi's times (end of the 18th and beginning of the 17th century B. C.), one of the best known slave centers was based at Eshnunna, about 20 miles northeast of modern Baghdad, between the important cities in the south and the hill country. The background of our scene is a section of that city, reconstructed by the American excavators from the Oriental Institute of the University of Chicago.

The prospective buyers include one (with the grooved cap) from as far west as Mari. To the left is seen a prosperous slave merchant extolling the qualities of a Subarian girl to an even more prosperous Babylonian woman.

The letter from which the quotation under the picture was taken was addressed to a woman. That the women of Mesopotamia often achieved considerable success in business is indicated by records dating from the third millennium.

To the right, a male Lullu slave is made to display his strength by carrying on his back a trussed-up bullock. This particular demonstration may never have been attempted in ancient times. Modern counterparts of the Lullu, however, have transported grand pianos in the same fashion.

It is doubtful whether their prodigious feats of strength will remain on display much longer, for not a few of the Lurs of Baghdad have been sending their sons to Oxford.

Painting by H. M. Herget

Early 17th Century B. C. "The Present Year Is a Leap Year. The Coming Month Shall Therefore Be Recorded as Elul II"— Administrative Correspondence of Hammurabi

The Great Hammurabi Keeps an Eye on Taxes

INTENSIVE cultural progress had characterized most of southern Mesopotamia for several centuries prior to the accession of Hammurabi, greatest ruler of the First Dynasty of Babylon. Great strides had been made not only in the study of law but also in language, literature, music, and several of the physical and natural sciences.

Among these was the science of astronomy, even in those days a close relative of mathematics, in which the Babylonian was especially adept. Astronomy had an important bearing on religion, agriculture, and, as we shall see presently, on administration. It is the notable achievement of Hammurabi that he knew how to consolidate and promote these manifold cultural gains and to employ them in the service of the state as a whole.

For the art of Babylon at the time of Hammurabi we have to look outside the capital, because at Babylon itself the Euphrates has proved a serious barrier to the recovery of the early levels. We have now, however, a brilliant illustration of contemporary painting, thanks to excavations by the Louvre Museum on the site of ancient Mari, on the Euphrates, about halfway between Baghdad and Aleppo.

Since Mari was strongly influenced by Babylon, with which it maintained close contact, we have used a portion of one of the Mari panels, as published in the French journal *Syria,* for the background of our illustration. Some such scene might well have adorned the throne room of Hammurabi, in which our subject has been placed.

The painting shows two symmetrical groups of three mythical animals each—a sphinx, a griffon, and a human-headed bull—arranged between a palm tree and another tree of more stylized design. Attendants are picking dates, while a goddess is advancing toward the center.

The king, seated on the throne, is giving instructions to his vizier. The reason for the audience is the court astronomer, who stands beside the throne. He can be identified by pendants representing Venus and the constellation Leo.

The king has been informed that the time for an intercalary month is at hand. Hammurabi orders the next month to be not Tishri, the seventh month of the Babylonian calendar, but the sixth month repeated, that is, Elul II.

The king makes plain to his vizier what this will mean administratively: "Instead of being due on the 25th of Tishri, as announced, the taxes shall be delivered in Babylon on the 25th of Elul II."

The order, translated from the same document from which the citation in the title of the plate was borrowed, will be promptly relayed to the two couriers standing by the massive stele on which the law code is inscribed. The couriers, in turn, will relay the message to others who will finally carry it to all the provinces of the realm.

The inscription on the stele is in shadow except for a few lines of the column at the top. Closer inspection would show that the discernible signs say "whose foundations are as firm as heaven and earth."

The sculptured part depicts Hammurabi receiving from the sun-god the rod-and-ring—twin symbol of authority. The facial features of Hammurabi have been copied from the stele and from other contemporary representations.

Painting by H. M. Herget

Sixteenth Century B. C. "Come In, Guardian of Health! Go Out, Guardian of Evil!"—Inscription on the Arms of an Assyrian Terra-cotta Figurine

Medicine Teams Up with Religion and Magic

The subjects here illustrated are not peculiar to one particular period in the history of Mesopotamia. They could be made to apply readily, and with only minor modifications of detail, to virtually any period.

Our scene has been laid in the 16th century B. C., in order to preserve a regular chronologic sequence and to record, at the same time, the presence of the Kassites in the country. This people from the Iranian highlands, who brought with them a language neither Semitic nor Sumerian, overran Babylonia shortly after the Hittites, another people neither Semitic nor Sumerian, had made a paralyzing raid on the capital and put an end to the First Dynasty of Babylon.

Weakened by these combined blows, the country remained under foreign rule for some five centuries, until about the middle of the 12th century B. C. But, as has happened so often in history, the conquering barbarians were soon vanquished in turn by the superior native culture.

The Kassites took over all the significant features and practices of the Babylonians, and even carried some of these to lengths not previously known. This applies particularly to magic and divination.

In this picture the painted wall decoration is based on the recent discoveries made by the Iraq Department of Antiquities in the Kassite center of Dur Kurigalzu. The same is true of the standing figure with back to the wall, and the seated figure with the liver model. Other details are derived from Kassite and Assyrian sources long known.

An anxious father stands by the sickbed of his son. Two priests dressed to resemble fishes—for symbolic association with the water god Ea—seek to expel the demons suspected of having caused the malady. One of the priests is seen holding a bowl which, no doubt, contains some magic fluid.

The boy's hands are held open, in a gesture of supplication, as are also the right hands of the fish-garbed priests; but the head is hidden by one of the standing figures. This bed scene, incidentally, is modeled after a section on a frequently reproduced Assyrian bronze relief which depicts in several registers the exorcism of a female demon.

At the table to the right, an omen priest is hard at work on an inscribed model of a sheep liver. It happens to be an authentic old Babylonian piece now in the British Museum. The inscriptions on this model list the diagnoses based on the livers of real sheep slaughtered in the past for purposes of the omen lore.

The shape of each minute detail on the fresh liver was linked by the omen experts with some memorable event of the past—say, a ruler's victory over his enemies, another ruler's death from an infected toe, or a king's sad fate after a ladder had fallen on him. Each of these instances, by the way, was actually recorded.

The right link furnished the prognosis for the problem at hand; for instance, "If the right lobe (of the liver) is carved out like a purse, it is an omen of (King) Ibbi-Sin, indicating disaster." The priest in our case appears to have discovered a startling answer.

The sides of the ceremonial table are decorated with carvings of symbols of various gods as they appear on numerous boundary stones of the Kassite period.

Painting by H. M. Herget

Fifteenth Century B. C. "No, No, Not a Word of It Is True!"—From the Records about the Trial of Kushshiharbe

Justice Catches Up with a Corrupt Magistrate

MESOPOTAMIA from remote prehistoric times was a magnet for many races and peoples. The story about the Tower of Babel could hardly have been inspired by any other country.

Previous scenes and their descriptions have dealt with proto-Sumerians and Sumerians, Semites and Elamites, Kassites and Hittites. Another significant element, different in linguistic stock and in much of its culture, is represented by the Hurrians, the Horites of the Bible.

Members of this group played important roles throughout the ancient Near East in the second millennium B. C. Hurrian influence on the Hebrews is now known to have been especially significant. In Mesopotamia the Hurrians were thickly settled in the region of the modern oil center of Kirkuk.

These settlements have yielded a distinctive type of painted pottery, a repertory of new designs on cylinder seals, a novel type of painted wall decoration, and a rich collection of written records which afford a vivid picture of Hurrian society and of individual Hurrian personalities.

The most productive Hurrian site known to date is that of Nuzi, 10 miles southwest of Kirkuk, excavated by a joint expedition of the Iraq Museum of Antiquities, the American School of Oriental Research in Baghdad, and the Harvard Semitic Museum.

The present scene takes place in the Nuzi courthouse, whose walls are adorned with brilliant frescoes of a type not previously found in Mesopotamia. A painted incense burner in the corner and painted goblets on the table provide additional examples of Hurrian forms and decoration.

Seated at the table are three judges, their heads covered with austere hoods, each man equipped with the individual cylinder seal with which he will certify his verdict. They listen attentively. A scribe is at pains to record the testimony.

The accused is the mayor of the city, who is to become notorious in the local annals as the corrupt Kushshiharbe. He is flanked by two constables who wear copper coats of mail recalling the scale armor of Goliath. The excavations have yielded one such armor in a good state of preservation, and many scattered metal scales from other similar pieces of equipment.

The mayor's accuser is one of his former henchmen turned state's witness. The charges include various instances of malfeasance in office: bribery, intimidation, kidnapings; and the mean magistrate had even caused water to be mixed with milk.

Most of the testimony of this and of previous witnesses had left the accused impassive. He is aroused, however, by an allegation involving the comely girl Humerelli, who stands demurely by. Against her will, it is charged, the girl had been dragged to the private residence of the mayor.

Kushshiharbe is vehement in his denial. But his words appear to have fallen on deaf ears, for generations later the trial of Kushshiharbe was still mentioned as a significant turning point in the history of the city.

That the chief magistrate of a city intrusted to his charge some 3,400 years ago should have been guilty of corruption and excesses is scarcely surprising. What is highly significant, however, is that he was tried and made to pay for his misdeeds. The nature of the penalty is not recorded.

Assyria Gains the Upper Hand over Babylonia

WHILE SUMER and Akkad and Babylon were making history in Lower and in Central Mesopotamia, a city on the middle Tigris was rising slowly to ever increasing prominence. Its name was Ashur, as was also the name of its chief god. The state that city came to control—one which developed eventually into a far-flung empire—is known as Assyria.

About the time of Hammurabi, Ashur enjoyed sufficient independence and power to make its influence felt in distant Cappadocia, an easterly area of Asia Minor. Later in the second millennium the city came under the domination of the Hurrians, but the relative balance of power which prevailed in western Asia in the 15th and 14th centuries B. C. gave the resolute native rulers of Ashur their chance to gain complete freedom.

From then on it was a story of constant rise, with the kings of Ashur becoming the equals of other monarchs. From the end of the second millennium down to almost the middle of the next they were leaders and finally masters of the Fertile Crescent.

Ashur's closest neighbor of any prominence was Babylon. The relations between the two were much like those that many centuries later characterized Greece and Rome. Babylon was the cultural center, but no match for its northern neighbor in war and politics. Ashur, on the other hand, was keenly resentful of its inferiority in culture. The resulting rivalry was acute and bitter.

Our scene seeks to capture that moment in history when the political tide had swung for the first time decisively in favor of Ashur. This occurred during the reign of the vigorous Assyrian king Tukulti-Ninurta I. The words which he uttered on humbling the captured Babylonian king, Kashtiliash IV (opposite page), were to become symbolic of the future status of these two states.

Tukulti-Ninurta I transferred his capital from Ashur to a near-by site, to which he gave his name. It was excavated by a German expedition under Walter Andrae, and the results of that work are ample for a reconstruction of the life of the period.

The great hall focuses upon a niche containing a sculptured stand bearing the statue of the chief deity, who holds in his left hand the rod-and-ring, used as a symbol of authority.

The king, clad in a rich fringed garment, has been copied from one of his reliefs. His sandaled right foot is placed on the neck of the Babylonian. In his right hand he holds the scepter with which he touches the skull of his prisoner, while his left clutches the ring, this time separated from the rod. The garment of Kashtiliash has the vertical folds which often distinguish the Babylonian dress from the Assyrian.

The scene is witnessed by the vizier, beside whom stands a Syrian emissary with an Anatolian observer wearing the typical pointed shoes.

The decoration has been selected from among the scenes uncovered on the walls of Tukulti-Ninurta's palace. One of these paintings has been utilized for a valance of woven material placed over the side door flanked by two soldiers. The design shows two mythological figures, back to back, one on red and the other on blue.

The left hand of each holds a basket or bowl of gold, with some substance which the right hand now places on the conventionalized palm to lend it greater fertility.

Painting by H. M. Herget

1243–1207 B. C. "His Royal Neck I Trod with My Foot, Like a Footstool"—Annals of Tukulti-Ninurta I

The Assyrian Military Camp Was No Place for Idlers

For all its youthful vigor, Ashur required several centuries to consolidate the position which had been carved out for it by Tukulti-Ninurta I and his predecessors. Then came a period of gradual expansion, principally toward Syria-Anatolia, Armenia, and Iran. The mountain districts in particular presented a constant threat and challenge.

The Assyrian state was forever at war, forcing a mounting burden on the people, conquerors and conquered alike, to support a military establishment. The ceaseless campaigns were successful, however, in terms of political and geographic expansion. With these successes came also advances in art, and especially in sculpture, which in some aspects attains a vigor never hitherto achieved and seldom equaled since.

If the vitality of a state may be measured not so much by its size as by its principal artistic expression, then the height of Assyrian power was reached in the first half of the 9th century B. C., under Ashurnasirpal II.

The present painting is laid against a background of war and chase, respectively the principal occupation and pastime of this king. Details are abundant, and they are derived not only from the numerous reliefs but also from the painted ceramics of the period. By using the device of a military camp, a common one on the reliefs themselves, it was possible to bring in a number of separate scenes which combine into a characteristic and authentic picture of the age.

The center of the camp is taken up by the royal canopy. Under it the king is seen performing his daily sacrifice. The king's face is known to us from the reliefs, as is also his sword with the double volute near the end.

The colors of the cloth cover on the table and the dark blue of the headdress are based on contemporary painted work; the same is true of the detail on the silver incense stand. Attention should also be directed to the chevron motif on the canopy, which is typical of Ashurnasirpal's age.

The typical chariot of this period was mounted on six-spoked wheels; later Assyrian wheels sported eight spokes.

Against the camp wall, to the left, an attendant is filtering and cooling water, employing the same system used by the servants in the author's archeological camp 10 years ago.

Behind the water boy stands the camp's baker. In the corner to the right an orderly is busy in an officer's tent making up his master's cot. Another servant is helping a warrior to a drink of water.

The remainder of the crowded interior of the camp is given over to a groom and his horses, a slaughterer, two soldiers at their meal, and two cooks.

The entrance to the camp is guarded by armed soldiers. One of them can be seen behind a tall shield held on the ground by the left foot inserted in a notch. The footgear consisted of sandals, which contrast with the half-boots used by the Assyrians of later periods.

Approaching the entrance is a group of men carrying a slain lion. They are accompanied by a boy with two thoroughbred hunting dogs straining at the leash.

Because lions did not disappear from this area until much later, we can obtain fine representations of these beasts from the sculptors of Ashurnasirpal and their disciples under Ashurbanipal, some two-and-a-half centuries later.

Painting by H. M. Herget

883–859 B. C. "Ninurta and Nergal, Who Love My Priesthood, Intrusted to Me the Wild Creatures of the Field, Commanding Me to Follow the Chase"—From an Inscription of Ashurnasirpal II

A Dead Assyrian Is Furnished with Provisions for the Beyond

Burial customs in Mesopotamia differed widely according to period and the particular cultural group involved. Bodies might be extended or flexed and put to rest in jars, wooden caskets, stone sarcophagi, or ordinary cloth wrappings.

The burial place might be a hole in the ground, a tomb lined with sun-baked bricks, or a large chamber with vaulted ceiling. Finally, throughout much of Mesopotamian history, burials took place in special areas set aside for cemeteries. In some instances, however, there were no formal cemeteries outside the inhabited section. The dead were interred within the residential precinct, on a mound that may have gone through numerous previous occupations, and frequently inside the property of the deceased.

The Assyrian graves of the first millennium B. C. reflected the view that the dead belonged inside the house which they had occupied during their lifetime. In this manner the spirit could remain close to the family and receive from the bereaved the care without which it would be doomed to restless wandering. Where the decedent had been well to do, his body was not placed directly under the floor, but was laid instead in a vaulted chamber, sealed off by a sturdy door that could be reached through a steep shaft.

Our scene depicts the interior of the house of an Assyrian nobleman just "gone to his fate." The details of the room are based on Walter Andrae's reconstruction of the so-called Red House in Ashur.

The solid wooden doors swing in; the poles rest in sockets lined with metal and are surmounted by ornamented knobs. The niche with the sacrificial table and an opening for a figurine of the house god is a place suitable for private devotions.

A service for the dead is being performed by the eldest son of the house. The master has just been removed from his deathbed and placed on the stretcher, on which he will be borne to his grave, his right hand resting on a plate filled with the food he will need in the hereafter. The widow's grief will probably not become vocal until the body has reached the vaulted tomb for the last rites.

The excavators of Ashur fortunately uncovered the burial vault of Ashurnasirpal II, together with his huge stone sarcophagus.

The floors were paved with large dolerite slabs, and the walls rested upon three layers of the same type of slab engraved with an inscription of the king repeated 18 times. The dolerite sarcophagus was about 12 feet long and some 6 feet in height and in width. It, too, carried on three sides an engraved inscription of the monarch.

Of special interest is the two-inch round opening in the massive lid of the sarcophagus. The Epic of Gilgamesh tells us that the hero's departed friend, Enkidu, appeared to Gilgamesh through an aperture in the earth. The opening was for the use of the spirit of the dead.

In addition to the plate with food, the body was buried with all the personal belongings of the interred: ornaments, weapons, favorite vessels. A small niche in the wall was for an oil lamp, to be left burning after the lid had been fastened down and the door of the chamber had closed forever.

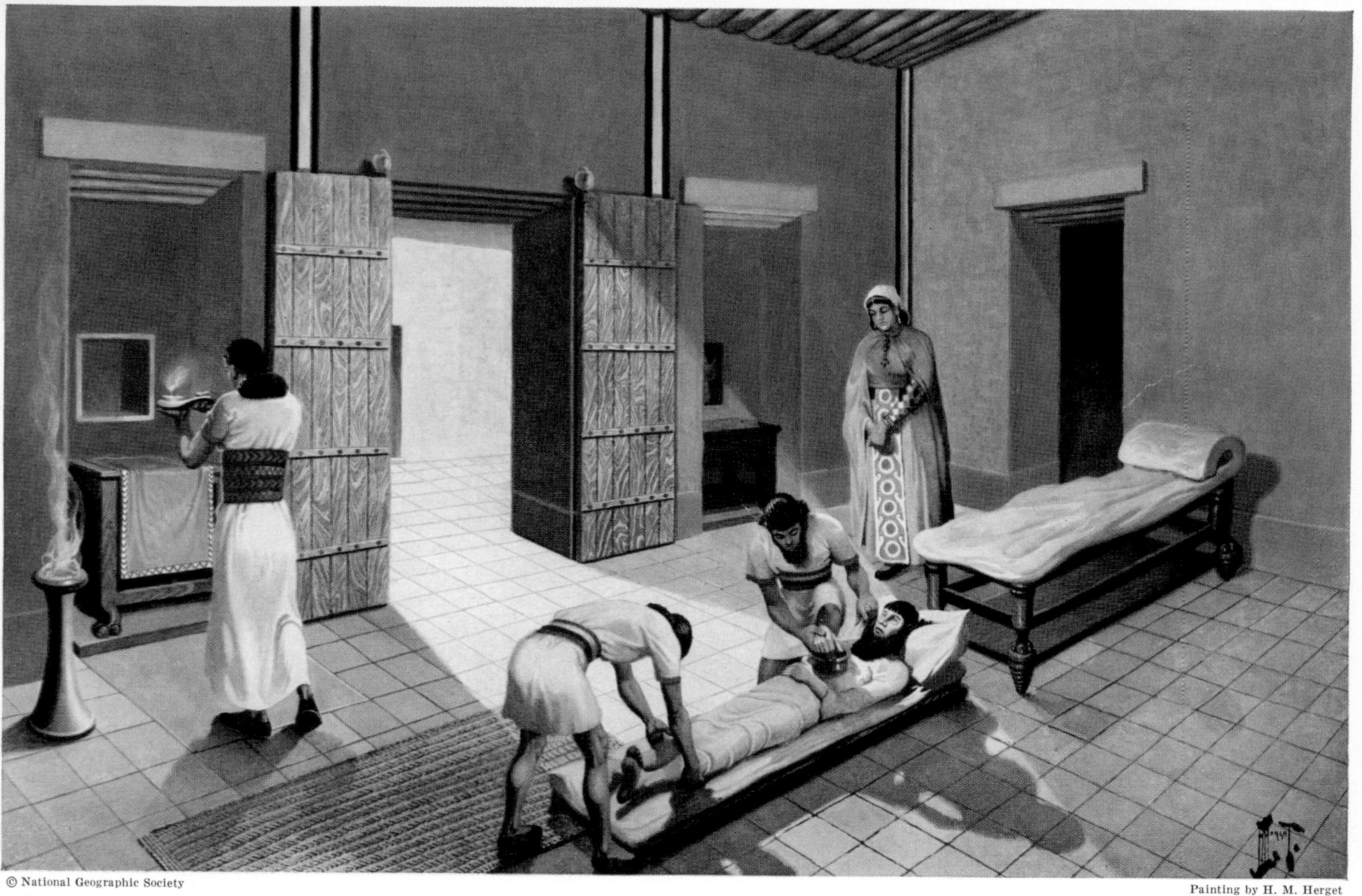

Painting by H. M. Herget

Ninth Century B. C. "The Canals Wail, the Watercourses Echo Them. Of Trees and Fruit the Face Is Darkened"—From an Assyrian Funeral Text

To the Victorious Assyrians Belong the Spoils

The expansion of Ashur northward brought with it successive transfers of the capital of Assyria, from Ashur to Calah (Nimrud), and later to Nineveh, where it was to remain till the fall of the empire, save for a brief interlude at Dur Sharrukin (modern Khorsabad).

These northward moves were already in evidence under Ashurnasirpal II (page 56). Yet throughout Assyrian history it was the city of Ashur that remained the religious capital of the state, the place where the rulers wished to be buried and where they sought the favor of the gods and protection from foes by building temples and fortifications.

Shalmaneser III, son and successor of Ashurnasirpal, was no exception to this trend. The exhaustive German excavations on the site have disclosed many phases of this king's care in keeping the whole city in good repair, and especially in strengthening its western portions, a section that until then had been particularly vulnerable to attack.

Our scene takes place before the west gate of Ashur, now a strong link in the massive chain that ringed the city from all sides. The spacious but well-protected interior of the gateway was broken up into two large halls with room for three pairs of heavy doors. These halls afforded ample space for guards. In one of these stood a large basalt statue of the king seated upon a cube-shaped throne.

No distraction must interfere with the brief intervals that were suitable for plowing. And the women might take a little time out from their daily chores and enjoy a quick bath—as they do in that district to this day—in a secluded spot where water had been left from the spring rains.

An Assyrian general has just returned from a successful campaign in the west. He stands at the foot of the ramp, ready to review his troops and survey the spoils.

Behind him stands an official dictating an account of the results to two scribes. One of these writes in cuneiform with stylus on clay, and the other, in Aramaic with pen on parchment. Both procedures have been recorded for us on the wall paintings uncovered by the French at Til Barsib.

The column is led by a horseman followed by three tribute bearers, one carrying a monkey and two others burdened with bows. Next comes an armed soldier escorting a group of women, Anatolian girls in embroidered coats and a desert woman in a fringed dress and with a shawl over her head. Following these are a battering ram, a detachment of the Assyrian infantry, and the first of a long procession of war chariots.

Shalmaneser III recorded his exploits and activities not only in the official annals of his reign and on reliefs of stone and bronze but also on the famous Black Obelisk of alabaster found at Calah. Fragments of another obelisk of the same ruler were recovered in Ashur.

Of the scenes depicted on this large monument, which stands well over six feet in height, perhaps the best known is the one that deals with the tribute of "Jehu, son of Omri," king of Israel. The monument was a record, in word and relief, of the king's military achievements down to the thirty-first year of his reign. But his account was not precise by modern standards; Omri was not the father of Jehu, but an Israelite king of another dynasty.

Painting by H. M. Herget

858–824 B. C. "To Rule and Subject in Anger the Foes of Ashur, He Sent Me Forth"—Annals of Shalmaneser III

The Ambassador from King Midas Marvels at the Wealth of Sargon's General

All the Assyrian rulers mentioned so far had been members of a single dynasty. The task of gradually raising the country to the status of a world power had apparently absorbed all the energies of its leaders and left little room for internal intrigue and revolt.

Toward the end of the 8th century B. C., however, the ancient dynasty had lost its grip on the land. Discontent was rife, especially in influential Ashur.

This was the juncture at which a forceful general stepped in to seize the reins and establish himself as king and head of a new royal house. Respecting tradition, he tried to make his subjects forget that he was a usurper. He manipulated his genealogy and took the name of Sargon (II), "The King Is Legitimate."

He sought to give his rule a fresh start by founding a new capital, about 12 miles north of Nineveh. He called the place Dur Sharrukin, or "Fortress of Sargon," Sargonburg.

Fate was kind to Sargon at first. In the year 721 B. C. had come the surrender of stubborn Samaria, the capital of the Kingdom of Israel. The land was converted into an Assyrian province and its name was to disappear as a political designation for nearly 27 centuries, until A. D. 1948.

The restless Sargon lacked the temperament to derive lasting enjoyment from his new title and his magnificent new capital. Within less than a score of years he was killed in battle, far from his native land.

He had managed in that short time to carry the might and the fear of Assyria to distant places which none of his predecessors had ever seen. Among these were the mountain fastnesses of Urartu, or Armenia, and the districts of Phrygia, ruled over by King Midas. Midas had to send a delegation to Assyria begging for peace.

Thanks to the recent excavations by the Oriental Institute of the University of Chicago at Khorsabad, the site of Dur Sharrukin, we now have many details from that impressive center unknown to the earlier excavators.

Of great importance are the wall paintings that were found in a residential building. The one here reproduced as the background for our composition is based on a reconstruction by the Oriental Institute. The residence in question was neither a part of the palace nor even the home of the vizier. It was merely the house of a high official.

The Assyrian's dress is amply attested on contemporary monuments, but the visitor's garb had to be pieced together from a number of scattered sources. He holds a straw fan in his right hand and a partly folded "foreign" cap in his left.

The painting that the Phrygian will talk about when he gets back home shows at the top a giant triad which consists of a god with rod-and-ring, receiving the homage of Sargon attended by one of his officials. The right hand of the king is raised and the forefinger extended in a characteristic gesture of supplication.

Winged genii of fertility form the inner border of the triad panel, much in the manner of borders on old Persian carpets. The same genii, but this time in kneeling position, fill two of the three registers in the lowest of the three friezes.

The middle register of the decoration is given over to representations of stylized animals.

Painting by H. M. Herget

721–705 B. C. "The Gods Who Dwell in Heaven and on Earth . . . Granted Me the Eternal Boon of Building That City and Growing Old in Its Midst"—Inscription of Sargon II

A Huge Guardian Statue Is Hauled Up the Slopes of Nineveh

Sargon's son and successor, Sennacherib, left a record of a vivid, versatile, and vindictive personality. Many proud cities felt the curse of his wrath, among them Babylon and Jerusalem. The echo of his Judean campaign still rings in our ears, thanks to the eloquence of Isaiah.

Because his relations with his stern father had been less than cordial, Sennacherib lost little time, on receipt of the news of Sargon's death, in abandoning Dur Sharrukin and erecting a new capital at Nineveh.

The result was a spacious center in which temples and palace were flanked by exotic parks. Although the Tigris flowed by the walls of Nineveh, Sennacherib got a steady supply of fresh mountain water for his capital by having his engineers construct an aqueduct from mountain springs 30 miles away.

The monumental buildings of Assyria were often guarded by gigantic sculptured demons. Set up in pairs against the side walls of the main entrance, these figures protected the building from all manner of evil influence.

Earlier types, from Ashurnasirpal's time to Sargon's, were shown in two views; from the front they appeared to be standing, but the side view showed them in motion. This dual position was achieved by means of a fifth leg.

Sennacherib's demons, as depicted on contemporary reliefs, reflect for the first time a more realistic treatment in dispensing with the fifth leg. Our scene attempts to sum up the story told by these reliefs.

At the foot of the Nineveh mound, near the confluence of the Khosar and the Tigris, is a large raft fastened to the right bank by long ropes. A sledge supporting a human-headed bull is being moved off the raft and up the slope.

Men standing on the raft pull at a huge wooden lever. Its lower end is wedged under the sledge by large rollers which are constantly being adjusted. The sledge itself is also on rollers. A bucket gang keeps the track wet.

Four long chains of captives are pulling the monstrous load of 40 tons up the slope. Each chain gang is directed by a supervisor and goaded by a man with upraised whip.

From the front of the raft the workers are urged on by one officer who claps his hands rhythmically, and another who employs a sort of speaking horn. The rich garb of the Assyrians contrasts sharply with the dress of the chain gangs.

Near the top of the slope stands the wheeled throne from which Sennacherib watches. The movable throne, held up by two beardless servants, is protected from the sun by a richly embroidered parasol attachment. A bearded official stands on one side, as two attendants with flywhisks are ready to act. All the Assyrians wear laced half-boots.

The king's guard consists of Greek shieldmen who can be identified by their helmets. They are armed either with lances or with bows and arrows. The lancers wear half-boots, but the archers have the sandals of earlier times.

Along the upper part of the slope moves a line of carts carrying props, spare rolls of rope, and other towering equipment. Down by the riverbank, water for the bucket gang is supplied by irrigation engines of a type still common.

The entire operation has attracted visitors from the opposite bank, who are using inflated skins to get across.

Painting by H. M. Herget

704–681 B. C. "White Limestone . . . the People of Enemy Lands . . . Quarried. I Turned It into Protective Bull Colossi for the Gates of My Palace"—Annals of Sennacherib

Queen Mother Naqiya-Zakutu Nips a Revolt in the Bud

In 809 B. C., when Shamshi-Adad V was as yet too young to discharge his duties as king of Assyria, the Queen Mother took over as regent for four years.

So impressed were her contemporaries with the performance of this woman—a feat unprecedented in the notably masculine social order of the Assyrians—that the fame of this queen, Sammuramat by name, eventually spread to distant lands. The Greeks made of her a composite character of some fact and much fable and handed her name down to posterity as Semiramis; but even their ready inventiveness failed to endow Semiramis with achievements equal to those of a later Assyrian queen, Naqiya-Zakutu.

We can tell from her name that Naqiya-Zakutu, one of the wives of Sennacherib, was of Canaanite origin, a native apparently of Palestine or Phoenicia. It may have been this marriage to an outsider that was responsible for Sennacherib's estrangement from his father Sargon. At any rate, Naqiya-Zakutu caused her royal husband to by-pass his older heirs by another wife, and appoint her own son, Esarhaddon, as crown prince.

For this favoritism Sennacherib paid with his life. His mother's counsel, however, helped Esarhaddon to crush the rebellion and later to extend Assyrian influence into another continent, by subjugating Egypt.

Nor did her amazing exploits cease with the death of her son. Her power reached down into the third generation, when her favorite grandson, Ashurbanipal, ascended the throne, once again ahead of an older heir apparent. It is tempting to speculate on what the matchless portrayer of Israelite King Saul or a Greek writer of genius might have done with a history of Naqiya-Zakutu's life and times.

Our scene brings together four members of the royal family in the palace garden, a place made familiar by the reliefs. The seated pair are Shamash-Shum-Ukin (the Saosduchin of the Greek sources), regent of Babylon, and his sister, the Princess Sherua-Eterat. They have been surprised by their grandmother, who is followed by their brother, King Ashurbanipal, as they were plotting the murder of their hated sovereign. The dowager queen will know how to put an end to such schemes.

Ashurbanipal is well known to us from his major reliefs, but there is also a less familiar plaque which shows us the two brothers together. The king's dress displays the rich embroidered folds of the north, whereas the regent wears the plainer garb of the Babylonians, characterized by its straight lines.

Both men have mustaches, following a fashion established in the preceding century. Their earrings, as well as those of the women, have been selected from among the many specimens of that period, for these ornaments changed with the times no less than other items of dress.

The attire of the women has been pieced together from sundry monuments. The features of the dowager queen had to be derived from imagination, which cannot but be stirred and stimulated by the fantastic career and the evident power and personality of the foreign-born queen, who could assert herself over three generations of kings that rank among the most illustrious monarchs of history.

Painting by H. M. Herget

Time of Ashurbanipal, 668–626 B. C. "You Who in Your Heart Are Hostile to Me, You Who Counsel and Discuss a Wicked Scheme . . . Concerning the Murder of Ashurbanipal!"—From an Assyrian State Letter

Painting by H. M. Herget

Time of Nebuchadnezzar II, 604–562 B. C. "By the Side of Ishtar of Babylon . . . All Babylon Goes Exultant"—A Babylonian New Year's Text

A Babylonian Procession Greets the New Year

With Assyria crushed and Nineveh razed to the ground, Babylon had at last the opportunity to regain the prominence and prestige that had been its lot more than a thousand years earlier, during the golden age of Hammurabi. Its fondest hopes were realized under the long and able rule of Nebuchadnezzar II.

The Old Testament remembers this king as the ruthless conqueror who destroyed Jerusalem in 586 B. C. Babylonian history, however, celebrates him primarily as the conscientious administrator and tireless builder who made his capital the greatest city of that time in the world.

To be sure, this brilliance was to be only temporary. Just as the end of Ashurbanipal's reign at Nineveh was separated by only a few years from that city's destruction, mainly at the hands of the Medes, so was Babylon's glory under Nebuchadnezzar to be followed by the triumph of another Iranian army, led this time by the great Persian king Cyrus, who occupied the ancient metropolis in 539 B. C.

The Babylon whose praises Herodotus sang was the Babylon that Nebuchadnezzar had fashioned. Among its many outstanding attractions was the famous Procession Street which passed under the unforgettably impressive Ishtar Gate. South of the Ishtar Gate, and along the west side of the great avenue, could be seen the fabulous "hanging" roof gardens and the seven-staged temple tower, the Tower of Babel, some three hundred feet tall.

The Procession Street got its name from the annual procession of the gods in connection with the New Year's festival. Assembled from all the provinces of the kingdom, the statues of the principal deities were first moved with solemn ceremony and in a rigidly observed order of precedence through the Ishtar Gate and out to the northern outskirts of the city. There they were transferred to boats and taken to the Garden Temple up the river.

Then followed the most dramatic part of the entire cycle, the consummation of the sacred marriage of the principal god and goddess, on which depended the fertility and prosperity of the whole land.

Our scene witnesses the joyous return of the procession, on the eleventh day of the month of Nisan, through the north side of the Ishtar Gate. The beautifully enameled decoration speaks for itself. The approximate dimensions of the north side of the Gate are 70 feet for the height of the towers and 35 feet for the height of the vaulted passageway; the width of the entrance was about 15 feet. The south end was considerably taller.

The gods are placed in so-called carriage boats, each decorated with gold, lapis, and carnelian. On the first boat rides Marduk, attended by four priests, one at each canopy post. Behind the first boat is the royal chariot drawn by three steeds; on it ride the driver, the king, and the parasol holder.

The second boat carries Marduk's consort, whose crown is surmounted by an eight-pointed star. Next comes a boat with the seated figure of the sun-god, Shamash. Hidden from view is a seemingly endless procession of other deities, whose name and rank are supplied by the texts.

The illustration is based on the carvings from Malatya, far north of Babylon. Each major city celebrated the festival in much the same way.

National Geographic Photographer B. Anthony Stewart

"I, Ramesses III, Won Victories in War and Sacrificed Richly to My Gods"

Such, in brief, is the context of the pictures and hieroglyphs with which he covered walls and pillars of his temple, now commonly called Medinet Habu, at Thebes. A wealth of gold, silver, and precious stones was also lavished on its ornamentation.

Daily Life in Ancient Egypt

By William C. Hayes

Department of Egyptian Art, the Metropolitan Museum of Art, New York

With 32 Paintings Illustrating the Life, Culture, and History of the Egyptians of the Three Periods from 3200 B. C. to 1788 B. C. by H. M. Herget, in Cooperation with the Author

IN THE last century and a half millions of cubic yards of the soil of Egypt have been moved and sifted, thousands of its native population have worked their lifetimes in its multitude of "digs," and hundreds of ships have sailed from its harbors, laden with antiquities for the museums and private collections of the five continents.

Yet today "the old mine" shows not the slightest sign of being exhausted. The records of the last 40 years of excavation are brighter than those of any previous period in the annals of Egyptian exploration.

"King Tut's" Tomb Opened in 1922

On November 4, 1922, one of the Earl of Carnarvon's workmen, under the direction of Howard Carter, uncovered in the Valley of the Tombs of the Kings at Thebes the uppermost of a flight of rock-cut steps leading down into the intact and fabulously rich tomb of King Tūt-ʿankh-Amūn.*

Eight years were required to clear the tomb of its magnificent contents. During this time as many as 400 persons a day—well-to-do Europeans and Americans—stood in line in the broiling heat of the royal valley for the privilege of peeping for two minutes into the half-empty sarcophagus chamber.

"King Tut" became a name familiar from Bering Strait to Timbuktu. To this day his much publicized "curse" is resurrected whenever one of the several thousand visitors to his tomb dies of old age or similarly suspicious causes.

Tūt-ʿankh-Amūn's treasures were still pouring out of his tomb when, in February, 1925, Dr. George A. Reisner, head of the Harvard-Boston Museum expedition at El Gîza (page 82), uncovered beside the Great Pyramid the tomb of the mother of its builder, Queen Ḥetep-ḥeres, wife of the great Snefru, founder of the Fourth Dynasty (2680-2560 B. C., pages 85 and 95).

Though the queen's beautiful alabaster sarcophagus was empty, her gold-mounted carrying chair and her canopy, bed, armchair, and jewel caskets, covered with finely chased gold, must be classed among the handsomest objects the valley of the Nile has ever yielded.

Meanwhile, at Saḳḳāreh (Saqqâra), 20 miles south, Cecil M. Firth, working for the Egyptian government, had begun to clear the huge and amazing architectural complex surrounding the step pyramid of King Djoser of the Third Dynasty. Here the visitor, wandering about the enclosure of this earliest of free-standing stone structures, may see the graceful wood and reed architecture of primeval times immortalized in glistening white limestone (pages 72, 74, and 92).

More than 30,000 Treasures Found

Entering the subterranean passages of the pyramid itself, one is hemmed in by tile-covered walls of a gorgeous turquoise blue. From these passages in 1936 James E. Quibell, Mr.

*** Notes on Symbols and Diacritical Marks**

ʿ (example Rēʿ) a guttural sound unknown to English (corresponds to Hebrew *ayin,* Arabic *ain*).

ḥ (example ḥotep) emphatic h (corresponds to Arabic ḥā).

ḳ (example Saḳḳāreh) backward k; rather like our q in "queen" (corresponds to Hebrew qōph, Arabic ḳāf); hence the map spelling Saqqara.

ṭ (example maṣṭabeh) a thick t, halfway between sharp t and th, spoken with the tongue pressed against the back of the front teeth.

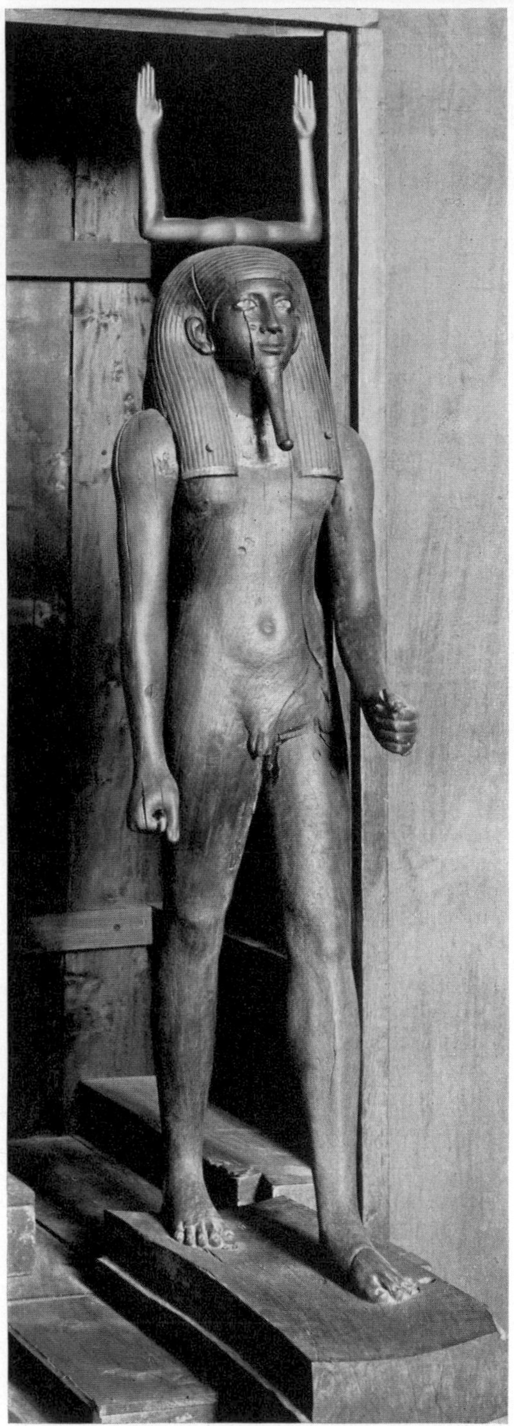
Metropolitan Museum of Art

Raised Arms Mean *Ka*, Spirit Double

They form a hieroglyph signifying the vital force the Egyptian believed was born as a counterpart with his body, lived with it, and accompanied it into the next world. This wooden statue of the *ka* of King Ḥor, co-regent of Amen-em-ḥēt III, was found in a pit tomb near the latter's pyramid at Dahshûr.

Firth's successor at Saḳḳāreh, extracted more than thirty thousand jars and bowls of alabaster and other fine stones—a small portion of the original contents of the plundered royal tomb.

For years the stupendous task of clearing and restoring the great temple of Amūn at El Karnak had been in progress, when in 1914 Monsieur Legrain of the Egyptian antiquities service began to investigate the internal filling of the temple's third huge pair of gateway towers. These towers, built under King Amen-ḥotpe III of the Eighteenth Dynasty, were found to be filled with hundreds of carved stone blocks from earlier structures.

In recent years Henri Chevrier, engineer of the antiquities service, has extracted from them the major parts of several magnificent buildings of the Middle Kingdom and early New Kingdom. The walls of these edifices are covered with yards of fine relief sculpture.

A few years ago the headlines told of a new Egyptian treasure found near Tôd, a little village in Upper Egypt. Here in the foundations of a little known temple Bisson de la Roque, of the Louvre, uncovered a set of copper caskets deposited four thousand years earlier by King Amen-em-ḥēt II of the Twelfth Dynasty. They contained Babylonian cylinder seals, silver cups, and ingots of gold, silver, and lead.

At Saḳḳāreh in 1930, Walter B. Emery, of the Egyptian government staff, began a truly epoch-making discovery—the enormous brick tombs of the kings and nobles of Egypt's First and Second historic Dynasties. From the chambers of these great structures Mr. Emery has already recovered more fine objects and more inscriptions of this little known period than had been found during the whole previous history of Egyptian excavation.

News from Ancient Egypt

More recently, important news from Egypt comes from Tanis (modern Sân el Hagar) in the Delta, where Professor Pierre Montet of the University of Strasbourg has run into a perfect nest of intact royal tombs of the Twenty-first and Twenty-second Dynasties, about a thousand years before Christ. Coming from these tombs, the solid silver coffin of King Sheshonḳ, who captured Jerusalem about 930 B. C.; the granite sarcophagus, gold mask, and gold vases of King Pa-sebkha'nu I; and the gold statuettes of King Amen-em-opet have graced the picture sections of our newspapers in the last two decades.

Readers of the Bible—First Kings and Second Chronicles—know Sheshonḳ as Shishak. Less sensational, but quite as important are the hitherto unknown prehistoric civilizations which have been brought to light in the west Delta, in the Fayyūm (Faiyûm), and in Middle Egypt by Professor Hermann Junker of Vienna, Miss Caton-Thompson of London, and Guy Brunton of the British School of Archaeology in Egypt.

For eight years, 1926 to 1933, an expedition, sent out by the University of Chicago, under the leadership of Messrs. Sandford and Arkell, scoured the desert regions adjacent to the Nile Valley, and gave us for the first time a clear picture of the Egyptians of the Old Stone Age and the conditions amid which they lived.

These few highlights of the last two decades of exploration in Egypt explain why public interest in the ancient dwellers along the Nile is as keen today as it was when James Henry Breasted was gathering the material for his *History of Egypt.*

Those Who Drink of the Nile Are Egyptians

Fourteen thousand years ago the rains which for centuries had made lush the tableland of northeast Africa were failing, and as a result game was becoming scarce on the plains on either side of the Nile.

This failure of Nature's bounty forced the prehistoric ancestors of the Egyptians to desert the plains and descend into the lower valley and rapidly forming delta of the great river. There they abandoned of necessity the nomadic life of the hunter and settled down to farming.

Ever since that time the distinctive national character of the Egyptian has been dominated by the 750 miles of broad, placid river which links the Nubian frontier with the Mediterranean Sea.

Boston Museum of Fine Arts

Men-kau-Rē's Queen Adds a Homely Touch to Royal Dignity

In the Museum of Fine Arts at Boston is this almost-life-size statue. It represents the builder of the Third Pyramid with his wife standing by his side. His tomb is the smallest of the three great pyramids at El Gîza. Sun-dried brick was substituted for granite in his mortuary temple. His handsome limestone sarcophagus was lost by shipwreck.

Staff Photographer B. Anthony Stewart

This Is the Oldest Free-standing Stone Structure in the World

Across the Nile from Cairo's fashionable suburban spa at Helwân, this 200-foot step-pyramid rises above the pebble-dotted sands of Saḳḳâreh. It started as a flat maṣṭabeh tomb (page 90), and passed through a series of developments to pyramidal form, thus marking the transition from the simpler to the more elaborate style.

Metropolitan Museum of Art

More than a Thousand Years of History Are Embraced in This One View at Thebes

In the foreground are tombs of the Ptolemaic period (page 167), from the time of Alexander to the day of Antony and Cleopatra. The site is that of a Ramessid temple, dating from the XXth Dynasty. The excavations are those of the Metropolitan Museum of Art during its 1935-36 season.

Here Are "Motion Pictures" Nearly 4,000 Years Old

This wrestling mural, found in the funerary chapel of Baḳet at Beni Hasan, could almost be cut into strips and mounted in a Zoetrope, the device which first showed the persistence of shifting images in the human eye.

"Egypt," declared the ancient oracle of the god Amūn, "is the land watered by the Nile in its course; and those who dwell below the city Elephantine and drink that river's water are Egyptians."

Egypt's prehistory, revealed by excavations of the last 55 years, began before 13,000 B. C. This date marks a point late in the North African Palaeolithic, or Old Stone Age.

From a primitive hunting people, equipped with a single crude flint implement, the Palaeolithic fist-axe, the early Nile dwellers required more than five thousand years to settle down into permanent encampments and to develop bone, shell, and flint implements of refined and diversified types.

The dawn of the Neolithic period, or New Stone Age, about 5000 B. C., brought with it, in addition to new types of stone tools and weapons, the manufacture of pottery vessels, the erection of light wood, reed, and mud houses, the cultivation and storage of cereal grains, the domestication of useful animals, and the establishment of fixed burial customs and funerary beliefs.

From here on the tempo was increased. By 3800 B. C. the Egyptian was producing decorated pottery, stone vessels and mace heads, bone and ivory utensils of many varieties, slate palettes for grinding cosmetics, beads and other items of personal adornment, and crude statuettes modeled in clay or carved in bone or ivory. He had even mastered the art of spinning and weaving linen cloth.

In the succeeding six hundred years metal tools and weapons, heretofore very rare, began to come into widespread use.

It was during this last period that the people of Egypt, hitherto divided politically into some twoscore small, independent districts, or "nomes," ruled by "nomarchs," united themselves into two clearly defined states—the Kingdom of Upper Egypt (the Nile Valley) and the Kingdom of Lower Egypt (the Delta).

Cultural and political differences had always existed between the people of the Delta and

From "*Beni Hasan*" by N. de G. Davies

They Decorate Tomb Walls of the Nomarch of the Oryx Province

By contrasting body colors of the Egyptian athlete and his negro opponent the ancient sports artist made clear the holds, many of which are identical with those used today. A similar match is depicted in color on page 116.

their hardier, but more backward, neighbors to the south; and by 3200 B. C. (the time represented in our first plate, page 88) the two kingdoms were locked in a long and bitter war for the control of the country—a war which, with the ultimate victory of Upper Egypt, about 3000 B. C., led to the birth of Egypt as a united nation and the inauguration—under Menes, the first true Pharaoh—of its 27 centuries of dynastic history.

Egyptians Are Africans

Like their neighbors and kinsmen, the Libyans, the Bedjas, the Somali, and the Galla, the Egyptians are, and always have been, Africans, members of the African or "Hamitic" branch of the brown, "Mediterranean" race. This long-headed, lightly built, brunet people, medium of stature and sparse of beard, are found throughout the whole of the Mediterranean area.

Toward the end of the Fourth Millennium B. C., just before the rise of the historic or "dynastic" period, there began to filter into Egypt, apparently from Asia, a broad-headed, "Armenoid" people, who did much to improve the native Nilotic stock physically and intellectually, but failed to alter to any appreciable extent its fundamental character.

Since this most important of all the influxes of outsiders, Egypt has been invaded by the representatives of a score of different peoples and nations: negroes, Asiatics, and Aegeans, Assyrians, Persians, Greeks, Romans, Byzantines, Arabs, and Turks.

Yet the native type, entrenched in its long, narrow river valley, has held out so tenaciously against all intruders that the Egyptian of today is to all intents the same man as the Egyptian of the 20th century B. C.

Contrary to the picture drawn of him by insufficiently informed and sensational writers of the last two thousand years, the ancient Egyptian was, like his modern descendant, a simple, cheerful, and thoroughly likable fellow. Though intelligent and quick to learn,

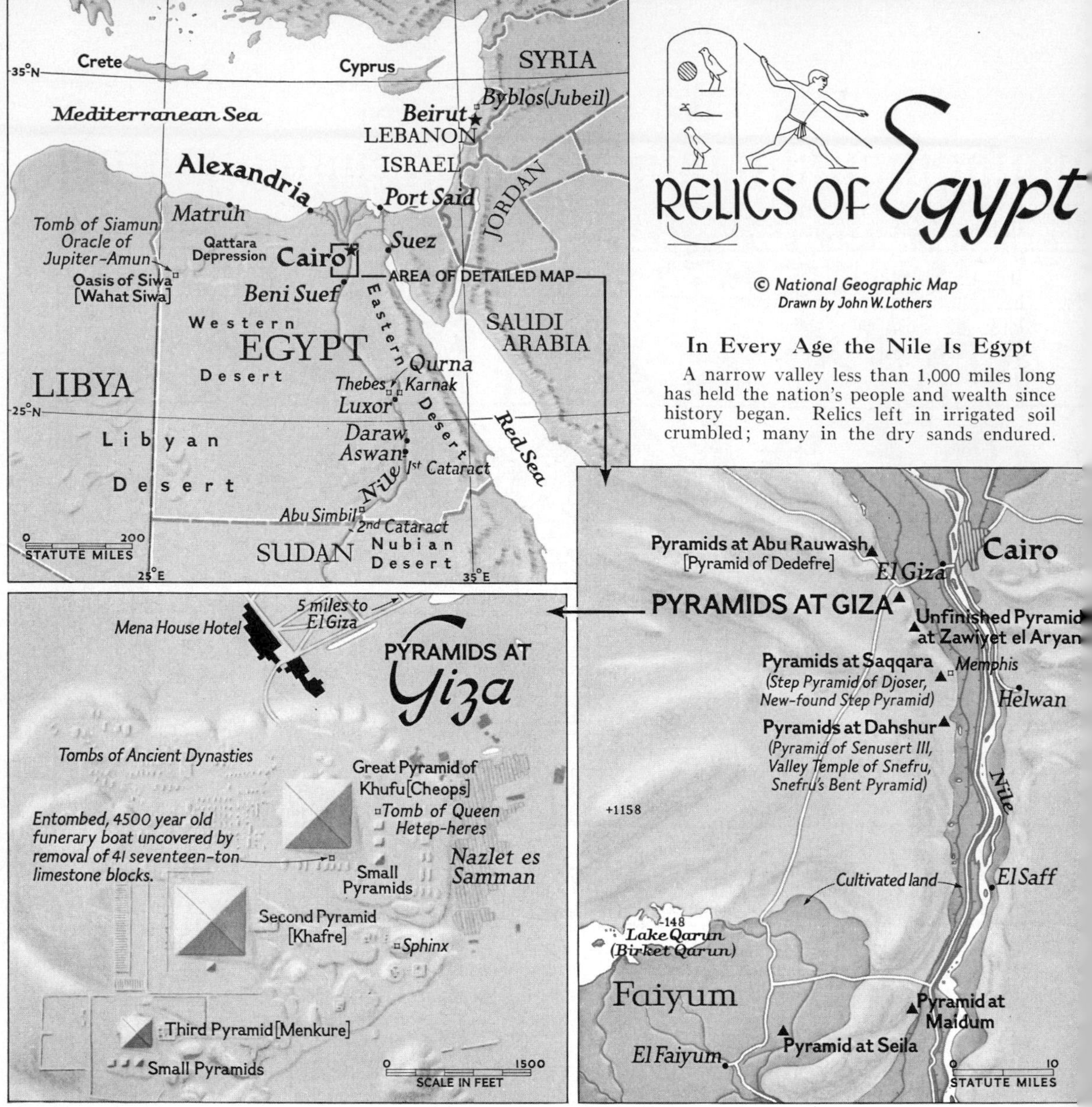

RELICS OF Egypt

© National Geographic Map
Drawn by John W. Lothers

In Every Age the Nile Is Egypt

A narrow valley less than 1,000 miles long has held the nation's people and wealth since history began. Relics left in irrigated soil crumbled; many in the dry sands endured.

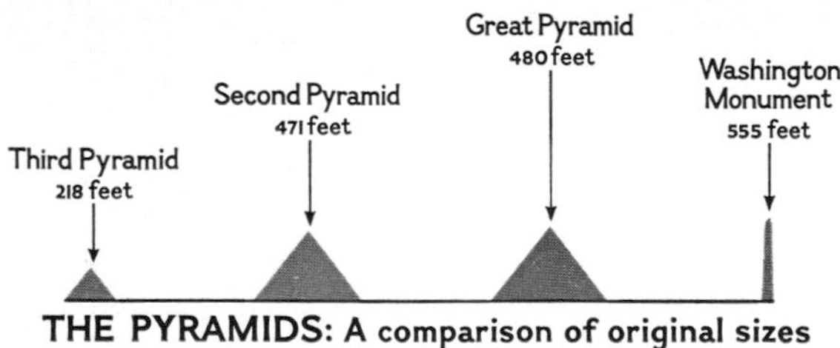

THE PYRAMIDS: A comparison of original sizes

he had a practical, unimaginative mind.

He was a materialist, not given to deep speculative thought and unable to evolve or to express a purely abstract idea. His profession and his natural talent for hard work made him perhaps the most industrious of all the peoples the earth has ever known.

Although he invented virtually nothing, the uses to which he applied the inventions of others permitted him to attain a dominant position among the nations of the ancient world for more than three thousand consecutive years, and to achieve a civilization which in many respects has remained unequaled until modern times.

His outstanding practical asset was his great talent for organization, exhibited primarily in the orderly and efficient marshaling of manpower and materials, and in the careful administration of the affairs of the home, the town, and the state.

The pyramids are the result of this talent—and not of the Egyptian's mechanical genius. His mechanical devices were few and crude, and remained so during the whole of his dynastic history. The dynastic Egyptian, for example, never knew the pulley or the block and tackle, and never developed them, although he employed ropes extensively.

The Egyptian's chief personal virtues have always been his essential gentleness; his devotion to family, friends, king, and gods; his tolerance; his utter lack of snobbishness; and his hearty sense of humor.

He has been, to be sure, at times illogical and inconsistent in his beliefs and thought processes, uninquisitive, ridiculously conservative, highly superstitious, frequently petty, and, when threatened by danger, likely to become panicky and vindictive and to indulge in outbursts of childish cruelty.

Ancient Egyptian Not Weird but Human

On the whole, however, his good qualities have outweighed his faults. If not the most brilliant, he was certainly the most human, the most understandable, and the most pleasant of the peoples of his time.

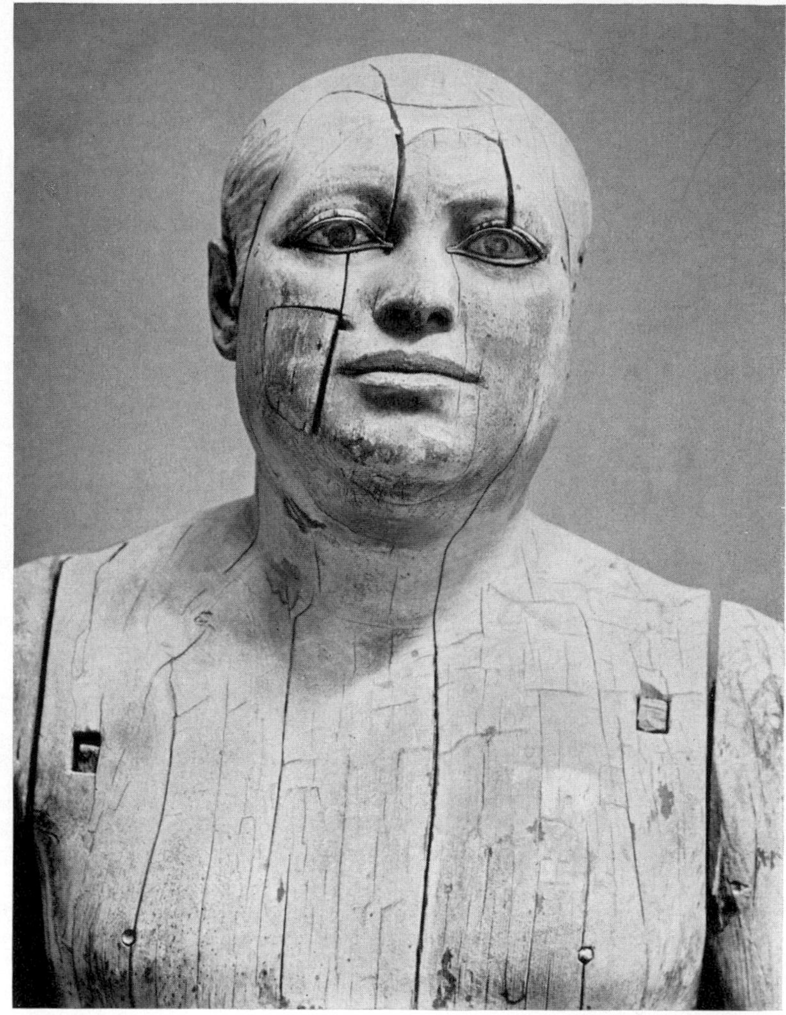

Metropolitan Museum of Art

To Modern Egyptian Diggers This Resembled Their Mayor

In 1860, when Auguste Mariette was combing Egypt for specimens for his new museum, archeology was largely treasure-hunting, and this superb wooden statue was a rich prize. It was recognized as a portrait figure of Ka Aper, a priest-reader, of the Vth Dynasty, 2560-2420 B. C. (page 103). When the quartz eyes, set in copper lids, appeared from the earth, the workers cried "Sheikh el Beled" (Chief of the Village) and thus the statue is popularly known today.

His greatest contribution to the world's culture was his art—the naïve and honest product of great technical skill used primarily to represent and record all that the Egyptian regarded as fine, interesting, or enjoyable in himself, his life, his deeds, his possessions, and his natural environment. The whole was governed and characterized by the sense of dignity, the charm, and the impeccable taste, which seem to have been inbred in the Nilotic artist.

The social and political organization of ancient Egypt presented something of a paradox. Outwardly an absolute, hereditary monarchy ruled by a king, who even during his lifetime was regarded as a god, it was actually a country in which personal merit and personal ability, almost unaided, could determine a man's social and political status.

Family in the modern social sense counted for little or nothing. Only during certain limited periods was there a true hereditary aristocracy.

Men born peasants could and frequently did raise themselves by their own efforts to the highest offices in the land, and on several occasions to the kingship itself.

Though intensely devout, the ancient Egyptian had neither the mental nor the spiritual equipment necessary to the creation or even the adaptation of a great religion.

An analysis of the Egyptian religion shows it consisted of at least four unrelated cults

Rolling Back the Desert, Diggers Open the Newly Discovered Step Pyramid at Saqqara

Built block on block so that the sides rose in giant stairs, the step pyramids preceded the Bent Pyramid (second from right) and true pyramid (right). This buried monument is believed to have belonged to King Sekhemkhet. It was found in 1952 by Zakaria Ghoneim of the Egyptian Department of Antiquities.

or phases, no one of which ever passed beyond what we should regard as a primitive stage.

The Egyptian's conceptions of resurrection and life after death were as many and as various as his religious cults and their accompanying mythologies. He had, however, two all-important convictions: (1) that he *was* immortal and that not only his spirit but his whole ego would continue to live on after his mundane existence was ended; and (2) that his life beyond the grave was to be a somewhat exalted version of his life on earth.

The first conviction, eliminating, as it did, much of his natural fear of death, combined with his sunny disposition to make him one of the most cheerful peoples in history.

The second led him to provide his spirit not only with a home in which to dwell but also with all the material possessions and surroundings which it had needed and loved during its earthly existence.

The line of great royal pyramids, stretching from Cairo some 60 miles up the Nile, is the most striking expression of this idea and at the same time a poignant witness to the futility of it all. Built to preserve the dead, at enormous cost to the living, these tombs have without exception fallen prey to the ever-present grave robber.

Both the Pharaohs and their treasures have been dragged from their resting places and only the empty stone monuments remain as memorials to man's belief. To this simple faith, however, the museums of the world owe their Egyptian treasures.

The dry climate of the valley of the Nile made Egypt a perfect storehouse for preserving the innumerable records which its people loved to collect and put away. Filmy linen, delicate furniture of reed and wood, textiles, papyrus, paintings, which would have perished in the damp climates of Greece and Italy, have survived 3,000 to 4,000 years in Egypt, with texture and color undimmed by time.

The language of the ancient Egyptians is related not only to those of the other Hamitic peoples of North and East Africa but also to the Semitic languages of western Asia. Its principal characteristics are its realism and nicety of expression, its large, rich vocabulary, its insistence on strict word order, and its tendency to be formal, rigid, and conventional.

Writing first appears in Egypt at the time of the first historic dynasty, about 3000 B. C. Already at a fairly advanced stage when we first encounter it, the written language developed rapidly during the Early Dynastic Period, and by the Old Kingdom had achieved the form to which it adhered, with surprisingly few changes, for 2,500 years (page 135).

They Knew Their Calendar Was Wrong

Carved or painted in monumental hieroglyphs or written cursively in the "hieratic" script, it was the ancient Egyptian's most highly valued asset. It was used constantly, extensively, and for every conceivable purpose, from tomb inscriptions to stories, songs, letters, deeds, labels, and lists of all kinds.

Most of the picture signs with which this language was written were used also with straight phonetic value. When so employed, each stood for one or a group of the 24 consonantal and vocalic sounds in the language, the quality and number of the sounds represented depending on the individual sign. Vowels were not written. Hence a diversity of spelling Egyptian proper names in modern languages.

During the dynastic period the Egyptian dated events by the reigns and regnal years of his kings. He had, in addition, a civil year of 365 days—three seasons of four 30-day months each, with five intercalary days tacked on at the end to fill out what he conceived to be a true solar year.

This calendar, standardized about 2780 B.C., the ancient Egyptian maintained throughout the whole of his history. He was aware of the error resulting from his omission of the extra day every fourth year but was unable to correct it and apparently indifferent to it.

The Graeco-Egyptian historian, Manetho of Sebennytos (280 B. C.) grouped the historic kings of Egypt into 30 dynasties. His record seems to have been based on reliable sources, and is still employed as a convenient method of dating. The word *dynasty* means a family.

Our first painting (page 88) pictures the time shortly before the first historic dynasty, the "Protodynastic Period" (3200-3000 B. C.).

Succeeding paintings portray a number of reconstructed scenes and incidents from the Ist Dynasty (Early Dynastic Period, 3000-2780 B. C.), the IIIrd, IVth, Vth, and VIth Dynasties (Old Kingdom, 2780-2270 B. C.), and the XIth and XIIth Dynasties (Middle Kingdom, 2160-1788 B. C.).

King Tut-ankh-Amun Went to His Tomb with This Brightly Painted Boat

Egyptians believed that magic restored their mummified kings to life, expanded their funerary craft into barges, and sped them along the celestial Nile. In 1954, three decades after Tut-ankh-Amun's tomb (14th century B. C.) at Thebes yielded its boat, a dismantled craft some 1,200 years older was uncovered at Khufu's Great Pyramid at Giza (map, page 78). These Americans view King Tut's boat in the Egyptian Museum at Cairo.

David S. Boyer, National Geographic Staff

Staff Photographer B. Anthony Stewart

Near Man's Hugest Monuments a Silent Sphinx Stands Guard after Forty-five Centuries

At the right is the Great Pyramid of Khufu; at the left the Second Pyramid, built by the king Khaʿ-ef-Rēʿ. Carved from living rock in the shape of a lion with the head of the king, the Sphinx looks down on stonework which has been freed repeatedly from sand drifts. To insure the safety of their bones and hence their grasp on eternal life, and to perpetuate their memories, the Pharaohs made the building of mighty pyramids Public Works Project Number One. Yet sacrilegious grave robbers soon emptied these vaults, and builders of Cairo found the casings of them handy quarries from which to obtain ready cut stone.

Boston Museum of Fine Arts

Close-packed Maṣṭabeh Tombs Are Seen from the Summit of the Great Pyramid

When the kings and queens began constructing pyramids, the nobles and lesser members of the royal families took over the older style of sepulture. These houses of the dead were laid out in rows to form streets like those of a village.

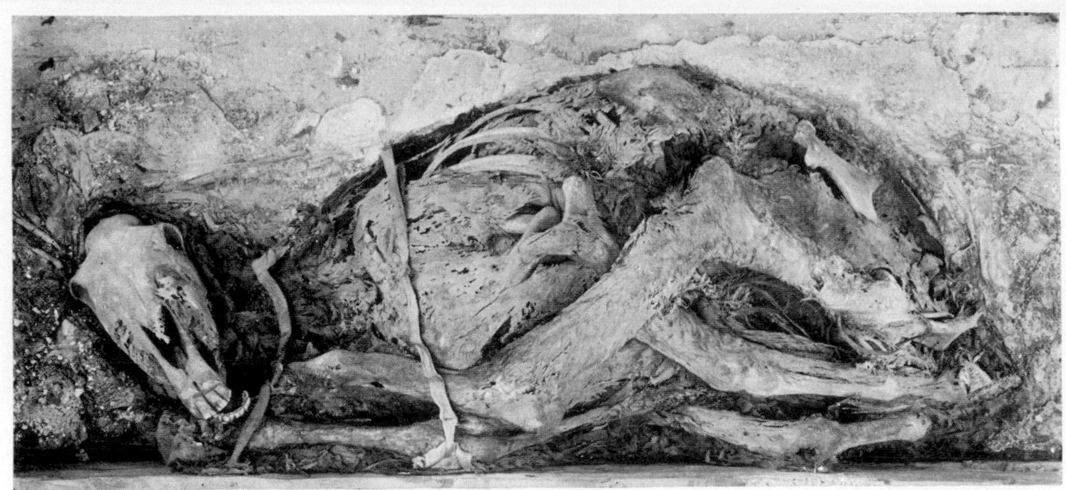

Metropolitan Museum of Art

About 1490 B.C. a Horse Was Given an Elaborate Burial

It was found near an XVIIIth Dynasty tomb wrapped in bandages and enclosed in a huge coffin. Soon after being introduced into Egypt by the Hyksos, these animals were considered so precious as to merit the highest honors. This one, of Arab type, was interred with its saddle. Note girths on neck and shoulders.

Metropolitan Museum of Art

In a Chariot with Rawhide Tires, Priest Yuaa Rode Out to Watch His Son-in-law's Stupendous Building Operations at Luxor

The horse had only recently been introduced into Egypt. Yet this light, graceful cart with its body sheathed with embossed leather, is a masterpiece of refinement. Although the animal shown in the burial above was interred with its saddle, the Egyptians were not riding enthusiasts. They preferred to travel by carriage. The owner's daughter was the wife of Amen-ḥotpe III.

Metropolitan Museum of Art

Ancient Egyptians Enjoyed Mechanical Toys

These ivory dancing dwarfs were spun by strings passing through the holes in the base. They were found in 1934 in a maṣṭabeh northeast of the Pyramid of King Se'n-Wosret I at El Lisht.

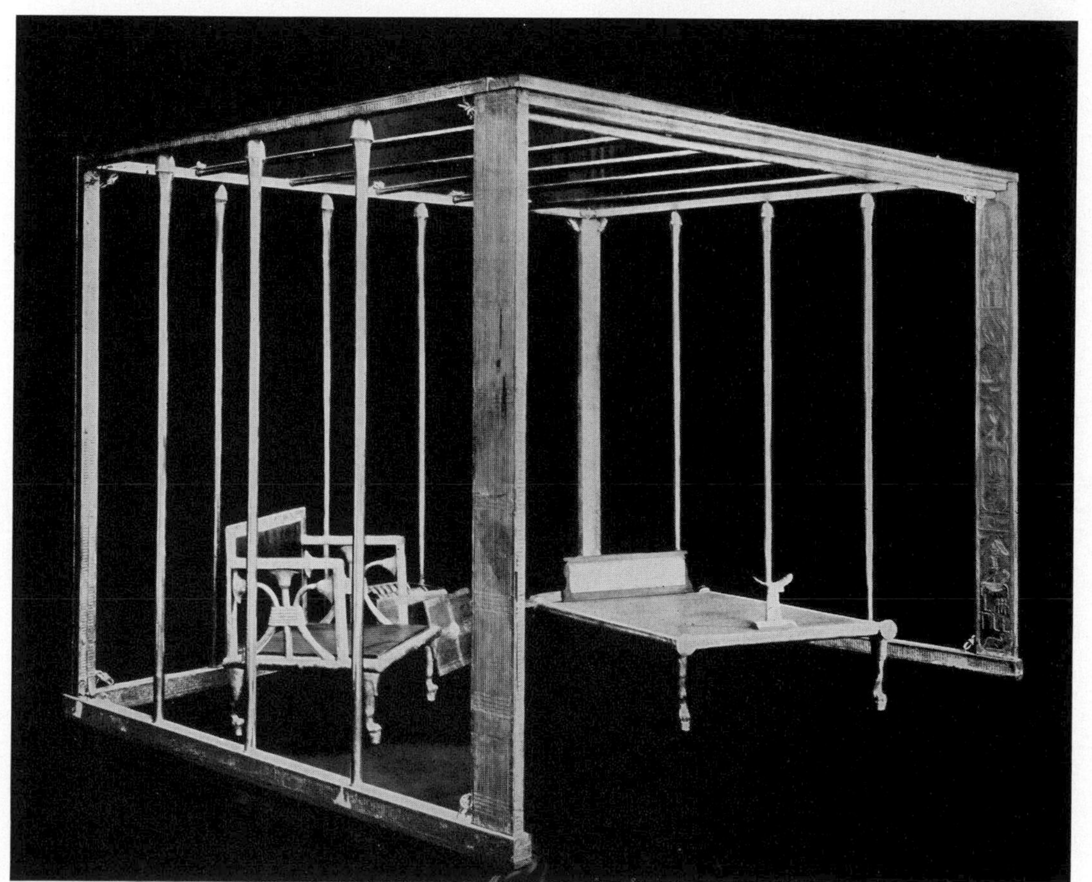

Boston Museum of Fine Arts

While Khufu Built His Pyramid, His Mother Slept under This Gold-plated Canopy

The names of her royal husband, Snefru, decorate the gold-covered wooden uprights of Hetep-heres' bedroom. On an alabaster headrest padded with fine linen, she laid her head. Papyrus plants curve in graceful patterns on her armchair. The Harvard-Boston Museum Expedition found this fragile furniture east of the Great Pyramid at El Gîza in 1925.

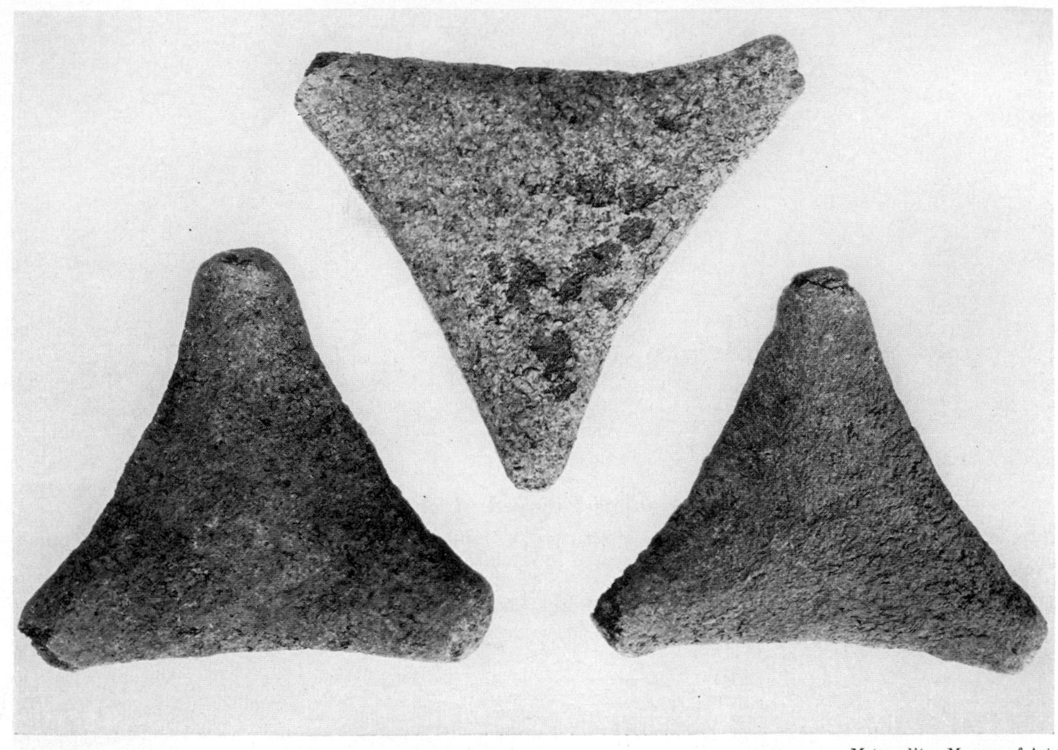

Metropolitan Museum of Art

These Loaves of Bread Are 3,500 Years Old

They were found in "digs" at Thebes and are now in the Metropolitan Museum of Art, New York. Made of coarse barley flour with the husks left in, they resemble in texture some of the "health" bakery products of today. Three and a half millenniums have rendered them exceedingly dry and hard, but they are not petrified. Aside from age-long staleness, they remain exactly as they were when they were baked. There is no truth, however, in widely circulated stories of seeds of grain recovered from the pyramids sprouting and producing plants when placed in watered soil. Numerous experiments have proved that the germs are dead.

Metropolitan Museum of Art

Three Pieces of This Ancient "Vanity" Are Treasured in Paris and London

Around the circular space in which cosmetics were prepared in prehistoric times, a spirited lion hunt has been going on for 5,000 years. The sculptured fragments were found by modern Egyptians and sold. One reached the Louvre, two the British Museum. In making the painting reproduced in color on page 88 the artist used for models the figures depicted on the ancient palette and thus obtained details which render the scene entirely accurate.

Bedouin Boosters Help the Visitor up the Great Pyramid's Jagged Slope

Many of the 2,300,000 blocks of this mightiest of monuments were quarried out and barged across the Nile from the Moḳattam (Muqattam) Hills. The ascent has been enjoyed or tolerated by generations of visitors. "Bakshish (tipping) is optional," says Baedeker, but the Arab helpers take up the option along with the climber.

Painting by H. M. Herget

". . . In the Time of the Primeval Kings"

Hunters of the prehistoric kingdom of Lower Egypt return to their town in the northwest Delta, bearing a slain lion. Their passing attracts the attention of a woman who has been working in an irrigated field and she gazes admiringly at them. (Protodynastic Period, 3200-3000 B. C.)

Life in Lower Egypt Before the Dawn of History

A BAND of protodynastic Egyptians, fresh from a successful lion hunt along the desert's edge, are returning to the town of Saïs, capital of an important nome, or district, in the northwest Delta.

The town, raised on its earth embankment above the partly inundated swampland which comprised most of the Kingdom of Lower Egypt, is surrounded by a stout mud wall, topped by a high reed parapet. In the center of the town stands the towered palace of the "nomarch" (prince of the district), and, behind this, the fenced enclosure and hoop-roofed shrine of the local goddess, Neït.

The standard of the goddess—a pair of arrows crossed behind an 8-shaped shield, the whole mounted on a tall pole—stands before the shrine. Emblem of the district as well as the divinity, the device surmounts a palace tower also.

Like the shrine, the houses of the town, ranged in regular streets around the central buildings, are of the typical Lower Egyptian form, with the curved roof and prominent corner posts, seen in stone buildings, coffins, and reliefs and paintings of the historic period. All the buildings are of light wood and wickerwork construction, their elaborately recessed door and window openings closed by strips of brightly colored grass matting.

In the cultivated field, water, dipped by hand from the irrigation canal, is being transferred in slow stages from one square compartment, or basin, to another by the breaching of the small dikes which separate the squares; men are furrowing the rich black soil with wooden mattocks; and a woman with an infant on her back is pausing from similar toil to view the hunters and their quarry. She is clad in a woven linen mantle and wears in her hair a carved ivory comb and hairpin.

The hunters, like their neighbors and kinsmen, the Libyans, are tattooed on their arms and legs and wear ostrich feathers stuck into their thick, wavy hair. The wolf tails, swinging from the backs of their short grass hunting kilts, were believed to endow them with the strength, fleetness, and ferocity of that animal. Their bows are of the long, recurved, African type, their arrows of reed with chisel-shaped, hard stone tips.

Their other weapons include the remarkably fine, curved flint knife produced at this period, the double axe, also of hard stone, the wooden throw-stick, or boomerang, the mace with the pear-shaped stone head, the flint-tipped lance, and the lasso of palm-fibre rope.

Their strange black dogs are of an extinct breed, the appearance of which is preserved to us in later representations of the animal of the god Anubis, the watchdog of the tomb.

In making this painting and those which follow, the artist has sought verisimilitude. With the aid of the author he has selected wherever possible and used as models authentic objects unearthed in the Egyptologists' "digs."

NOTE: The quoted capline accompanying each painting is in every case an excerpt from the writings of the ancient Egyptians themselves, as preserved either in their papyri or in the monumental inscriptions in their tombs and temples.

Painting by H. M. Herget

"A Smasher of Foreheads Is He . . . He Spares Not and There Is No Remnant"

The "Horus" Na'r, King of Upper Egypt, "mops up" in one of his most notable victories over the peoples of the Delta—victories which led to his complete conquest of Lower Egypt and his welding together of the Two Kingdoms into one united nation. (Beginning of the Ist historic Dynasty, 3000 B. C.)

A King of Upper Egypt Conquers the Delta and Unites the Two Kingdoms

ABOUT 3000 B. C. the long war between the Two Kingdoms, or, as the Egyptians called them, "the Two Lands," was brought to an abrupt and permanent end. An Upper Egyptian king, whose official name as the earthly representative of the god Horus was *Naʿr,* finally led the armies of the federated nomes of the south to a series of decisive victories over the north.

He invaded and subdued the whole of the Delta, and proclaimed himself "King of Upper and Lower Egypt," uniting the two parts of his country under one central rule and founding the long line of its prehistoric kings.

It is highly probable that this Naʿr, whose personal name is unknown, is Egypt's great legendary hero, King Menes the Thinite, reputed founder of the Ist Dynasty.

In our plate we see Naʿr and his Upper Egyptian army, already near the end of their successful campaign, routing in battle the hosts of the Waʿ-shi, a west Delta folk, apparently of considerable importance. The right of dispatching the wounded enemy chief has been reserved for the king himself, and his heavy mace, with its alabaster head and gold-plated handle, is about to descend on the skull of the helpless man.

Naʿr's short linen garment is girdled at the waist by an elaborate beadwork belt, supporting a bead sporran, each pendant of which is topped by the gold cow head of the goddess Ḥat-Ḥor. From the back of the belt hangs an animal's tail, from now on one of the regular attributes of Egyptian kingship. Naʿr wears on his head the tall, white, helmet-like crown of Upper Egypt, which he is soon to unite with its counterpart, the red, wicker-work crown of Lower Egypt.

On the king's left is his vizier, or prime minister, clad in a panther skin, and behind him stands his orderly with his sandals and oil jar.

Outlined against the sky, above the companies of archers and spearmen, appear the standards of the more important nomes of Upper Egypt, among which we may recognize the hawks of Hierakonpolis and Idfu and the wolf of Asyût.

The more effectively to govern his newly subjugated northern domain King Naʿr Menes moved his capital and residence from the south to a site a few miles above the apex of the Delta. There, according to ancient tradition, he founded the great city of "White Wall," more familiar to us under its Greek name, "Memphis." The hoary antiquity of the city of Memphis has recently been attested by the discovery nearby of a royal cemetery dating from the First Dynasty and containing, among others, the tomb of Naʿr's immediate successor, the Horus ʿAḥa.

© National Geographic Society

Painting by H. M. Herget

"It Will Be Thy Counsel That Causeth the Work to Be Accomplished . . . My Majesty Desired"

King Djoser and his architect, the great I-em-ḥotep, survey the royal pyramid at Saḳḳâreh (Saqqâra) from the east wall of its enclosure. (IIIrd Dynasty, reign of Djoser, 2780-2762 B. C.) The buildings in the court are replicas in stone of the primitive dwellings and shrine appearing on page 88.

King Djoser and the Wise I-em-ḥotep Usher in the Old Kingdom

During the reigns of the 18 kings of the Ist and IInd Dynasties the development of the newly united nation was rapid. When, about 2780 B. C., Djoser, the Memphite, came to the throne as the first king of the IIIrd Dynasty, the Egyptians already possessed the political and administrative organization, the material equipment, and the cultural background requisite to the inauguration of that great era which we know as the Old Kingdom.

It was Djoser's chief counselor, the same I-em-ḥotep, who, by his grandiose achievements in architecture and the allied arts and sciences, reaped the fruits of the preceding centuries of development; and, in doing so, established the standards and conventions which from now on governed Egyptian life, culture, and art.

Though the king was evidently a strong and able ruler, his fame has been almost completely overshadowed by that of I-em-ḥotep, a man renowned from his own day to this as an architect, a physician, a priest, a magician, a writer, and a maker of proverbs. Twenty-five hundred years after his death "he had become a god of medicine, in whom the Greeks who called him Imouthes, recognized their own Asklepios."

I-em-ḥotep's outstanding accomplishment as an architect is the step pyramid and extensive funerary complex which he built for Djoser at Saḳḳâreh (Saqqâra) south of modern Cairo and near the ancient capital city of Memphis. The pyramid, the earliest free-standing stone structure known, towers 190 feet above the desert plateau and is surrounded on all four sides by a vast walled enclosure, containing an elaborate group of shrines, storehouses, altars, courts, gateways, and secondary tombs—a veritable city in itself, planned and executed as a single unit and built throughout of fine white limestone from the near-by Muqattam Hills.

These remarkable buildings, excavated in recent years by the Egyptian government's expedition at Saḳḳâreh, are replicas in stone of the light wood, reed, and brick structures of earlier times, their columns, roofs, cornices, and walls preserving every structural and ornamental detail of the primitive and traditional house and temple forms.

On page 92 we stand with the king and his architect on the east girdle wall at Saḳḳâreh and gaze across the court of the *ḥeb sed,* or royal jubilee festival, at the pyramid (page 74).

The striped linen cover of Djoser's massive wig, is one of numerous henceforth traditional forms of headdress worn by the kings of Egypt. His artificial beard, another of the common insignia of kingship, derives from the smaller but genuine chin beards affected by the earliest Pharaohs (page 90). I-em-ḥotep wears the leopard-skin uniform proper to one of his many offices—that of priest.

Painting by H. M. Herget

"Mother of the King of Upper and Lower Egypt, Follower of Horus, Guide of the Ruler, Favorite Lady"

The Dowager Queen "whose every word is done for her, daughter of the god of his body, Ḥetep-ḥeres," pays a call on her son, King Khufu, builder of the Great Pyramid. These quotations are inscribed on the back of the queen's carrying chair, now in the Cairo Museum. (IVth Dynasty, reign of Khufu, 2656-2633 B. C.)

The Builder of the Great Pyramid Receives a Visit from His Mother

The time is the early IVth Dynasty, about 2650 B. C.; the place, a corridor leading into the throne room, or audience hall, in the king's palace at El Gîza.

On the throne dais at the rear of the hall sits the King of Upper and Lower Egypt, Khufu, the builder of the largest and most enduring tomb monument in history: a pyramid 767 feet at the base, 479 feet high, and containing 3,277,000 cubic yards of solid masonry—some 2,300,000 blocks of stone, each weighing on the average of two and a half tons.

Khufu, or, as the Greeks called him, Cheops, wears the Red Crown of Lower Egypt and is attended by his two fan-bearers and his master of ceremonies, the Overseer of the Audience Hall, seen advancing to meet the cortège.

The queen-mother, Ḥetep-ḥeres, widow of the great Snefru, founder of the IVth Dynasty, is borne into the presence of her son in her gold-mounted carrying chair, raised high on the shoulders of four courtiers and followed by a group of fashionably dressed ladies of the royal harīm. Her pet dwarf waddles along under the chair, a picture of licensed impudence—ancient Egyptian counterpart of a medieval European court jester.

The student of ancient Egypt will immediately recognize the composite quality of this picture. The queen's carrying chair and silver anklets we know to have been the property of Ḥetep-ḥeres; for they were found in February, 1925, by the Harvard-Boston Expedition in her tomb on the east side of the Great Pyramid, together with a quantity of other splendid items of her personal property—all now in the Egyptian Museum in Cairo.

The gold tiara which the queen wears, on the other hand, is borrowed from another IVth Dynasty woman, whose tomb was recently discovered at El Gîza. Her wig is from the well known and nearly contemporary statue of the Princess Nofret.

The faience "matting" tiles in the corridor and the doorway into the audience hall are taken from the tomb of King Djoser of the preceding dynasty. The diorite stand to the right of the doorway—now in the Metropolitan Museum in New York—belonged to Khufu's son, King Khaʿ-ef-Rēʿ (Chephren).

The palm columns in the hall (here of wood) are from the mortuary temple of King Saḥu-Rēʿ of the Vth Dynasty, the throne dais from a relief in the mortuary temple of Queen Nēït of the VIth Dynasty. The types, clothing, coiffures, and jewelry of the figures have been faithfully copied from IVth and Vth Dynasty tomb reliefs.

The Egyptian Farmer—Winter Sowing in the Pyramid Age

The receding waters of the yearly Nile flood have left the damp fields at El Gîza ready for the planting of the winter crop of barley or wheat, and the steward of a large Old Kingdom estate has drawn the baskets of seed from the granary and rounded up his lord's serfs for the task of sowing. The steward himself may be seen in the middle distance, accompanied by the ever-present scribe, checking the distribution of the baskets of seed.

The sowers walk slowly across the muddy fields, turning to drop the seed as they go. The plows, drawn by teams of long-horned African cows, are used to turn the seed under, their shallow wooden shares being admirably suited to the purpose.

The heavy hooves of the draft animals are as important in this operation as are the plows themselves. Both are assisted in the task by the herd of goats, which bring up the rear of the procession, lured from in front by a handful of grain and driven from behind by the twisted rope whips of their herdsmen.

In the background appear, to the right, a temporary reed windbreak, used as a camp by the farmers during their weeks in the fields, and, to the left, a cluster of adobe houses and domed grain bins.

On the desert plateau beyond—remote as were their owners from the dirty, sweaty world in the foreground—rise the pyramid tombs of three great kings of the IVth Dynasty, Khufu (or Cheops), Khaʿ-ef-Rēʿ, and Men-kau-Rēʿ, father, son, and grandson.

Although the farming group is all drawn from a well-known Vth Dynasty tomb relief, it is characteristic of Egypt during most of its history, and, except for the garments of the men, might pass for a present-day scene. Certainly, the agricultural methods and equipment—notably the plow and the baskets—have changed very little in the last 4500 years. The ancient farmer would feel at home in modern fields.

The conservatism and lack of inventiveness of the ancient Egyptian is nowhere else so well illustrated as in his continued use of the crude agricultural implements and irrigation machinery of his remote ancestors. In view of the fact that farming (with the accompanying problem of artificial irrigation) was his principal occupation and livelihood, it is surprising to note that such essential aids to agriculture as the well-sweep, the water-wheel, the Archimedes screw, and the disk thresher did not come into use in Egypt until relatively late times and then only as importations from abroad.

The well-sweep is shown in the color plate on page 147; but the water-wheel—a Graeco-Roman importation—was unknown to the dynastic people of Egypt and is therefore not portrayed in the paintings accompanying this article.

Painting by H. M. Herget

"I Was One That Produced Barley and Loved the Grain God"

Peasant-farmers of the Old Kingdom sow seed in the fields near El Gîza within sight of the three great pyramids. The Nile floods have receded, leaving the fertile soil ready for the planting of the crops which made Egypt a prosperous land. (Vth Dynasty, 2560-2420 B. C.)

Supplies of Food for a Resident of the City of the Dead—an Old Kingdom Maṣṭabeh Field Near Memphis

When, early in the IIIrd Dynasty, the kings (and, subsequently, the queens) of Egypt adopted the pyramidal form for their tomb monuments, the earlier "maṣṭabeh" type was taken over by less important members of the royal family, nobles of the court, and well-to-do officials of the kingdom, remaining popular until the end of the Middle Kingdom.

The rectangular, flat-topped mass of masonry with steeply sloping sides is a direct development from the crude mound of sand or mud heaped over the prehistoric grave. The one or more pits to the subterranean burial chambers pass vertically down through the body of the maṣṭabeh, which is usually solid except for a small chapel, a smaller statue chamber, and one or two other tiny rooms built into its stone or brick core.

Like the homes of the living, these abodes of the dead were laid out in regular streets and form extensive "towns" grouped about the pyramids of the kings.

In the plate opposite there spreads out before us part of such a maṣṭabeh town. Several types of maṣṭabeh appear in the group, but the one in the center, with the two "false doors" in its east façade and the chapel portico in its northern end naturally draws our attention.

To this tomb comes a long and motley procession of servants of its deceased owner, bringing the "raw materials" for his periodical funerary banquet: beef, butchered, and on the hoof, game, fowls of every description, vegetables, fruits, bread, beer, wine, and flowers for garnishing the tables. A scribe, with his pen-case and water jar slung over one shoulder, herds the bearers along, and at the entrance to the maṣṭabeh chapel the mortuary priest receives and disposes of the offerings.

Along the street in front of the maṣṭabeh a funerary statue of the dead noble is being dragged upon a sledge over a track liberally "sloshed down" with water.

At the right of the scene a cemetery guard sleeps peacefully beneath his awning, while his small son brings up his daily supply of water on donkeyback.

In the distance stand the three Vth Dynasty pyramids at Abusīr (Abu Sîr) and, farther to the south, the pyramid of Snefru and that of Huni of the IIIrd Dynasty at Dahshûr.

Painting by H. M. Herget

". . . And Homage Done to This Excellent Noble's Lordly Soul, Now That He Is a God That Liveth Forever, Magnified in the West"

Food offerings are here brought to a "maṣṭabeh" tomb in the Memphite necropolis. This was a scene often enacted in ancient Egypt. The people believed that after death they would continue to use and enjoy all the comforts they had known in life. (Vth Dynasty, 2560-2420 B. C.)

Netting Wildfowl in the Marshes

Fowling with the ancient Egyptians was both a sport and a means of livelihood, entered into with equal zest by the rich man out for a few hours' amusement, by the peasant in search of a succulent meal, and by the professional fowler, whose whole time was devoted to supplying the larders and stocking the poultry yards of his employers or clients.

Small land birds were caught in little spring traps of ingenious design; but the chief victims of this combined pastime and business were the wild goose, the pintail duck, and the widgeon, which during the migratory seasons swarmed over the pools and waterways of Egypt in apparently countless thousands.

Of the several devices used for catching these birds alive one of the most common and certainly the most spectacular was the large "clap-net" of the type shown in our painting. It appears to have been operated somewhat on this order:

A small pool, known to be frequented by wildfowl, having been selected and baited, the two halves of the net were spread out flat on either side of it, their inner edges "hinged" on staked cords, their outer edges provided with securely anchored draw-ropes, as shown.

The five fowlers manning the draw-rope squatted low in the tall grass of the marsh, leaving only the look-out, his cranium camouflaged by a cap shaped to resemble a duck's head, peering over the top of his blind. When enough birds had alighted on the pool to satisfy the watcher that a good catch would be made, this man sprang up suddenly, throwing his arms wide and spreading his white sash across the back of his shoulders.

His companions, taking the signal, straightened up and, with a mighty heave which landed them all on their backs, swung the wings of the net up, over, and down on the already rising birds, flattening them against the surface of the pool and snaring many in the meshes of the trap.

At this point the small boys, waiting in the background with the empty crates, went into action and captured a dozen or so live ducks for the roasting spit or the poultry farm.

The clap-net is frequently represented in tomb reliefs and paintings, especially those of the Old Kingdom. Because of the often puzzling conventions of drawing used by the Egyptian artists, the exact form and the exact method of manipulation of the net has presented something of a problem to the modern student. The reconstruction shown is one of the several accepted ones. It is, however, not unlikely that the netting extended, in triangles below the draw-ropes, beyond the limits of the rectangular frames.

Painting by H. M. Herget

"It Is Good, However, When the Net Is Drawn and the Birds Are Made Fast"

Fowlers operate a clap-net in the marshes near Abusīr (Abu Sîr). The flora of this characteristic Egyptian swampland includes clumps of palm trees, long swamp rushes, the tall papyrus, and the Egyptian lotus, or water lily. In the left background appears the great solar obelisk and sun temple built by King Ne-Woser-Rēʿ of the Vth Dynasty (2515-2486 B. C.).

The Egyptian Scribe and His Equipment

THE career of "scribe" in ancient Egypt was as exacting in its requirements as it was honorable and profitable in its rewards. A young man fortunate enough to have passed through the great school of scribes at Memphis or, later, at Thebes was expected not only to be able to read, write, and draw with a skill approaching perfection but also to have a thorough knowledge of the language, literature, and history of his country.

Furthermore he must be well versed in mathematics, bookkeeping, law, management and maintenance of personnel, general administrative procedure, and even such subjects as mechanics, surveying, and architectural design.

Once a man had qualified as a scribe, he automatically became a member of the educated official class. This status exempted him from menial labor of any sort, and he could rise through a series of recognized stages to the very highest offices in the land.

The scribe of page 103, seated with his fellows in the chancellery of a great estate of the Vth Dynasty, is engaged in making an inventory of his lord's linen supply. He is assisted in the task by a fat under-treasurer, who is reading off to him the distinguishing marks written on a corner of each sheet.

The writer sits cross-legged, making the tightly stretched front of his linen kilt serve as a desk. He writes from right to left in a fine "hieratic" hand, using a slender brush composed of a reed with a carefully frayed and trimmed tip.

His excellent paper is made of narrow strips of the pith of the papyrus reed, crossed in two directions, pressed together, and subsequently burnished. His writing pigments—black and red—are contained in the two bowls of an alabaster palette, or ink-stand, which may be seen lying on the floor by his right knee.

To the ring on the end of the palette is attached a pointed piece of rag or other substance, which serves as an eraser. Next to this is the hard stone slab and grinder for pulverizing the pigment.

The scribe's bronze basin, containing the water for mixing his pigments, rests on the leather trunk, in which he keeps his rolls of fresh papyrus. The small inscribed cylinder, suspended from his neck, bears his master's name, and is used for sealing documents, cases of goods, and other items pertaining to the estate.

Linen cloth, as we have seen, was woven in Egypt from remote prehistoric times. Usually of excellent quality, it varied in texture from a coarse burlap-like cloth to the finest, gossamer cambric. Ordinarily the cloth was woven in long sheets, or bolts, finished at one end with a long fringe, and having a selvage edge and short selvage fringe along the sides.

In addition to weavers' marks, woven into the fabric, the sheets were often marked at one corner with a short ink inscription, giving the name of the individual, estate, or government department to which they belonged. The latter marks are similar in appearance and, to some extent, in purpose to the modern laundry marks. Dated sheets, found on mummies, have been valuable aids to researchers who have sought to reconstruct some of the more obscure periods in Egyptian history.

Painting by H. M. Herget

"But the Scribe Directeth the Work of the People"

"For him there are no taxes, for he payeth tribute in writing." A staff of professional scribes works in the administrative office of a large Old Kingdom estate. (Vth Dynasty, 2560-2420 B. C.) The brightly colored lotus columns—so seemingly out of place in a business office—bespeak the ancient Egyptian's love of floral ornament.

A "Dwarf of the Divine Dances from the Land of the Spirits" as a Gift to the Boy King of Egypt

IN THE second year of the reign of King Pepy II of the VIth Dynasty a caravan led by Prince Ḥar-khūf, Lord of Elephantine and Governor of the South, reached the First Cataract of the Nile, having journeyed far to the south to the distant country of Yam. It had returned with a rich cargo of gold, ostrich feathers, ebony logs, panther skins, ivory, and, last but not least, a dancing pigmy from Central Africa as a gift to the pharaoh.

Since "the Lord of the Two Lands, the King of Upper and Lower Egypt, Nefer-ka-Rēʿ, the Son of Rēʿ, Pepy" was eight years old at the time, he was considerably more elated over the pigmy than he was over the material addition to the national treasury. When Ḥar-khūf was about to board ship for the journey down the Nile to Memphis, he received a long and excited letter from his king, urging him to take every precaution to see that the little creature arrived safely.

"When he goes down with thee into the vessel," wrote Pepy, "appoint excellent people who shall be beside him on each side of the vessel . . . lest he fall into the water. When he sleeps at night, appoint excellent people who shall sleep beside him in his tent; inspect ten times a night."

Ḥar-khūf's ship, its two-legged mast unstepped and its Nubian crew bending lustily to the oars, is seen speeding downriver against the prevailing wind. Unlike those of the freight boat, which is passing up river under sail, the steering oar of the governor's ship is equipped with the newly invented rudder post and tiller.

Ḥar-khūf sits before his comfortable, leather covered cabin, his bodyguard and traveling trunks on his right, his orchestra on his left, and roars with laughter at the antics of his small charge. The latter is in the direct care of a full sized compatriot—presumably an "excellent person"—who, as can be seen, is taking no chances of losing the little dancer in the Nile.

Since Ḥar-khūf proudly inscribed the account of his trip and a copy of the now famous letter on the façade of his tomb opposite Elephantine, we may assume that both the ship and the king's present reached their destination in good condition.

The First Intermediate Period (2270-2160 B.C.) and the Middle Kingdom (2160-1788 B.C.)

Throughout the Vth and VIth Dynasties the power of the landed nobility had risen steadily until, toward the end of the VIth Dynasty, it threatened to overshadow that of the king himself. During the short reigns of the weak rulers who succeeded Pepy II this threat became a reality. The central government was disrupted or ignored; the country broke up into a series of petty states; and the Old Kingdom came to an ignominious end in dissension, internal strife, local feuds, and general disorder.

These conditions existed for more than a century, with first one princeling and then another claiming sovereignty over the land. During this period there rose and fell in rapid succession the VIIth and VIIIth Dynasties of Memphis and the IXth and Xth Dynasties of Herakleopolis, now Ihnâysa el Madîna.

About 2160 B.C., the warrior nomarchs of Thebes, by defeating the Herakleopolitan confederacy, reestablished firmly the pharaonic rule, and as kings of the XIth Dynasty founded what we know as the Middle Kingdom.

Painting by H. M. Herget

"Come Northward to the Court Immediately and Bring This Dwarf with Thee"

Prince Ḥar-khūf, governor of Nubia, travels down the Nile with a pigmy as a gift to King Pepy II. The figure of the dancing pigmy is taken from a little ivory statuette found at El Lisht in 1933 by the Egyptian Expedition of the Metropolitan Museum in New York. (VIth Dynasty, 2nd regnal year of Pepy II, 2331 B. C.)

An Ancient Egyptian Brewery

The Middle Kingdom has been characterized truly as Egypt's "feudal age", and, if under the XIIth Dynasty the country rose to new heights of greatness, it was because the kings of this dynasty were strong enough and wily enough to dominate the powerful nomarchs, to gain their loyalty, and to turn their vast resources to the uses of the crown and of the nation.

Beer was the ancient Egyptian's favorite beverage, and on the estates of the great lords of the Middle Kingdom the brewery ranked next in importance to the granary and the bakery, on both of which it was dependent.

The brewery of page 107 is taken from a wooden funerary model found at Thebes in the tomb of the Chancellor Meket-Rēʿ, a wealthy official of the XIth Dynasty.

In it we see the complete process of brewing the simplest and apparently the most common of the several types of beer consumed in ancient Egypt. Barley or wheat, brought in baskets from the granary, is first cracked in a stone mortar, then ground to coarse flour on the limestone mill (left). This arduous task was regularly reserved for a woman.

The flour scooped out of the catch-basin of the mill passes to the man in the left background, who works it into dough on his kneading tray, adding to the new dough the yeasty residue from the last baking of bread. The loaves of dough are placed on the low stove next to the kneading table and heated until they have fully risen.

They are then crumbled up and thoroughly mixed with a large quantity of water in the great jars in the right background. In the mixing process a man steps into the jar and treads the mash with his feet.

After several days' fermentation the thick, lumpy liquid is strained through a sieve into the specially designed brewer's vat in the foreground. The spout of this vat is so placed that it allows the beer to be poured off, leaving the barm at the top of the vat and the dregs in its bottom. The beer is "bottled" in pottery jars stoppered with hemispheres or cones of Nile mud.

The resulting beverage, except for the absence of malt, resembled the modern Egyptian wheat beer, or "booza", a liquid with the consistency of thin gruel, averaging around 7 per cent in alcoholic content.

The hard, greenish white pottery, of which the ancient beer jars were made, is still the favorite material of the potters of the modern province of Ḳeneh (Qena) in Upper Egypt. Here are produced from the same pale desert clay the present-day "zīr," "gulleh," and "ballas"—water jars par excellence—, the last much photographed on the heads of the slender daughters of modern Egypt.

Painting by H. M. Herget

"Beer Is Brewed for Him on the Day of His Festival"

By the doorway of a Middle Kingdom brewery stands the portly brewmaster, his scepter of authority in his hand, and the workers bend to their tasks though there is no threat in the attitude of their overseer. The funerary model from which this group was derived is in the Metropolitan Museum in New York. It was found at Thebes by the museum's Egyptian expedition in the spring of 1920. (XIth Dynasty, reign of King Mentu-ḥotpe III, 2060-2015 B. C.)

An XIth Dynasty Carpenter's Shop

Lack of good native timber woods and metal fastenings combined to make the Egyptian carpenter a past master in his craft. He learned to produce sizable boards and beams by the patient and artful piecing together of the short and narrow cuttings obtainable from his scrubby local trees—sycamore fig, acacia, tamarisk, sidder, and willow.

Using as fastenings only tapered and straight hardwood pegs, he managed by skillful joinery to construct coffins, shrines, boxes, sledges, doors, and articles of furniture, many of which remain strong and rigid to this day.

At an early period the Egyptians began importing wood, the timber fleet plying between the Delta and the Syrian coast bringing cargo after cargo of cedar, cypress, fir, and pine from the Lebanon. The caravans and boats of the upper Nile also supplied the workshops with Sudanese ebony and other tropical woods.

Good wood, however, remained a costly luxury and was always used with the utmost care, considerable labor and skill often being expended to obtain a fine, massive effect with the minimum outlay of material.

The sides and ends of the coffin under construction on page 109, for example, are tapered in thickness from top to bottom, so that the visible top edges of the finished box will display a massiveness suggesting the presence of almost twice the amount of wood actually used.

In addition to the pegged tenon and overlapped mitre joints appearing in this coffin, the Egyptian carpenter was acquainted with most of the devices known to the modern cabinetmaker, including the various rabbet, dado, and lap joints, and the dovetail.

His bronze cutting and boring tools—saw, adze, axe, chisel, knife, scraper, and bow drill—were equipped with hardwood handles. His mallet and square were of hardwood, and his whetstone usually of quartzite.

The "plane" used by the man in the center of the picture is a lump of sandstone with a carefully plattened abrading surface. Other abrasives, such as fine sand, were employed for giving the wood surfaces a smooth, even finish. A glue, much like modern carpenters' glue, and a coarse "crack filler" were also used by the ancient Egyptian worker in wood.

When finished, the coffin and its lid will be coated inside and out with a thin layer of stucco, painted in brilliant colors, and inscribed with appropriate funerary texts. Prominent on its left side will be the great pair of painted eyes, through which its deceased occupant may gaze forth each morning toward the east and the rising sun.

Painting by H. M. Herget

"Many Artificers Built It, and All Its Woodwork Was New Appointed"

In a carpenter's shop of the Middle Kingdom, one of the heavy, rectangular coffins typical of this period, is in process of construction. The simple but serviceable tools are employed by the hands of master craftsmen and the pieces of lumber are joined with wooden tenons and pegs. (XIth Dynasty, 2160-2000 B. C.)

Painting by H. M. Herget

"I Would Build for Thee a New Mansion . . . Planted with Trees upon Every Side of It." "Thy Young Folk . . . Shout for Joy Over Thee"

Children at play in the garden of a country estate of the Middle Kingdom demonstrate the happy, carefree life of the early Egyptians, who were ever a human and jolly folk. Represented in tomb reliefs as early as the Old Kingdom, the boys' game is usually labeled "Going round four times." (XIth-XIIth Dynasties, 2160-1788 B. C.)

The Formal Gardens and Informal Children of Ancient Egypt

IN LAYING out and planting the walled parks surrounding their pleasant country villas, the Egyptians displayed the conventionality, orderliness, and love of symmetry which are outstanding in their art and, indeed, in their whole life.

Before any extensive orchard or garden was actually started, sketches were made and from these finished plans were drawn, showing the distribution of pools, trees, and avenues, and containing written notations of the more important distances and spacings.

The pools, all shallow, were for ornament, not for bathing. Though Egyptians could swim, there is no record of their going in for swimming as a sport. Crocodiles were too numerous in the Nile.

The installation and upkeep of the park was entrusted to a staff of professional gardeners, headed by an "Overseer of the Garden", who evidently regarded himself as a person of no small importance. The excellent taste of the ancient Egyptian and his very real love and understanding of nature invariably produced most happy results.

From his high-roofed front verandah, with its brightly painted lotus-bud columns, the country gentleman of page 110 looks out over his large rectangular lotus pool, stocked with fish and bordered by regularly spaced clumps of flowers and flowering shrubs: mandrakes, oleanders, jasmine, bindweed, cornflowers, and dwarf chrysanthemums. Around this aquatic and floral centerpiece are ranged rows of sycamore fig trees, and, behind these, the tall date and dōm palms.

The great man's children and their friends, idolized by their proud and indulgent parents, have the run of the garden. The boys, with their heads shaven except for the braided side lock of "youth", are unhampered by clothes. The girls, clad in simple one-piece dresses, wear their hair in "pigtails."

The more or less self-explanatory games in progress are chosen from a score or so of children's pastimes depicted on the walls of Middle Kingdom tombs. Even the cat and the ridiculous little dachshund-like dog are authentic XIIth Dynasty types. The painted wooden "paddle" doll, well known in the XIth Dynasty, though not originally designed as a child's toy, could and probably did serve as such.

Most interesting are the balls, with which the girls are playing. With cores of tightly packed barley husks and stitched leather covers, they resemble the modern baseball.

The verandah, pool, and garden are from a miniature produced by an Egyptian model-maker of the Third Millennium B. C. The model, with its high wall, brightly painted little columns, and tiny wooden trees, is in the Metropolitan Museum in New York. The oxidized copper lining of its small pool shows that the latter was once filled with water.

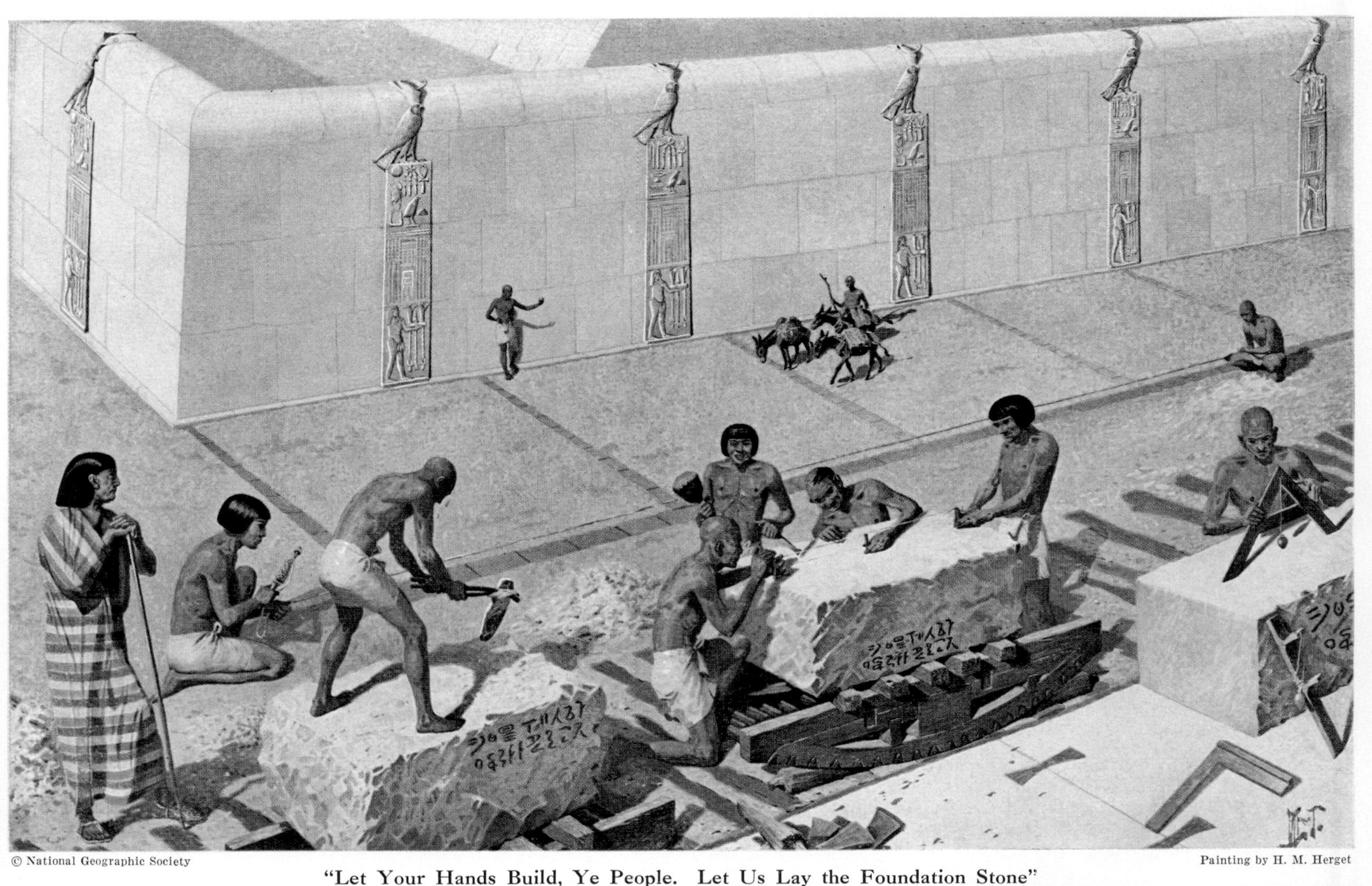

© National Geographic Society

Painting by H. M. Herget

"Let Your Hands Build, Ye People. Let Us Lay the Foundation Stone"

Stonemasons work in the outer enclosure of the pyramid of King Se'n-Wosret I at El Lisht. The heavy blocks of limestone can be turned easily by means of the wooden rockers on which they rest. (XIIth Dynasty, reign of Se'n-Wosret I, 1980-1939 B. C.)

The Egyptian Stonemason and His Craft—Construction Work on a XIIth Dynasty Pyramid Site

The scene shifts from the cool shade of an Upper Egyptian garden to a section of the sun-baked desert plateau on the west side of the Nile some thirty miles south of modern Cairo; and we find ourselves, on page 112, in the outer enclosure of the pyramid of King Se'n-Wosret I, the second pharaoh of the XIIth Dynasty, who ruled Egypt with a strong hand between the years 1980 and 1939 B. C. Across the back of the scene stretches the limestone inner enclosure wall of the pyramid, bearing the elaborately carved name panels of the king.

In the foreground construction is in progress on the girdle wall of one of the many small pyramids which surround that of the monarch. Masons are dressing and laying the rough blocks of limestone, newly brought from the quarry. The transport inscriptions recently painted on the sides of these blocks, are dated to the 12th Day of the 1st Month of the season of Shōmu, in the 12th Regnal Year (of Se'n-Wosret I), in other words, mid-September, 1969 B. C.

The blocks are being handled on stout wooden stone-rockers, which can be swung around with ease, tilted to any desired angle, and, by means of a series of heavy wooden hand wedges thrust under their runners, raised vertically as much as two or three feet. To prevent them from sinking into the sand, the rockers are operated on a track of heavy timber balks.

The man on the left-hand block is rough-dressing its surfaces with a hard stone maul.

Those about the right-hand block are checking the final dressing of its joint surfaces with a set of "boning rods": three rods of equal length, over the tops of two of which a cord is stretched from edge to edge of the surface being tested. The third rod, moved back and forth with its top always under the tightly stretched cord, serves to locate "high spots" in the surface. These are then dressed away by the man with the chisel and mallet.

The chisel is of bronze, hardened by prolonged hammering.

The blocks are laid in a coarse white gypsum mortar; and those in the foundation course of the wall are held together by stout wood "cramps".

Elsewhere in the scene we see, either in the hands of the men or lying about in the foreground, the mason's reel and line—used here to check the alignment of the leveling bricks of the court—and the mason's level, plumb, and square.

© National Geographic Society

Painting by H. M. Herget

". . . In Order to Prevent Any Negro from Passing It by Water or by Land"

Egyptian soldiers of the Middle Kingdom question a negro merchant in the river narrows below the southern frontier fort at Semna. The ram's head standard on the fort indicates that its garrison is composed of a battalion of the Regiment of Amūn. (XIIth Dynasty, reign of King Se'n-Wosret III, 1887-1850 B. C.)

An Ancient Egyptian River Fort on the Sudan Frontier

For some distance below its second cataract the Nile, forcing its way through outcrops of hard, crystalline rock, forms a series of narrow rapids, which, though navigable in antiquity by light, shallow-draft boats, exposed traffic to blockades and attacks by partly subjugated savages.

To protect their own commerce with the south and to control the native traffic both by land and water, the Egyptian kings of the XIIth Dynasty built a line of forts along these rapids on both sides of the river. The best known and best preserved of them are the pair flanking the Semna rapids, 50 miles south of Wadi Halfa.

The west fort at Semna, shown reconstructed on page 114, though founded originally by King Amen-em-ḥēt I, was named "Powerful-is-King-Se'n-Wosret III", having been greatly enlarged and improved by the latter pharaoh (1887-1850 B. C.). Its great L-shaped plan was enclosed within massive walls of sun-dried brick, 15 to 25 feet thick and more than 30 feet high.

The walls, strengthened by longitudinal and transverse timbers and equipped with towers, buttresses, and battlements, were built on an embankment of granite rubble.

In addition to the towered north and south gates, there were, on the river side, a small postern gate and a covered stone stairway leading down into the Nile. This well protected stairway enabled the soldiers who were defending the garrison to obtain a constant supply of water even in times of the closest siege.

The fort was a canny piece of military architecture, perfectly adapted to the rocky prominence on which it was built and so devised that all approaches to it were difficult and hazardous. Early in its history it withstood a siege of several months.

The 150 to 300 Egyptian soldiers stationed in the fort lived with their women and children in a small town, built inside the walls and including, among sundry other buildings, several little brick temples.

On page 114 a detail of typical Middle Kingdom soldiers, in charge of an officer, is halting for inspection, a negro trader, who, with his family and heavily laden papyrus canoe, is en route northward. By decree of the pharaoh, the only negroes who were permitted to pass the forts at Semna were those on "official business" or those headed for the Nubian trading post at Iḳen.

Besides ivory, wild animal skins, and other cargo the negroes' canoe carries a dog-headed baboon (cynocephalus ape) of a well known breed, evidently a pet.

Painting by H. M. Herget

"Making Every Visitor Welcome, Forwarding Travelers North and South"

Prince Thūty-ḥotpe, lord of the "Hare" nome, provides entertainment for a visiting Bedawīn sheikh and his family. Wrestling was an immensely popular sport among the Egyptians of the Middle Kingdom, and many hotly contested bouts are depicted in detail on the walls of the great tombs at Beni Hasan esh Shurûq, Mîr and Deir el Barsha. The nomarch's dogs are Sudanese greyhounds. (XIIth Dynasty, reign of King Se'n-Wosret III, 1887-1850 B. C.)

An Egyptian Nomarch Entertains a Bedawīn Sheikh

Although the Egyptians always regarded as barbarians, the dwellers in the deserts to the east and west of the Nile and the Asiatic tribes farther to the north, they carried on a lively commerce with these peoples. More often than not during the Old and Middle Kingdoms, the trade was conducted on an entirely friendly basis.

It is therefore not surprising to find the "Prince, the Confidential Friend of the King, the Great Chief of the Hare Nome", Tḥūty-ḥotpe, extending the hospitality of his verandah to a desert prince and his family—little knowing that within a few hundred years these same people, the "Hyksos", were to invade and to subject to their warlike rule the whole of northern Egypt.

The Hyksos Abshai—for that is the sheikh's name—has just delivered a shipment of galena, used by the Egyptians as an eye cosmetic, to Prince Khnūm-ḥotpe, ruler of the Oryx Nome, whose domain was situated in Middle Egypt, immediately to the north of that of Tḥūty-ḥotpe. On his way home he has stopped to pay a state call on the latter.

For the amusement of his guest Tḥūty-ḥotpe has staged a series of wrestling matches such as those depicted in detail in the famous wrestling sequence found at Beni Hasan (pages 76 and 77). These contests of skill and strength will be followed by some acrobatic dancing, performed by the girls seen standing on the left of the crowd in the courtyard.

Next to the nomarch sits his wife, Ḥatḥor-ḥotpe, arrayed in her best and holding a rotating fan of colored matting. Tḥūty-ḥotpe, himself, wearing the distinctive robe and pectoral of a vizier, toys with an ivory handled flywhisk.

The Bedawīn, whose gaudy woolen mantles and crude possessions contrast sharply with the refined attire and accessories of their hosts, seem enthralled with the simple spectacle. Their enthusiasm is shared by the Egyptians in the courtyard, among whom are a number of local celebrities—notably the tall, scrawny herdsman, well known to students of ancient Egypt as "the thin man of Mîr".

The painted tombs of the great XIIth Dynasty lords of Middle Egypt at Mîr, Deir el Barsha, and Beni Hasan esh Shurûq, are veritable treasure houses of information for students of life in the Middle Kingdom. Most familiar to travelers are those at Beni Hasan, famed for the so-called "proto-Doric" columns of their rock-cut façades.

Though these columns, the shafts of two of which appear in our painting, superficially resemble the Greek Doric column, there is no real basis for the association, some 1300 years separating these from, for example, the Parthenon.

Painting by H. M. Herget

"And His Majesty Loved Her Exceedingly"

The Princess Sit-Ḥatḥor-Yūnet was daughter of King Se'n-Wosret II, sister of King Se'n-Wosret III, and aunt of King Amen-em-ḥēt III. The Metropolitan Museum in New York possesses the greater part of the jewelry and other possessions of this lady. (Latter part of the XIIth Dynasty, about 1890-1840 B. C.)

A King's Daughter and Her Personal Possessions

When, in 1887 B. C., King Se'n-Wosret II of the XIIth Dynasty died and was buried beneath his pyramid at El Lahûn, he left behind him, in addition to his son, Se'n-Wosret III, three daughters, the second of whom, Princess Sit-Ḥatḥor-Yūnet, outlived her brother and died in the reign of her nephew, King Amen-em-ḥēt III. As a favored relative of three great pharaohs, this petite and doubtless charming woman was well provided for. When, in February, 1913, the expedition of the British School of Archaeology in Egypt cleared her tomb beside the pyramid of her father at El Lahûn, they found in it a treasure of jewelry and other feminine equipment, which in beauty of design and refinement of execution has remained unsurpassed to the present day.

In our portrait we have caught the princess "making up" her eyes with black cosmetic contained in a small gold-mounted jar of polished obsidian, and applied with a slender ebony stick. Her silver mirror has a handle of obsidian, mounted with gold, electrum, carnelian, lapis lazuli, and green paste, and adorned with gold faces of the goddess Ḥat-Ḥor. Sit-Ḥatḥor-Yūnet's jewelry is of gold, electrum, and silver, "molded and chased with microscopic accuracy" and cunningly inlaid with blue and green paste, carnelian, lapis lazuli, turquoise, amethyst, and garnet. The beads in her necklaces, girdles, and bracelets are of amethyst, turquoise, lapis, carnelian, and gold.

The pectoral, which Sit-Ḥatḥor-Yūnet wears, was a gift from her father, King Se'n-Wosret II, and bears his cartouche in the center of its design. Her bracelet, as the inlaid inscriptions on their clasps show, were given her by her nephew, King Amen-em-ḥēt III.

On the dressing table of the princess is the larger of her two ebony jewel caskets, paneled in ivory, gold, blue faience, and carnelian, and bound in gold and silver. Beside it lie a silver rouge dish, a bronze razor with gold handle, two bracelets of gold and semi-precious stones, an unguent jar of alabaster, and two others of obsidian, mounted with gold.

With this attractive representative of one of the greatest and most luxurious phases of Egypt's history we take our leave of "the Older Period".

Aided by our paintings, we have coursed lightly through some 11 millenniums of human development, 1,200 years of which fall within the period of recorded history. We have seen the Egyptian as a shaggy hunter of the Old Stone Age, roaming the gravel terraces of an incredibly ancient Nile. We have followed him through his long formative stage to his first high point in the Pyramid Age of the Old Kingdom.

We have seen him falter at the end of this period and rise again to new cultural and artistic heights in the Middle Kingdom. Beyond the stage represented by the ultra-sophisticated lady of El Lahûn it would seem impossible for him to go.

We have, however, not yet reached what many students regard as the full bloom of Egyptian culture—the New Kingdom. To this we turn in the second part of this article.

Mighty Cliffs Back the Temple of Ḥat-shepsūt, Female "King" of Egypt

The ardent feminist is pictured in a more tender mood on page 138. On page 142 a priestly procession moves against the splendid background of the memorial to one of the first great women of history. But as one comes over the barren steeps from the Valley of the Tombs of the Kings at Thebes, this is the view of the colonnaded structure.

Daily Life in Ancient Egypt: *The Later Period*

WITH the passing of the XIIth Dynasty in 1788 B. C. the Middle Kingdom, the second great period of Egyptian history, came to an end.

During the reigns of the feeble kings of the XIIIth Dynasty of Thebes and those of the apparently contemporary XIVth Dynasty of Xois in the Delta, political, economic, and cultural conditions in the country went from bad to worse. About 1730 B. C. Egypt was subjected for the first time in its recorded history to the indignity of a foreign overlordship.

The northern part of the country was seized by the princes of an Asiatic people, or group of peoples, known to us as the Hyksos. From their fortified capital at Avaris in the northeast Delta, these foreigners ruled the whole of Lower Egypt and exacted tribute from the native rulers of the south.

The Hyksos Introduce the Horse

Since many of the important changes in the life and culture of the Egyptians of the New Kingdom, as contrasted with those of the Old and Middle Kingdoms, can be attributed, either directly or indirectly, to their contact with the Hyksos, it will be useful to summarize briefly what little we know of this intensely interesting people.

The name "Hyksos" appears to have been derived from the title *ḥeḳau khasūt*, "Princes of the Uplands," applied by the Egyptians to the sheikhs, or tribal leaders, of these foreigners.

Traces of the Hyksos occur in Egypt as early as 1900 B. C., and their seizure of the country in the late 18th Century B. C. seems to have been the result of the rise to political power of a foreign element long resident in the land, rather than of a sudden invasion from without.

The origin and race of the Hyksos are still unsolved problems, but it is clear that they were basically of Semitic stock and that they filtered into Egypt from Palestine, which for several centuries was their home, or at least their base of operations. They were both warlike and highly civilized, expert metallurgists, makers of fine pottery, and builders of well planned and efficiently fortified towns.

They were the first people with whom the Egyptians came in close contact who knew and used the horse, and they were undoubtedly responsible for the introduction of this enormously important animal into Egypt.

For more than a century two successive lines of Hyksos kings, the XVth and XVIth Dynasties, exercised authority over the country, with only mild resistance from their vassals, the Egyptian rulers of Thebes. Shortly before 1600 B. C., however, the weak XIIIth Dynasty having given place in Upper Egypt to the much more vigorous XVIIth Dynasty, these native "Princes of the Southern City" began to fight back in earnest.

In the time of the Hyksos king Apōpy III the Theban Seḳen-en-Rēʿ Taʿo II was slain in a battle against the foreigners, the crushed head and mutilated body of his mummy attesting the violence of his death.

Taʿo's elder son, King Wadj-kheper-Rēʿ Ka-mosĕ was more successful. Rallying his vacillating henchmen, he besieged and captured the hostile town of Neferūsi in Middle Egypt and inflicted several other serious reverses on the Hyksos armies.

Ka-mosĕ's younger brother and successor, King Nebpeḥty-Rēʿ Aʿḥ-mosĕ, finished the job, destroying Avaris after a long siege and driving the Hyksos back into Palestine. There for some years he continued to harry them and sack their towns.

Thus, with Aʿḥ-mosĕ I, the founder of the XVIIIth Dynasty, Egypt in 1580 B. C. once more became an independent and powerful nation and embarked upon those centuries of glorious achievement and high civilization which we know as the New Kingdom.

Egypt Becomes a Great Empire

The considerable plunder which Aʿḥ-mosĕ I brought back from his raids on the Hyksos cities in Palestine aroused in the Egyptians a lust for conquest. Recent years of practice in the art of war and the possession of a well armed, well trained and highly mobile army now enabled them to gratify this desire.

No longer content with simply policing their northern and southern boundaries, the kings of the XVIIIth Dynasty campaigned farther and farther into both Asia and Africa. At the death of Aʿḥ-mosĕ's great-great-grandson, Tḥut-mosĕ III, Egypt controlled and levied tribute on an empire which stretched southward to the Fourth Cataract of the Nile and northward to the farther shore of the Euphrates.

In addition to the vast wealth in slaves, animals, raw materials, and finished articles, an immense supply of gold poured into the Nile Valley. It was drawn as tribute from provinces and vassal states and extracted in a steady stream from the rich and constantly worked royal mines in Nubia.

Gold now became the outstanding medium of barter. By controlling the bulk of the gold supply of the then known world, Egypt was able for centuries to hold the balance of power among the nations of the Near East and to

Metropolitan Museum of Art

Nefret-īty, of Graceful Beauty, Had a Mind of Her Own

When priestly pressure caused Akh-en-Aten to be false to his name, his pretty wife, here pictured, forsook her husband and remained true to the "living Aten," symbolized by the sun. The life-size limestone bust from which this

Metropolitan Museum of Art

Egyptians Accepted, but Seldom Rode the Horse

About a century after the Hyksos introduced the animal into Egypt, this painted wooden statue—now in the Metropolitan Museum of Art—was made. Pharaohs are pictured riding in chariots but this groom goes astride his mount to the royal stable (page 136).

Metropolitan Museum of Art

Menena's Ancient Tomb at Royal Thebes Is Still a Happy Hunting Ground

In the wall decorations which pictured his life, and so continued it beyond the grave, the "Scribe of the Fields" surveys his lord's property, prays to Osiris, and welcomes his relatives. But he is also pictured decoying ducks to his boomerang while his wife, with an armful of lotus flowers, admires his skill. Beyond the papyrus hedge the official spears fish while his daughter steadies his stance with a protecting hand. The paintings retain their perfect color after about 3,500 years.

Metropolitan Museum of Art

Princess Khenmet Wore This Circlet 3,800 Years Ago

Tiny blossoms are strung on gold wire, inlaid with green feldspar and carnelian between larger lotus flowers.

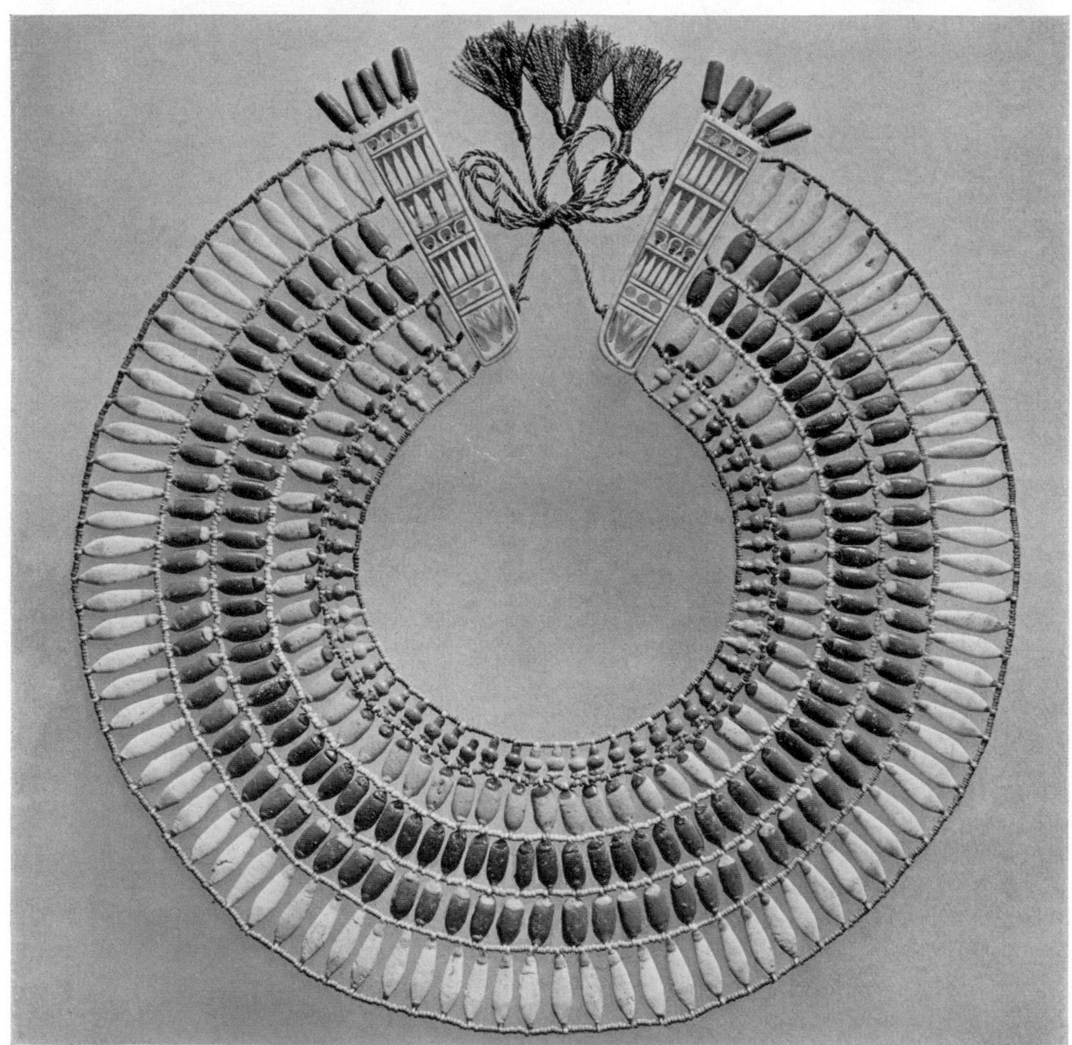

Metropolitan Museum of Art

Fruits and Flowers of Glazed Frit Formed the Costume Jewelry of 1386-1356 B. C.

A fine example of such modest decoration is this bead broad-collar in red, yellow, blue-gray, and white.

A. W. Cutler

Beyond Lesser Pillars in the Hypostyle Hall at El Karnak Loom Huge Shafts

Every one of the 12 columns flanking the central aisle of Thebes' greatest temple supports an enormous open capital. Two of these are visible (upper left) just behind the crosspiece of the first arch. On the tops of these 70 feet above the ground a regiment could stand, a hundred soldiers to each platform.

Metropolitan Museum of Art

With Incense and Libations, King Seth̲y I Wins the Favor of Falcon-headed Sokar, God of the Underworld

On the fine-grained limestone walls of the ruler's temple at Abŷdos, Egyptian low-relief sculpture appears at its best. Just below the double cartouche, showing his throne and personal names and with vulture-headed Nekheb protecting him with her wings, the pharaoh pays his tribute. The hieroglyphs over the head of the god mean "I give thee all strength: I give thee all power." In his right hand the deity holds the *ʿAnkh,* or sign of life, in his left the *Was,* scepter of "well-being."

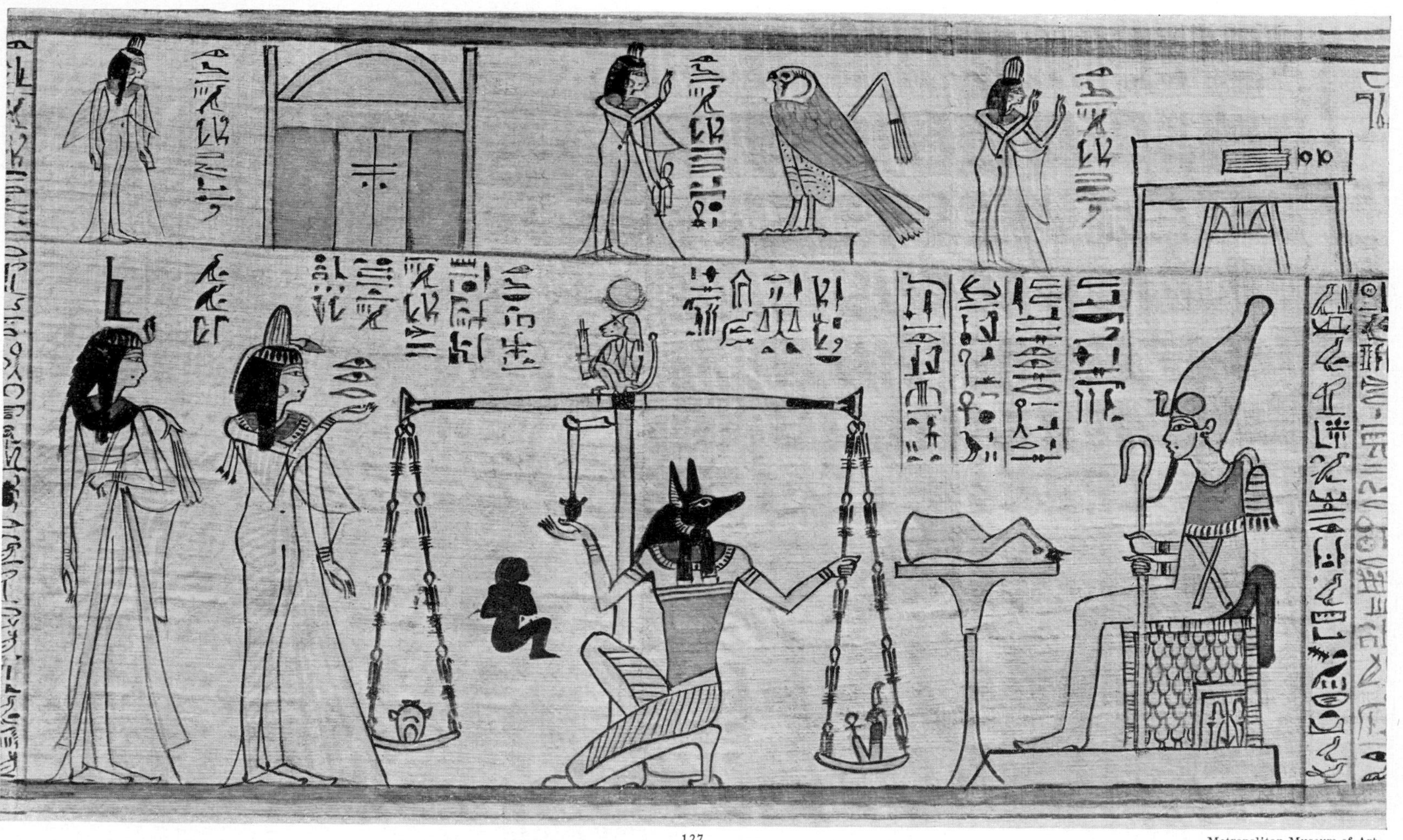

Metropolitan Museum of Art

Now a Museum Piece in New York, This Papyrus Was Princess Entiu-ny's Open Sesame Through the Underworld

Once the spells forming the Book of the Dead were painted inside the coffin. In the New Kingdom, they were inscribed on a papyrus roll and buried with the mummy. Here before Osiris, judge of souls and god of the deceased, the dog-headed Anubis weighs the heart of the candidate against a figure symbolizing truth. Behind the slender princess in her diaphanous gown stands Isis, sister of Osiris.

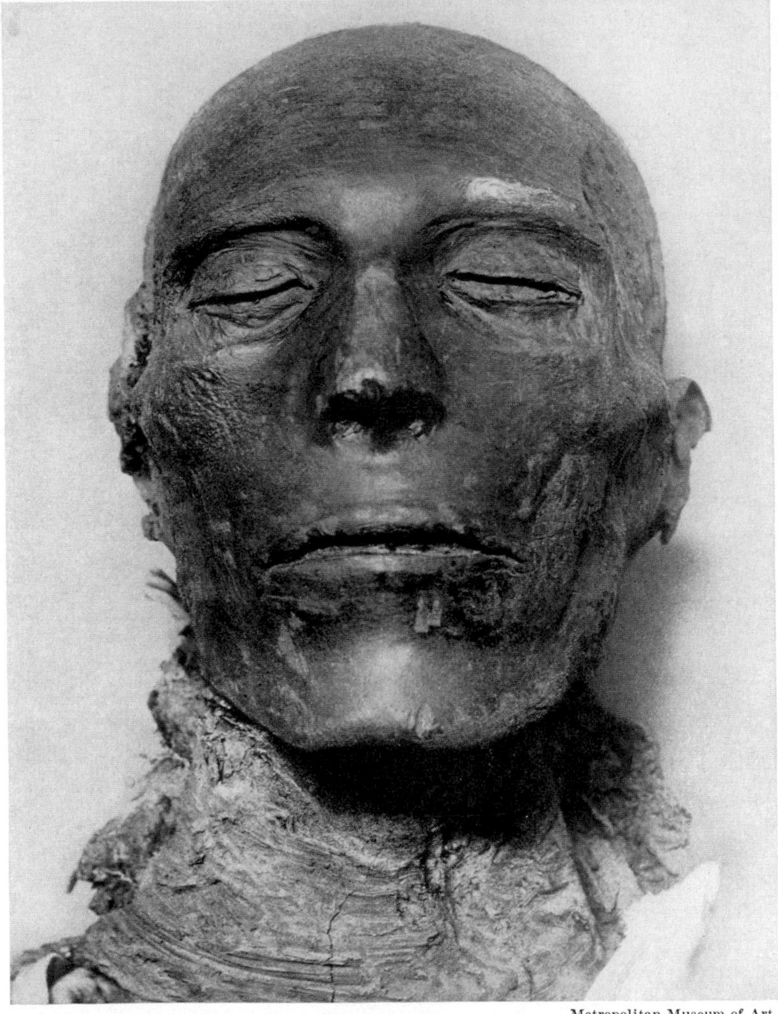

Metropolitan Museum of Art

Sethy's Well-preserved Mummy Survived Adventures Worthy of the Living Pharaoh

Buried in 1298 B. C. in the finest of the tombs of the Kings at Thebes, it was plundered, recovered, reburied, found by peasants, and finally rescued for the Egyptian Museum at Cairo. This king invaded Asia Minor, repulsed the Bedouin, fought at Armageddon, and took Tyre. Having signed a treaty with the Hittites, he devoted himself to peace and the arts. His battle reliefs are among the most imposing of those which have survived.

maintain her dominant position long after she had lost those sturdy virtues through which she had achieved this position.

Even more influential than these material riches in molding the character of the New Kingdom was the host of new ideas with which Egypt's political expansion brought her into contact. Though conservative to the end and ever reluctant to alter its traditional mode of existence, "the land watered by the Nile" nevertheless became in the centuries following 1600 B. C. less and less an isolated African community and more and more a component part of the eastern Mediterranean world.

Into the art of Egypt there creep those graceful and vivacious forms and concepts which we recognize as characteristic of the pre-Greek peoples of the islands and littorals of the Mediterranean. Semitic cults and the at least superficial effect of contact with Semitic modes of religious thought appear in the Egyptian religion.

It was, however, in the realm of cultural improvements of a more practical nature that Egypt's debt to her more inventive neighbors to the north and northeast was greatest.

The Pharaoh Was an Absolute Ruler

There can be no doubt that such New Kingdom innovations as defensive body armor, the compound bow, the scimitar and the long sword, the wheeled vehicle, and the well-sweep—the first and only piece of irrigation machinery used by the dynastic Egyptians—were direct importations from Asia.

Over this new, opulent, and highly cosmopolitan state, in which numerically the foreign population of slaves, artisans, mercenary soldiers, and merchants bulked almost as large as the native Egyptians, the pharaoh ruled in absolute power, surrounded by his bodyguard of picked troops and his coterie of royal favorites.

The landed nobility, so prominent in the Middle Kingdom, had been completely suppressed, and their place taken by an army of officials of the crown. At the head of these, directly under and responsible to the king himself, there were now two viziers, one for

Upper Egypt and one for Lower Egypt, and two chief treasurers, whose reports to the monarch were important features of the daily administrative routine.

The southern vizier, the more powerful of the two, in addition to his functions as chief magistrate and head of the judiciary branch of the government, also controlled the vast estates and personnel attached to the service of the new chief god, Amūn. Except for that granted by royal decree to the god, all land was the property of the crown, and was worked by the king's serfs or was bestowed "as a favor of the king's bounty" on his officials.

The principal government activities, in which every citizen played a part, either voluntarily or by compulsion, included, in addition to the almost yearly military campaigns, the exploitation of quarries and mines, the opening of trade routes through the deserts, the excavation of waterways and irrigation canals, and the erection of new and, as time went on, increasingly stupendous public buildings.

Staff Photographer Maynard Owen Williams

Checked Against His Mummy, This Superb Statue of Ṭhut-mosĕ III Proved to Be a Faithful Portrait

Though forced for twenty years to submit to the will of Ḥat-shepsūt, his aunt and co-regent, he came to be one of the greatest of the Pharaohs. Victor in many campaigns, he showed a streak of littleness by masking the inscribed bases of Ḥat-shepsūt's obelisks with brick walls and obliterating, so far as possible, her name and memory from the rolls of history.

The chief beneficiary of the pharaohs' extensive building operations was the god Amūn of Thebes. As patron of the nation's new capital and the special divinity of Egypt's ruling family, this deity had risen to unchallenged supremacy.

The temple of Amūn at El Karnak (page 164)—to name only the principal "house of the god"—is in itself a monumental history of the New Kingdom and the Late Dynastic Period, for there was scarcely a king of Dynasties XVIII-XXX who failed to enlarge or embellish this greatest of shrines. To the service of this and the numerous other temples of the god there was diverted much of the nation's wealth in gold, lands, serfs, and cattle.

The priesthood of Amūn, as time progressed, absorbed more and more of the country's manhood, and the administration of the god's huge estates required a host of stewards, treasurers, overseers, and scribes almost as numerous as those in the employ of the king.

As was the case with the preceding periods of Egyptian history, our knowledge of life in the New Kingdom is derived largely from the contents and the decorated walls of the tombs of the dead. At Thebes, where the majority of the great personages of the New Kingdom

Metropolitan Museum of Art

Tūt-ʿankh-Amūn's Burial Mask Has Been Shorn of Its Kingly Beard

Above his forehead are the royal insignia of vulture and serpent. A solid gold coffin (page 131) one-eighth of an inch thick sheathed the masked mummy. Outside that were two wooden cases overlaid with gold, a rose-granite sarcophagus, and four shrines, the outer one 17 feet long, 11 feet wide and 9 feet high.

were buried, the tombs were rock-cut in the sides of the precipitous cliffs that border the Nile Valley throughout Upper Egypt.

The maṣṭabeh tomb disappeared, and the pyramid, no longer the special prerogative of the royal dead, was greatly reduced in size and relative importance.

Deep into the western cliffs at Thebes winds a long and tortuous valley, its boulder-strewn way ending in a secluded natural amphitheatre. Here, far from prying eyes, King Tḥut-mosĕ I about 1520 B. C. had his architect Ineny excavate for him a secret tomb.

The job was done, as an inscription in Ineny's own tomb tells us, with "no one seeing, no one hearing"—which may possibly mean that "dead men tell no tales," for it must have required a considerable gang to excavate and clear the underground passages and chambers of the tomb. After the royal burial the small and simple entrance way, nestled against the base of the precipitous rock wall, was filled in with débris and thus obliterated from view.

The example of Tḥut-mosĕ I was followed by his successors, the kings of the XVIIIth, XIXth, and XXth Dynasties; and the deserted bay in the western cliffs became what we now know as the Valley of the Tombs of the Kings, a site familiar as the resting place of Egypt's royal dead.

Funerary beliefs were now dominated by magic, as typified by a series of spells, designed to assure the comfort and well-being of the deceased in the world beyond the tomb, and known collectively as the "Book of the Dead." Exemption from the penalties likely to be exacted for a not altogether blameless existence could be purchased, and the morality of the individual and the nation suffered accordingly.

This and the other unhealthy conditions latent in the new order of things, however, did not seriously affect the unparalleled prosperity of the country until after the fall of the second of the great dynasties discussed on pages 136-167, the XVIIIth (1580-1320 B. C.) and the XIXth (1320-1205 B. C.).*

* See NATIONAL GEOGRAPHIC MAGAZINE articles: "Fresh Treasures From Egypt's Ancient Sands," by Jefferson Caffery, November, 1955; "Kayaks Down the Nile," by John M. Goddard, May, 1955; "Safari From Congo to Cairo," by Elsie May Bell Grosvenor, December, 1954; "Sinai Sheds New Light on the Bible," by Henry Field, December, 1948; "By Felucca Down the Nile," by Willard Price, April, 1940; "At the Tomb of Tutankhamen," May, 1923, and "East of Suez to the Mount of the Decalogue," December, 1927, both by Maynard Owen Williams; "Land of Egypt," by Alfred Pearce Dennis, March, 1926; "Along the Nile, Through Egypt and the Sudan," by Frederick Simpich, October, 1922; and others listed in the NATIONAL GEOGRAPHIC MAGAZINE Cumulative Index.

Metropolitan Museum of Art

Tūt-ʿankh-Amūn's Mummy Lay under Wings of Gold Cloisonné

Innermost of three coffins was this golden shell. The headdress vulture is Nekhebet, goddess of Upper Egypt; the cobra Buto, goddess of Lower Egypt.

Imperial Airways, Ltd.

The Colossi of Ramesses at Abû Simbil Look Their Best from the Air

The visitor on foot, staring up at the 65-foot statues, finds the Pharaohs' knees stricken with elephantiasis, the royal heads remote. But as the plane circles north over ... the carvings have better perspective. The figures' pose seems designed for the flyer, not the Nile sailor.

Ewing Galloway

Wife and Children, More than Life Size, Are Calf-high Figures on the Ramesses Colossi

Between the ankles of the headless statue stands Prince Amun-her-khepesh-ef (page 134). Each day's morning sun briefly floods through the door into the 200-foot chamber carved from living rock, lighting other great Ramesses carvings inside. A smaller temple close by honors Nefertari, Ramesses' queen. The Aswan High Dam, begun in 1960, will raise the river level 190 feet, drowning these Nubian treasures unless a preservation plan is implemented.

Metropolitan Museum of Art

A Tiny Son Clings to the Accordion-pleated Kilts of Egypt's "Great" Pharaoh, Ramesses II

On forests of granite obelisks and acres of warlike temple carvings, the ruler boasted of his might. But in this black granite statue, now in Turin, the authority of the shepherd's crook, symbol of power, modified by a tightly gripped handkerchief, and fine linen gives a foppish touch to the war helmet.

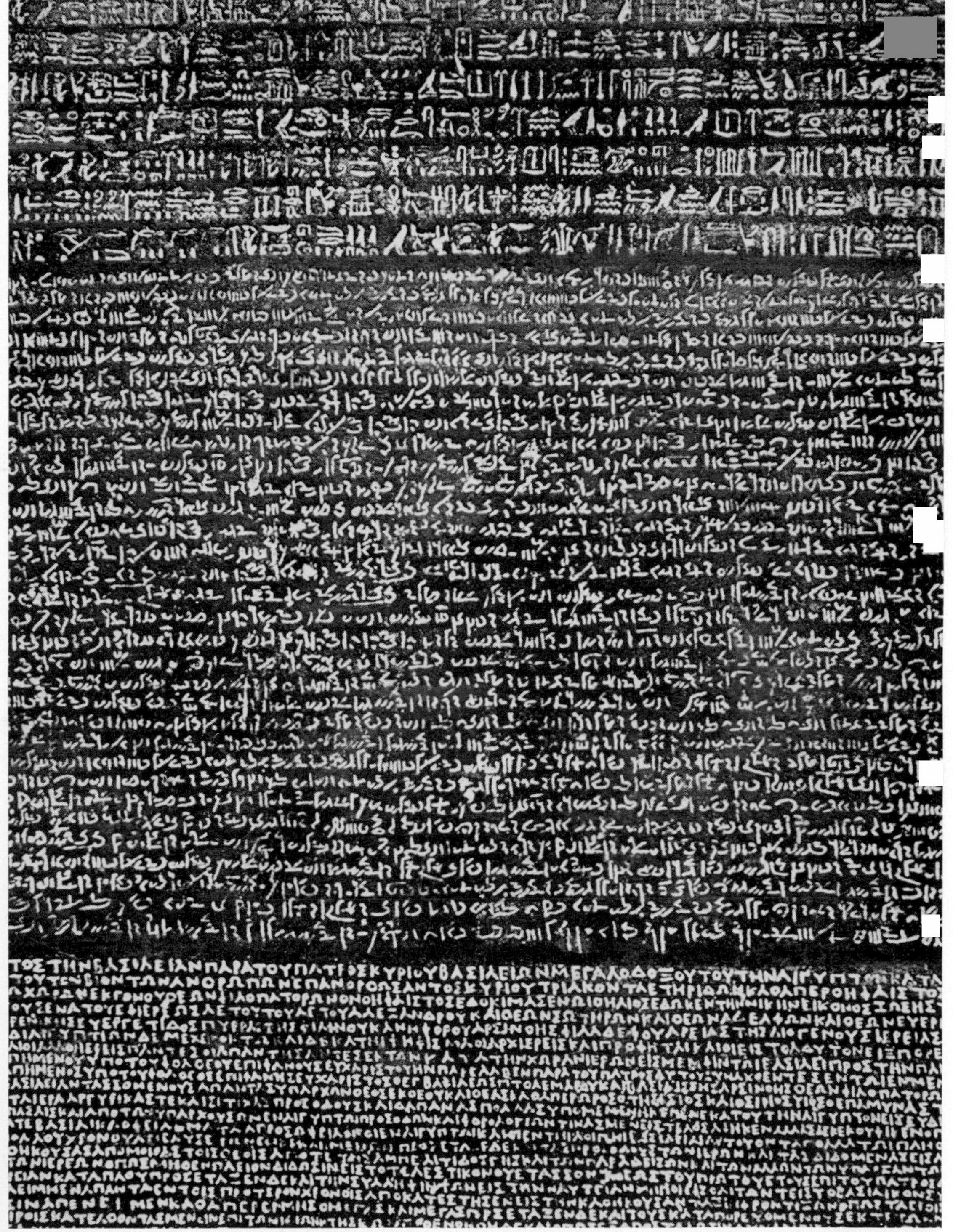

© British Museum

Best Clue to the Language of the Ancient Egyptians Was the Rosetta Stone

About 193 B. C. a 15-year-old Pharaoh was supported by the priests of Memphis. Their decree was inscribed in three forms (top to bottom); the sacred writing or hieroglyphics of the priesthood; the demotic writing of the demos, or people; and the Greek, which was a common tongue of the eastern Mediterranean. In A. D. 1799 one of Napoleon's officers found the basalt block while digging trenches.

© National Geographic Society

Painting by H. M. Herget

"The Entire Land Shall Acclaim Me the Victorious Ruler Within Thebes"

"Ka-mosĕ, who protects Egypt," the last king of the XVIIth Dynasty, with his brother, Aʿḥ-mosĕ, the founder of the XVIIIth Dynasty, and their grandmother, the dowager queen Teti-sheri, inspects a team of chariot horses. (Beginning of the New Kingdom, about 1590 B. C.) See page 75.

The Founders of the New Kingdom

A PAUSE in his successful campaign against the Hyksos has given the Pharaoh Ka-mosĕ an opportunity to return to his capital and enjoy a brief reunion with his family. Against a background formed by the Nile and, in the distance, the well known cliffs of western Thebes, we find the warrior king discussing with his younger brother, Prince Aʿḥ-mosĕ, and his grandmother, Queen Teti-sheri, the merits of a team of horses, destined for the royal stables.

The Egyptians, thanks to the example set them by the enemy, had recently begun to import these hitherto unknown animals from Asia and to use them with epoch-making results in the newly inaugurated chariot division of the army—a branch, which through its mobility and its deadly efficiency was soon to help transform the naturally peaceable inhabitants of the Nile Valley into world conquerors.

Our portrait of King Ka-mosĕ is taken from his man-shaped coffin, unearthed at Thebes in 1857. The elements of the armlet which the Pharaoh wears on his right arm—a cartouche flanked by a pair of small gold lions—were found among the wrappings of his badly decayed mummy. A poniard with a silver handle of the old lenticular pommel type was tied on the left arm of the mummy in Nubian fashion.

The dagger actually shown in Mr. Herget's painting, also the property of Ka-mosĕ, is of Hyksos design, as is also the bronze war axe which the king holds in his right hand. The most interesting of Ka-mosĕ's weapons is his two-handed sword, its bronze blade inscribed with the king's names and titles, its handle delicately inlaid in gold.

The weapons and jewelry worn by Prince Aʿḥ-mosĕ are the most famous products of Egyptian minor art of the early New Kingdom. With the exception of the inlaid silver diadem, all are from the burial of Aʿḥ-mosĕ's mother, Queen Aʿḥ-ḥetpe, discovered at Thebes in February, 1859.

The axe, of copper with a cedar handle, is completely overlaid with gold and electrum, the blade adorned with designs inlaid in carnelian, turquoise enamel, and lapis lazuli.

The figure of the griffin appearing on the blade is a Helladic motif, borrowed directly from the island of Crete, with which Egypt at this time maintained close and friendly relations. There is, indeed, some evidence of a military alliance between the two nations, directed against their common enemy, the Hyksos.

Teti-sheri—"Little Teti"—we know chiefly from a statue in the British Museum, which represents her, not as we see her in the company of her distinguished grandsons, but as a fragile, charming girl, newly married to their grandfather, Prince Taʿo I.

During her long life Queen Teti-sheri played an important rôle in the varying fortunes of her husband, sons, and grandsons, and, revered and beloved, "lived to see Thebes transformed from a little provincial court into the capital of a great empire."

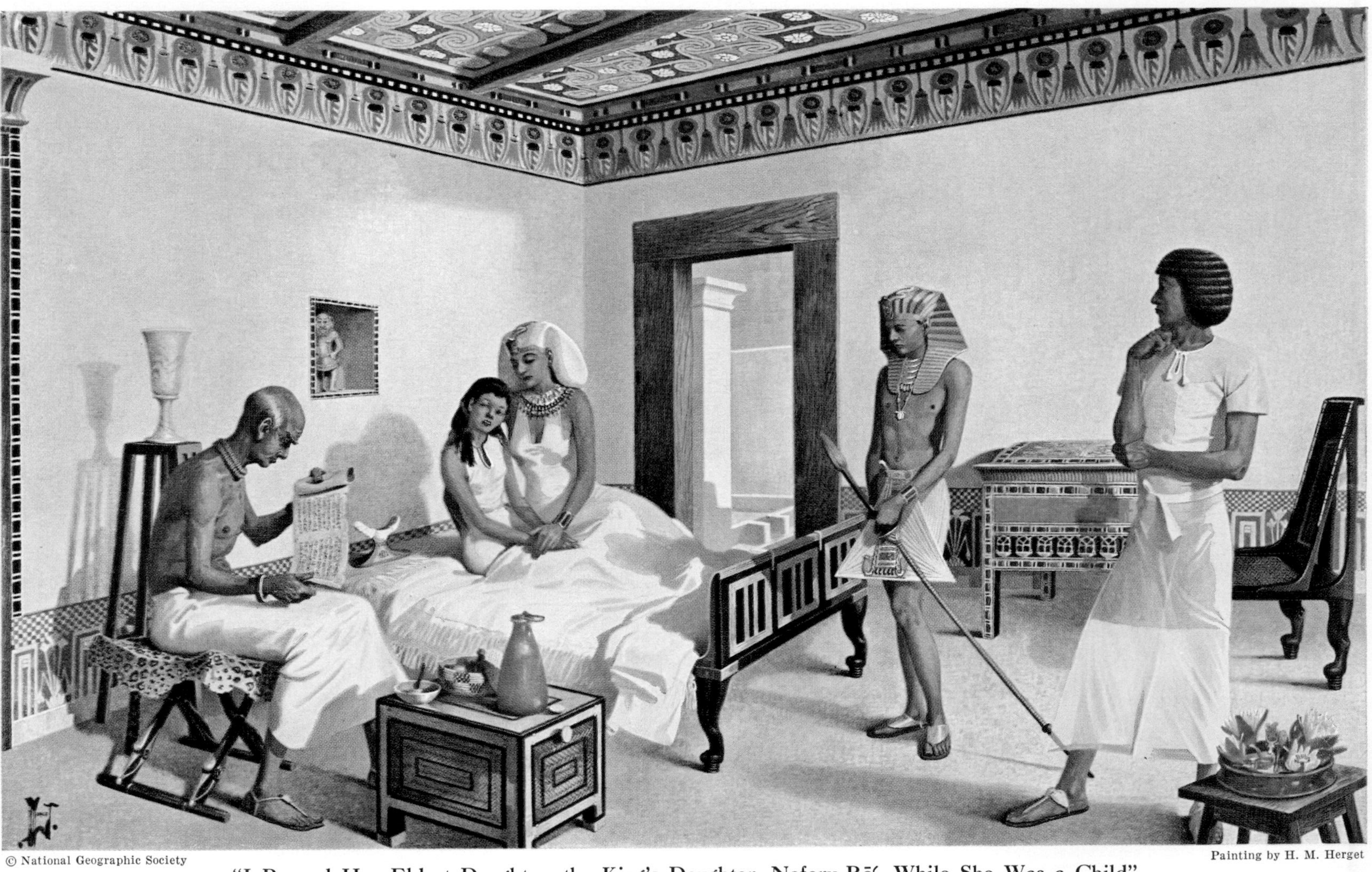

Painting by H. M. Herget

"I Reared Her Eldest Daughter, the King's Daughter, Neferu-Rēʿ, While She Was a Child"

The young princess Neferu-Rēʿ lies ill in her bedroom in the royal palace at Thebes, attended by her mother, Queen Ḥat-shepsūt, her half-brother, King Thut-mosĕ III, and her tutor, Sen-Mūt, the great Steward of Amūn. At the left, the royal physician is consulting his medical papyrus preparatory to mixing a remedy from the ingredients on the inlaid casket before him. Through the doorway at the right can be seen part of the bathroom with its limestone bathing slab and [illegible] joint reign of Ḥat-shepsūt and Thut-mosĕ III, 1501-1480 B. C.)

The Family of King Tḥut-mosĕ I

About 1520 B. C. Tḥut-mosĕ I, king of Egypt and grandson of Aʿḥ-mosĕ I, died and left as his heirs his son, Tḥut-mosĕ II, born to him by one of his secondary wives, and his daughter, Ḥat-shepsūt, the child of his queen.

To strengthen his right to the throne, Tḥut-mosĕ II was married to his brilliant and strong-willed half-sister, and for 18 years the two ruled the country as king and queen. Two daughters, Neferu-Rēʿ and Meryet-Rēʿ Ḥat-shepsūt, were born to the couple.

Tḥut-mosĕ II's only son, Tḥut-mosĕ III, had the misfortune to be the offspring of a harīm girl, named Isis. At his father's death in 1501 B. C. this boy, ten or twelve years old at the time, inherited the throne and the full titles and regalia of kingship.

However, as the courtier Ineny astutely observed, it was "the God's Wife, Ḥat-shepsūt, who managed the affairs of the Two Lands according to her own devices, and Egypt was made to labor with bowed back for her."

In the seventh year of what was, technically, the reign of Tḥut-mosĕ III, Ḥat-shepsūt, in a swift and apparently bloodless *coup d'état,* broke the age-old tradition which had held that only a male could be the ruler of Egypt, and had herself formally proclaimed "king." One of the few women ever to hold that position, she assumed all the titles, attributes, and other paraphernalia of the pharaonic office.

In this startling gesture she was supported by a group of faithful and most able officials, foremost among whom was her special favorite, Sen-Mūt, Chief Steward of the estates of Amūn and tutor of her daughter, the Princess Neferu-Rēʿ.

For fourteen years more Tḥut-mosĕ III, who had been allowed to retain a nominal position as co-regent and had been married to his half-sister, Neferu-Rēʿ, was forced to subject his own proud spirit to the will of his aunt (Ḥat-shepsūt); but from the sixteenth year of his reign onward he began to come into his own.

In this year or shortly afterwards Neferu-Rēʿ died, presumably the victim of an illness, and two or three years later Sen-Mūt fell or was forced out of royal favor. In 1480 B. C., having dominated the first twenty-one years of the reign of her nephew and having stirred in the breast of that spirited young man a hatred for herself which beggars description, Ḥat-shepsūt died or was thrust out of the way.

Thus, Tḥut-mosĕ III at last came into his birthright, and during the remaining 33 years of his long life performed those deeds of high prowess which have justly earned for him a reputation as one of Egypt's greatest pharaohs.

Painting by H. M. Herget

"The Arrival of the King's Messenger in God's Land, Together with the Army Which Is Behind Him, Before the Rulers of Pūnt"

Queen Ḥat-shepsūt's naval expedition, sent to the land of Pūnt on the Somali coast to procure myrrh trees for the garden of the god Amūn, is greeted there by the chief of the country and his deformed wife and daughter. (XVIIIth Dynasty, 8th year of the joint reign of Ḥat-shepsūt and Tḥut-mosĕ III, 1493 B. C.)

A Sea Voyage to a Remote Land

IN THE 8th year of the reign of Tḥut-mosĕ III a fleet of five sailing ships, each about sixty feet in length, unmoored from the bank at Thebes and stood out into the middle of the Nile, headed for the distant and half-legendary land of Pūnt. Dispatched by Queen Ḥat-shepsūt, the expedition was to bring back to Egypt living myrrh trees, to be replanted in the garden of the state god, Amūn.

Pūnt, it is generally agreed, was situated somewhere along the coast of Somaliland. To reach it Ḥat-shepsūt's ships had to sail northward almost as far as modern Suez, cross over by canal into the Red Sea, and then undertake the long and rarely attempted voyage southward.

It is greatly to the credit of the queen's unnamed admiral that the fleet returned safely to Thebes in the following year. It had brought back, in addition to the potted myrrh trees, rich cargoes of ebony, ivory, gold, electrum, aromatic woods, cosmetics, and panther skins, not to mention apes, dogs, and natives of Pūnt.

The land of Pūnt and the entire progress of the expedition are pictured and described in detail in a set of painted reliefs, which, most happily, are preserved in Ḥat-shepsūt's temple at Deir el-Baḥri at Thebes (page 142).

Our plate on page 140, drawn in its entirety from these reliefs, portrays the arrival of the fleet at Pūnt. The flagship has already touched shore, its sail is furled, and its mooring stake is being driven into the sand of the beach by two muscular members of the crew.

The Egyptian admiral, accompanied by a detachment of marines, has landed and is about to ingratiate himself with the natives by means of a modest present of Egyptian weapons and cheap trinkets. These he has laid out on the small table before him, hoping that their glittering appearance will please those who have come to meet him.

Peʿ-reʿ-hu, the tall, thin chief of Pūnt, and Eʿty, his fat, sway-backed wife, were too striking a pair to have been overlooked by the Egyptian artist, who evidently accompanied the expedition, and in the temple reliefs referred to they are depicted to the life.

These reliefs have, in fact, supplied us with nearly every detail of our painting: the Egyptian ships, their rigging, and their crews; the curious domical pile-dwellings of Pūnt; the local flora and fauna; the facial types, clothing, coiffures, and ornaments of the Pūntites; and even the mongrel pup, which barks a welcome to the visitors from afar.

Racially and even culturally the Pūntites and the Egyptians appear to have been related—a fact which seems in no way to have lessened the intense curiosity with which the two peoples regarded each other.

Painting by H. M. Herget

"Thou Seest Amūn in His Beautiful Festival of the Valley, Thou Accompaniest Him into the Shrines and Temples"

The procession of the barque of the god Amūn leaves the temple of Queen Ḥat-shepsūt at Deir el-Baḥri. From the upper, balustraded ramp of the temple, it has passed to the second terrace. Pillars of the third portico, above, show painted limestone statues of Ḥat-shepsūt in the form of the god Osiris. To the right is the shrine of Anubis and the famous "proto-Doric" colonnade. (XVIIIth Dynasty, later part of the joint reign of Ḥat-shepsūt and Tḥut-mosĕ III, 1485-1480 B. C.)

Amūn-Rēʿ, "King of the Gods," Pays His Yearly Visit to Queen Ḥat-shepsūt's Temple in Western Thebes

Ḥat-shepsūt's mortuary temple, designed and built for her by Sen-Mūt, occupies an imposing bay of the western cliffs at Thebes, three miles back from the bank of the Nile and almost immediately opposite the great temple of Amūn at El Karnak. Nestled into the base of the precipitous rock walls of the cliff and admirably adapted to its magnificent natural setting, this unusual building, even in its present ruined state, is a monument of great charm.

From the level of the desert plain the courts of the temple, each fronted by a beautifully proportioned colonnade, rise in wide, retreating steps, the upper court and the central sanctuary cut back into the living rock. Leading from the river bank to the temple there was in ancient times a walled avenue, three miles long, bordered by trees and flanked along its entire length by brightly colored sandstone sphinxes of the female "king."

Once a year, on the occasion of the "Festival of the Western Valley," the image of the god Amūn was ferried across the river from El Karnak in the great state barge "Powerful-is-the-Front-of-Amūn." It was borne up this avenue in the richly adorned portable boat of the god, and deposited for a short time in the sanctuary of the temple, where the god would receive tribute (page 120).

After accepting the prescribed offerings from the royal patron of the temple, the god, still in his barque, was borne down the ramps to the plain, and for two days made visits to temples on the west bank before returning to El Karnak.

The barque was carried on the shoulders of thirty-two priests, who paused to rest from time to time at stations provided at regular intervals along the way. A motley procession of standard-bearers, fan-bearers, censers, soldiers, musicians, singers, and priests preceded the barque.

Outside the temple precincts the procession was joined by the townspeople of Thebes, for whom this festival, like the many others celebrated throughout the year, was a never-ending source of delight.

The details of the barque and the procession are drawn chiefly from the somewhat later reliefs which the young King Tūt-ʿankh-Amūn caused to be carved in the temple of Amūn at Luxor. The reconstruction of Ḥat-shepsūt's temple we owe largely to long years of work and study by the Egyptian Expedition of New York's Metropolitan Museum.

Egyptian Chariots at Armageddon

THUT-MOSĚ III's first act, upon finding himself sole ruler of Egypt, was the attempt to erase every trace and destroy completely the memory of Ḥat-shepsūt. Her inscriptions, wherever visible, were covered over or mutilated, her statues were smashed to pieces, and her name was stricken from the roll of the Egyptian royal family.

Having vented the accumulated rage of twenty years on the monuments of his detested co-regent, the young king immediately put into operation his plans for the re-conquest of the Egyptian empire. He directed his first blow at Syria, where the local dynasts, profiting by the two decades of Ḥat-shepsūt's womanly rule, were in full revolt.

On the 15th of May, 1478 B. C., the Egyptian army, descending from the heights of Carmel, fell upon the Syrian allies in the plain of Esdraelon, driving them back into the strategically important and heavily fortified city of Megiddo, which was promptly invested and soon forced to surrender.

Tḥut-mosě III's arrogant disdain for military strategy in this and in most of his other battles was more than compensated for by the efficiency of the Egyptian war chariot as a fighting machine. Of strong, but very light construction, these vehicles were capable of attaining great speed instantly. They could be maneuvered with the utmost ease, and, thanks to their long axles and large, springy wheels, were usable over almost any type of terrain.

Unarmored and partaking of none of the qualities of the modern "tank," the chariot was intended solely to provide a movable platform from which the crack Egyptian archer could pour a murderous rain of arrows upon a less mobile enemy force.

More often than not in the early New Kingdom each warrior managed his own chariot, as shown in our plate. Later, however, we find the chariot crews consisting of two men, a charioteer and a fighter.

During the ensuing eighteen years Tḥut-mosě III led no less than sixteen expeditions into Asia, setting out in the spring of each year and returning in the fall, flushed with new conquests and laden with plunder and tribute. When, in the 43rd year of his reign, the now aging monarch turned his face from the north and concentrated his always vigorous attention on his Nubian provinces and on matters at home, he had reduced hither Asia to abject servility and given the eastern Mediterranean world a beating that it did not forget for centuries to come.

Painting by H. M. Herget

"His Majesty Went Forth in a Chariot of Electrum, Arrayed in His Weapons of War"

King Tḥut-mosĕ III, leading his chariot division, charges the host of the Syrians in the plain before Har Megiddo, the Biblical Armageddon. He wears the Blue Crown, or royal war helmet, and about his chest is bound a gold-overlaid leather corselet. His heavy compound bow can drive bronze-tipped arrows through a thick sheet of metal. Javelins, and extra arrows and bows are in cases strapped to the vehicle. (XVIIIth Dynasty, 23rd regnal year of Tḥut-mosĕ III, 1478 B. C.)

The Vintage of 1400 B. C.

On page 147 it is no longer spring on the blood-drenched field of Armageddon, but late summer on the Egyptian estate of the Royal Scribe, Khaʿ-em-ḥēt. The purple grapes, hanging ripe from the extensive arbor of the wealthy official, are being harvested by Khaʿ-em-ḥēt's farm hands. Among the laborers we can recognize, besides the native Egyptians, a negro from Central Africa, a bearded Semite from the district of the Lebanon, and a blond Caucasian from the northern shores of the Mediterranean—a rather cosmopolitan crew.

Carried in baskets to the pottery (?) wine press, the grapes are trodden by a singing group of men and boys, who, to prevent themselves from slipping in the juicy mash, are clinging to ropes suspended from a framework.

The new wine is scooped from the catch-basin and promptly "bottled" in large pottery amphorae, the interiors of which have been coated with a non-porous film of resin. The jars are capped with heavy mud stoppers, pierced with vents to prevent the fermenting liquid from bursting its containers or "blowing the cork."

The stoppers, while still damp, are stamped in several places with the name of the estate or its owner, and on the sides of the jars is written the date of bottling. The transportation of each of the heavy vessels to the wine cellar is accomplished by means of an intricately netted pot-sling, carried on a stout pole by two men.

In the arbor we see a man pouring water into the trenches from which spring the roots of the vines. At the right a peasant is irrigating the near-by field with the aid of a "shadūf," or well-sweep, a Mesopotamian invention, introduced into Egypt in the XVIIIth Dynasty and still in common use.

Second in popularity only to beer, wine was manufactured and consumed on a large scale by the ancient Egyptians from at least as early as the first historic dynasty (3000 B. C.). In addition to the domestic grape, palm, date, and pomegranate wines, foreign vintages, imported in bulk from Asia, were also much in favor with the discerning drinkers of the dynastic era.

Always a farmer at heart, the wealthy Egyptian official seems never to have let his love for his country estates wane during the centuries of Egyptian history. Over and over again in their sculptured or brightly painted tomb-chapels at Thebes great men like Khaʿ-em-ḥēt are shown inspecting all the activities of their farms, frequently taking their lunches with them and making a day of it.

Painting by H. M. Herget

"Causing the Vintage to Be Pressed"

At the grape harvest and the making of wine on the estate of the Royal Scribe, Khaʿ-em-ḥēt, Khaʿ-em-ḥēt in person appears (left), dressed for a tour of his fields. His leather shin-guards are to protect his legs from brambles and the like. The roof of the typical New Kingdom house in the background is fitted with large ventilators to catch whatever breeze may be blowing during the scorching Egyptian summer. (XVIIIth Dynasty, reign of King Amen-ḥotpe III, 1400-1375 B. C.)

A Family Outing in the Papyrus Pools

THE courtier Menena, like most other Egyptian husbands and fathers, was an indulgent man, and, when his job as "Scribe of the Fields of the Lord of the Two Lands" permitted him a little time off for duck hunting, he took his whole family with him. His making a family outing of the hunt was perhaps because the joy of merely being out on the cool water in his skiff of bundled papyrus reeds outweighed either the desire or the necessity of bringing in a large bag of ducks.

Menena is, however, tending strictly to business, his two decoy birds—small herons—held high in his left hand above the towering papyrus, into which the skiff has been nosed, his boomerang poised in his right hand for the throw.

The boomerang, or throw stick, was a favorite sporting weapon in Egypt from the earliest times, and so expert did its users become that they were capable at close range of knocking down a bird as it was rising in flight.

The pintail ducks, seen rising to the right, will be one fewer when this expert marksman has made his cast. Promptly the stunned bird will be retrieved by the light-footed cat which stands in the bow of the skiff beside Menena's son.

The two daughters are less interested in their father's sport than in the gathering of lotus flowers for decorating either themselves or their home; but Menena's wife, in addition to holding his spare boomerangs, is showing the proper zeal.

The family, with the exception of the younger daughter, may seem a bit over-dressed for a picnic in the papyrus thickets, but this is the way they are all represented in the famous painting in Menena's tomb at Thebes.

The papyrus plant, here shown serving as a natural blind for an amateur duck hunter, played a dominant rôle in ancient Egyptian life, art, and industry. Bound together, its sturdy seven-foot stalks formed supports for the roofs of the Egyptians' earliest houses, and from these primitive uprights developed the graceful papyrus column of the type, which, carved in stone at a colossal scale, upholds the roofs of the great temples of the New Kingdom.

From roped bundles of papyrus the Egyptian built his first boats, similar to the skiff shown here. The fibres of the pith of the reed provided him with the material for his writing paper, and from the tough outer bark he made baskets, hampers, crates, and furniture of all sorts. As the emblem of Lower Egypt, where it grows thickest, and as a constantly employed heraldic and decorative motif the plant is well known in its conventionalized form to anyone acquainted with Egyptian art. Few plants have played so outstanding a part in the life of a nation as did the papyrus in the ancient land of the Nile.

Painting by H. M. Herget

"Amuse Thyself with Field Sports; the Water Fowl Has His Moment of Death Reckoned for Him"

The courtier Menena, accompanied by his family, enjoys a pleasant day fowling in the papyrus thickets. The skiffs and their occupants waited silently behind the natural blinds formed by the papyrus until the birds, attracted by the decoys, came within range of the throw-stick. (XVIIIth Dynasty, reign of King Tḥut-mosĕ IV, 1420-1411 B. C.)

At Home with the Average Egyptian and His Wife

Any general account of ancient Egypt is, of necessity, largely taken up with the splendor of its rulers, the wealth of its great officials, and, at the opposite end of the scale, the simple poverty of its peasants. Thus we are prone to forget that, as in every great country, there existed at all times in the Nile Valley a large and, for the most part, well-to-do middle class—good, solid citizens, individually of no particular importance, but, collectively, the backbone of the nation.

Two such people appear on page 151. The man is, let us say, a clerk in a branch of the royal treasury, his wife a singer in the temple choir of Amūn. Their clothes, their few articles of jewelry, and the furnishings of their home, though hardly magnificent, are of good quality.

In addition to their house and small garden they probably own a little farmland, on which they pay the required taxes. It is likely that out of their modest living expenses they have saved enough to send their son to the school of scribes at Thebes and so assure him of respectable and well paid employment when he comes of age.

Just now the couple are amusing themselves with one of their most prized possessions—a game-box of cedar, inlaid with panels of blue faience. The top and bottom of the box carry the squared lay-outs, or "boards," for the two most popular Egyptian draughts games, the game of Senīt on the top, the game of Tshau ("Robbers") on the underside.

The faience playing pieces, which are the same for both games, were kept, when not in use, in the drawer in the end of the box. The set of four carved wands was used in place of knuckle-bones or dice, the way in which they fell, crossed, or pointed, when cast by a player, determining the moves that player was allowed to make.

The game in progress, Senīt, was played on a board of thirty squares, the squares laid out in three rows of ten. Certain key squares are inscribed as being advantageous or disadvantageous to the player landing on them.

Six pieces (usually conical or spool shaped) were used by each player, the object of the game being, not to take the opponent's pieces, but, apparently, to pass through them and return to the original starting point, at the same time blocking the other fellow's moves as much as possible.

The prominent rôle played by such games in the lives of the ancient Egyptians is indicated by the fact that a picture of a draughtsboard was one of the oldest and most common signs used in their written language, and that the games played on it are mentioned repeatedly in their funerary and religious literature.

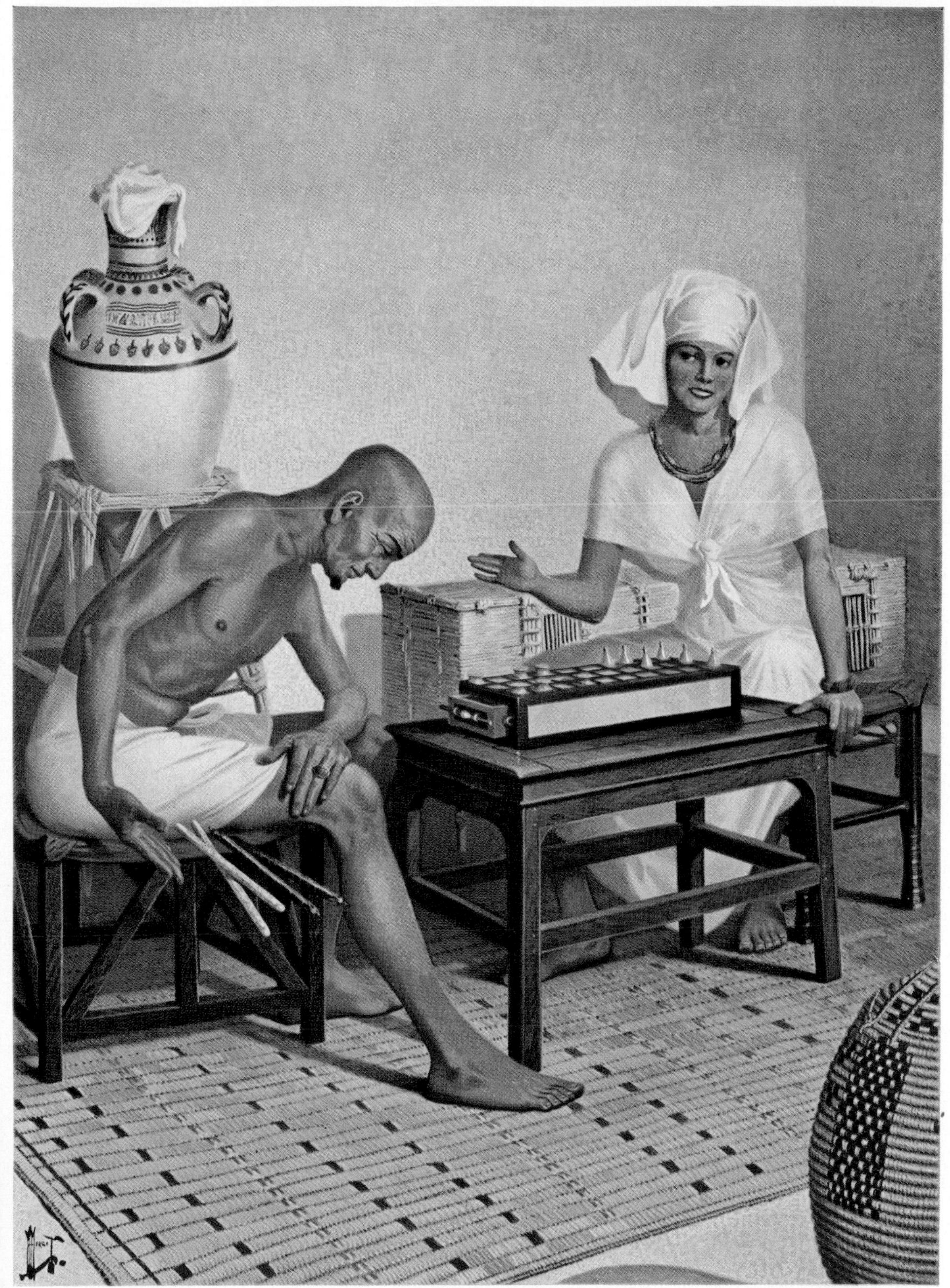

 Painting by H. M. Herget

"Sitting . . . , Playing Draughts, and Finding Twofold Contentment"

A middle-class Egyptian couple enjoy playing "Senīt," one of several popular table games of the dynastic Egyptians. In play it resembled modern parchesi and backgammon. The moves were determined by the manner in which the set of four sticks, or wands, fell when cast. (Mid-XVIIIth Dynasty, 1500-1400 B. C.)

The Aten Shines, King Akh-en-Aten Dreams, and the XVIIIth Dynasty Draws to a Close

As the XVIIIth Dynasty passed into its third century, Egypt, imbued with Asiatic ideas and Asiatic blood, which now flowed even in the veins of the royal family, turned momentarily from its old traditions and its old gods, and set up a new religion devoted exclusively to the worship of the vital force emanating from the disk of the sun, "the living Aten."

Simpler and more general in its appeal than the old Amūn cult, which it attempted to replace, this monotheistic solar religion concerned itself not at all with morality, but placed its emphasis on "harmony," joy of living, love of nature, intellectual liberty, individualism and spontaneity. Brief as was its existence, its effect on Egyptian life, and particularly on Egyptian art, endured for many centuries after the "heresy" itself had been forgotten.

The chief exponent of the worship of the Aten was King Amen-ḥotpe III's effeminate son, Amen-ḥotpe IV, who came to the throne of Egypt in 1375 B. C. For four years this sensitive idealist ruled at Thebes, and then, accompanied by his beautiful wife, Queen Nefret-īty, and a large group of devoted courtiers, withdrew to the quiet isolation of Tell el-ʿAmārneh (El ʿAmârna), some two hundred miles down the Nile, where he caused to be built for himself and for his god a wonderful new city, named Akhet-Aten, "Horizon-of-Aten."

Here, having changed his own name to Akh-en-Aten ("Spirit-of-Aten"), the pharaoh dreamed away the remaining fifteen years of his reign, while the empire of his fathers, ignored and forgotten, fell slowly to pieces and disorder, and lawlessness overran the land of Egypt.

Before he died, Akh-en-Aten attempted to reconcile himself with the much persecuted, but still powerful, priesthood of Amūn, and in so doing incurred the displeasure of Queen Nefret-īty, who removed herself to a palace in the extreme southern section of Akhet-Aten, and took with her thither her second daughter, ʿAnkh-es-en-pa-Aten, and the latter's husband, young Tūt-ʿankh-Aten.

Following the brief reign of Akh-en-Aten's elder son-in-law, Semenkh-ka-Rēʿ, Tūt-ʿankh-Aten came to the throne, moved the royal residence back to Thebes, altered his name to Tūt-ʿankh-Amūn, and permitted the old religion and the old order of things to be restored.

At the end of a short and otherwise insignificant reign, Tūt-ʿankh-Amūn—famous principally because his tomb miraculously remained intact until its discovery in 1922—died at the age of eighteen, and was himself succeeded by the same Ay who appears in the foreground of the plate on page 153, now a decrepit old man.

Ḥar-em-ḥab and the XIXth Dynasty

Ay did not last long, and about 1340 B. C. the government was taken over by the Quartermaster-General Ḥar-em-ḥab, a man of great vigor, experience, and administrative ability, who during his twenty years as pharaoh repaired most of the damage wrought during the "ʿAmārneh (ʿAmârna) Period" and died leaving Egypt and the Empire once more sound and prosperous.

At the death of Ḥar-em-ḥab in 1320 B. C. the throne passed to his old companion-in-arms, General Pa-Ramessu, better known as King Ramesses I, founder of the XIXth Dynasty.

© National Geographic Society

Painting by H. M. Herget

"Lo, His Majesty Appeared Like the Sun in His Palace . . ."

King Akh-en-Aten and Queen Nefret-īty, standing on the "Balcony of Royal Appearances" at Tell el-ʿAmārneh (El ʿAmârna), publicly award the "gold of honor" to a favored courtier, the Priest Ạy, later king of Egypt. Ạy is surrounded by his wife, friends, and children. (Late XVIIIth Dynasty, reign of Akh-en-Aten, 1375-1357 B. C.)

A Wealthy Theban Is Buried in His Tomb in the Western Cliffs

In 1318 B. C. the aged Ramesses gave way to his son, the brilliant Sethy I, who, after twenty-one years as king, was replaced by *his* son, Ramesses II—probably the best known of all Egypt's pharaohs (page 134).

The kings who followed Ramesses II—including Mer-en-Ptaḥ, often identified as "the pharaoh of the Exodus"—sink into insignificance beside his titanic figure; but it was not until many years after his death that the New Kingdom came to an end and dynastic Egypt entered upon its last, long drawn out death struggle.

With this briefest of historical outlines as a background, we are now ready to resume our inspection of the existences of the people who experienced life and death under the pharaohs just named. Let us start with a death.

The funeral procession, leaving the city of the living on the east bank of the Nile, has crossed the river, wound deep into the western cliffs, where lie the "eternal dwellings" of the dead, and halted before the portico of a freshly prepared tomb. The ox-drawn hearse, reproducing in its form the barque of the sun-god Rēʿ, stands empty at the left of the picture, and behind and past it come the bearers of the tomb furniture and other funerary equipment.

Beyond the hearse we see the "Canopic" chest, also mounted upon a sledge, and containing, in four stone jars, the four vital organs of the dead man, removed from his body during the process of mummification. At the left end of the portico the "Muu," a pair of mummers, wearing burlesque crowns of reeds, are performing their curious funeral dance.

The body of the dead, enclosed in a coffin made in the form of the god Osiris, has been stood upright before the door of the tomb, supported by a masked priest, impersonating the dog-headed god Anubis, the divine embalmer.

The "Sem," or chief mortuary priest, wearing the leopard skin of his office and assisted by a group of other priests, is "opening the mouth" of (i.e., restoring speech to) the deceased by touching the lips of the coffin with a ceremonial instrument shaped like an adze.

This act of magic, one of the final rites in the burial service, is witnessed in gloomy silence by the male relatives of the dead man, who sit brooding at the right of the scene. It is greeted with wails of anguish and violent gestures of grief by the female mourners, many of whom are undoubtedly professionals hired for the occasion.

The sorrow of the woman who clings to the legs of the coffin, however, is genuine, for she is the widow of the deceased, and even her conviction, that, in dying, he has but passed to a new and better life, is small comfort.

High above on the capstone of the pyramid the spirit of the dead man is depicted singing the morning hymn to the sun-god, Rēʿ, a song of praise repeated each dawn as the first rays of the sun warm the granite pinnacle of the tomb.

Painting by H. M. Herget

"A Funeral Procession Is Made for Thee on the Day of Burial"

At a New Kingdom funeral in western Thebes, the tomb chapel, its columned portico built of limestone blocks, its interior hewn out of the living rock, is surmounted by a small pyramid of brick, covered with stucco and capped by a granite pyramidion. In the porch may be seen the stela and two funerary statues of the deceased, and in the court before the chapel, the mouth of the secret burial shaft. "The mummy-shell is of gold, with head of lapis lazuli; the cover is (closed) over thee and thou art placed upon a sledge. Oxen drag thee and the dance of the Muu is performed for thee at the door of the tomb." (XVIIIth-XIXth Dynasties, 1500-1200 B. C.)

User-ḥēt Entertains

Complacent in his assurance of a blessed immortality, the ancient Egyptian was unawed by the prospect of death. His hearty version of the motto, "Eat, drink, and be merry, for tomorrow we die," was said, as it has always been intended to be said, carelessly and cheerfully. His talent for enjoying the good things of this life was enormous, and his often elaborate parties were rollicking affairs indeed.

Prodigious consumption of spiced wine and beer featured these banquets, and guests were urged repeatedly to drink long and deeply. Rich and heavy perfumes filled the banquet hall, and garlands and bouquets of fresh flowers were everywhere to be seen. Brightly painted wine jars, and cups, bowls, and vases of gold, silver, and alabaster added a note of gaiety and opulence.

Music was provided by orchestras of thinly clad girls, playing the double reed pipe, the three-stringed lute, the six-stringed lyre, and the twenty-two stringed harp, and beating out the time on big rectangular tambourines.

As the feasts, formal and decorous at the outset, gathered momentum, the tinkly rhythms increased their tempo, and the dancers passed from slow, dignified posturings to wilder and more exciting movements, often culminating in a series of leaps, somersaults, back flips, and hand-springs.

All the while an army of butlers and serving girls circulated among the guests, plying them with food of every description, flavoring their drinks with spices poured out of little silver pitchers, supplying them with fresh garlands and fresh cones of perfume, rearranging their elaborate, but often disordered clothing, and helping them in other ways.

At the end of the party some of the participants had to be assisted, or even carried, to their homes; but this was regarded as a compliment to the hospitality of the host.

Urging his master to make the most of the fleeting hour, a harper at such an ancient Egyptian feast once sang:

"Put unguent and fine oil together to thy nostrils,
And garlands and lotus flowers on the body of thy beloved,
As she sitteth beside thee.
Set singing and music before thy face.
Cast all evil behind thee and bethink thee of joy,
Until that day cometh when one reacheth port
In the land that loveth silence."

Painting by H. M. Herget

"Spend the Day Merrily, O Priest!"

User-ḥēt, Chief Priest of the Royal Spirit of King Tḥut-mosĕ I, gives a formal banquet in the central hall of his town house at Thebes. The host and hostess are seated together in the right foreground. The cones of perfumed fat, perched on the heads of the banqueters, will in the course of the long, hot afternoon melt and run down over their persons. (XIXth Dynasty, reign of King Sethy I, 1318-1298 B. C.)

Painting by H. M. Herget

"And There Was Made for Me a Tomb in the Midst of the Tombs"

"The masons that hew tombs marked out its plan; the master-draughtsmen designed in it; the master-sculptors carved in it; and the master-architects who are in the necropolis bestowed their care upon it." It was customary to plaster and paint each part of a tomb as soon as it was cut, even though the adjoining portions might be still in the process of excavation. In this scene at Thebes artists are laying out the decoration of the transverse forehall of the private tomb chapel, while masons and basket boys are at work in the as yet unfinished longitudinal passage. (XVIIIth-XIXth Dynasties, 1500-1200 B. C.)

Preparation of a Painted Tomb-chapel—The Egyptian Artist and His Methods

A T-SHAPED tomb-chapel, hewn out of the side of a hill in the Theban necropolis, is nearing completion. The rock-cut walls of the forehall of the chapel have been given a thick coating of plaster and, being now ready to receive their decoration, have been turned over to a learned scribe and his staff of painters and draughtsmen.

The latter are engaged in transferring to the walls a series of scenes and inscriptions, already planned and drawn up at small scale on flakes of limestone. To insure accurate enlargements of the original drawings and to maintain the strict canon of proportions, under which the Egyptian artist always worked, proportion squares are laid out on both the sketches and the walls, the lines which form the squares being "snapped" on by means of a cord coated with red pigment.

The man marking off the spacing of the lines is using a measuring rod, one royal cubit (20.6 inches) in length, divided into 7 "palms" of 4 "digits" each. On the squared "grid" so prepared there is made a full-size preliminary sketch in red outline and, over this, the finished drawing in black outline, a fine reed brush being used to lay in both drawings.

In coloring the drawings, the inscriptions, the borders, and the backgrounds, the painters will use blue, red, yellow, and green pigments, ground to powder on the spot and mixed with beeswax, albumin, gum, or a similar vehicle. Their paint brushes are palm sticks with carefully frayed ends, or bundles of grass lashed tightly together with grass cord.

Meanwhile the excavation of the longitudinal passage of the chapel is progressing rapidly. The stream of limestone chip, falling from the heavy bronze chisels of the stonecutters, is being run out of the tomb by an endless line of basket-boys; and already the plasterers are at work, smoothing over the walls at the forward end of the passage. Presiding over all this part of the work is the gang foreman, armed with his symbol of office—a heavy whip, impressive and formidable in appearance, but probably rarely used.

Many tombs at Thebes and elsewhere were pressed into service while their decoration and often even their excavation was in an unfinished state. Such tombs have provided the modern student with invaluable information as to the methods used. This information has been swelled by the discovery near several tombs of the work records and other memoranda, written down day by day on potsherds and flakes of limestone by the scribes in charge of the work.

Discarded by the ancient writers as soon as they had served their purpose, these short notes give us a vivid picture of the daily progress of the work, of the number and types of artisans employed, of the materials, food, and clothing supplied to the gangs, and of the amusing small details which cropped up during the course of the job.

Painting by H. M. Herget

"Lo, His Majesty Was at the City, Called 'House-of-Ramesses-Beloved-of Amūn' . . . There Came the King's Messenger . . . to Crave Peace"

Ramesses II, enthroned in the audience hall of his Delta palace, receives a delegation of Asiatics, headed by the envoy of Khattushili, king of the Hittites, with whom he subsequently concluded a treaty of peace. On the pharaoh's right stands his eldest son, Prince Amūn-ḥer-khepesh-ef, and, drawn up beside the throne dais, are members of the king's Sardinian bodyguard, as well as native Egyptian troops. The lion is a royal pet. (XIXth Dynasty, 21st year of Ramesses II, 1277 B. C.)

Ramesses "the Great"

WHETHER or not the second of the twelve kings of Egypt named Ramesses was entitled to the epithet now commonly applied to him is an open question. There can, however, be no doubt that, if not actually "great," he was one of the most remarkable—or, better, "incredible"—rulers the earth has known. A few statistics will show what is meant.

Ramesses II, born in 1318 B. C., came to the throne in 1298 and reigned the amazing total of 67 years, dying in 1232 at the ripe age of 86.

The names of seven of his queens, seventy-nine of his sons, and thirty-one of his daughters have been preserved to us, but this probably does not begin to represent the total number of his wives and children.

Buildings erected, enlarged, or completed in his reign include the Ramesseum—his great mortuary temple and palace in western Thebes—, the temple of Amūn at Luxor, the hypostyle hall and other structures at El Karnak, his own and his father's temples at Abŷdos, his father's temple at El Qurna, the temple of Ptaḥ at Memphis, several large buildings at Tanis, a palace at Ḳantīr (Qantir) and two imposing rock temples at Abû Simbil in Nubia (pages 132-133).

By virtue of his own gigantic building activities and his constant usurpation of the monuments of earlier kings, his name appears on almost every ancient building in Egypt and on literally hundreds of lesser monuments.

As a warrior he was less distinguished than as a builder. He did, however, conduct allegedly successful campaigns against the Nubians, the Libyans, the Syrians, and the Mediterranean islanders; and managed to check for the time being the rising power of the Hittites of Asia Minor. His outstanding military exploit was his inconclusive victory over the Hittites and their allies in the battle of Kadesh, where, whatever else may be said of him, he did undoubtedly display great personal valor.

Personally Ramesses II was every inch a king: tall, handsome, majestic in his bearing, and utterly reckless, both on the field of battle and in civil life. His vitality has probably never been surpassed, and this, coupled with his undoubted popularity, permitted him to accomplish deeds, which a nobler and more intelligent ruler might well have found impossible.

His greatest faults were his insatiable desire for publicity and his unparalleled talent for boasting—faults which have too often caused posterity, unimpressed and thoroughly bored by his endless self-eulogies, to dismiss him as an empty and pompous "blowhard," unworthy of serious consideration.

Painting by H. M. Herget

"Captivity Which His Majesty Brought, for the Works of the Temple of Amūn"

Foreign captives, among whom may be recognized several men of Semitic race, are engaged in making bricks for a construction ramp used in building the temple of Amūn at El Karnak. The scene, though taken from an XVIIIth Dynasty tomb painting, shows precisely the kind of work exacted from the Hebrews by the XIXth Dynasty "pharaoh of the oppression." The network loincloths worn by the laborers are of slit leather. (XVIIIth-XIXth Dynasties, 1500-1200 B. C.)

The Manufacture and Use of Brick in Ancient Egypt

THE average dictionary or encyclopedia derives the word *adobe* from the Spanish *adobar,* "to plaster," and lets it go at that; but *dobe,* meaning "brick," was a common word in ancient Egypt fifty centuries before the Spaniards invaded the Western Hemisphere, and, as the Arabic *ṭuba,* survives to the present day.

Nor have the methods of making and using the Egyptian sun-dried mud brick changed one iota since the prehistoric period. The modern brickmaker uses the same simple wooden mold seen in our plate, "strikes" his bricks in the same manner as did his remote ancestor, and leaves them to dry on the same flat mud surface under the same scorching sun. Only the size of the brick itself has changed, the New Kingdom bricks (14 x 7 x 4½ inches) being larger than the modern product.

The mud used for making bricks has always been the dark gray Nile alluvium, mixed with sand or chopped barley straw, and kneaded with water into a thick paste. The straw, though helpful as a binder and a drying agent, is by no means essential, many excellent bricks having been turned out, using only sand as a binder, or, if the clay content of the mud was high, with no binder at all.

For six thousand years sun-dried brick has been the principal building material of the Egyptians, far surpassing in the extent of its use cut stone. The latter, first employed in the IInd Dynasty, has been confined almost entirely to the construction of funerary and religious monuments, every other type of building—dwellings, city and temple walls, forts, storehouses, ramps, etc.—being of brick.

At an early period the Egyptian not only learned the secret of the arch and barrel vault, but mastered methods of laying and bonding brick, which enabled him to construct walls and embankments of enormous thickness, as, for example, the 80-foot girdle wall of the city of Tanis.

Without construction ramps, buttresses, sand-chambers, and temporary scaffoldings of brick, the pyramids at Gîza and the temple of Amūn at El Karnak could never have been built, and it is therefore to the ancient Egyptians' knowledge of the uses of the humbler material that we owe the existence of these greatest of all stone monuments.

Decline of Egypt in the Late Dynastic Period

A civilization like that of ancient Egypt cannot be wiped out in a day. It required, in fact, almost nine hundred years—from the XIXth Dynasty to the Macedonian conquest in 332 B. C.—for the dynastic era to pass out of existence.

During most of this period the country appeared outwardly as sound as ever and at times seemed to have recovered much of its old splendor—notably, in the reign of Ramesses III of the XXth Dynasty and during the brilliant, if fleeting, revival fostered by the Saïte kings of the XXVIth Dynasty.

Actually, however, Egypt was on its last legs: priest-ridden, economically unsound, sapped of its native vitality by centuries of luxury and self-indulgence, overrun by foreigners, and depending for its defense on an army composed almost entirely of mercenary troops.

In its weakened condition it was an easy mark for the new and powerful neighboring states, with which it now found itself surrounded; and the story of the end of dynastic Egypt is one of a long succession of foreign rulers, interrupted at intervals by the short-lived and, for the most part, local governments set up by petty, native dynasts.

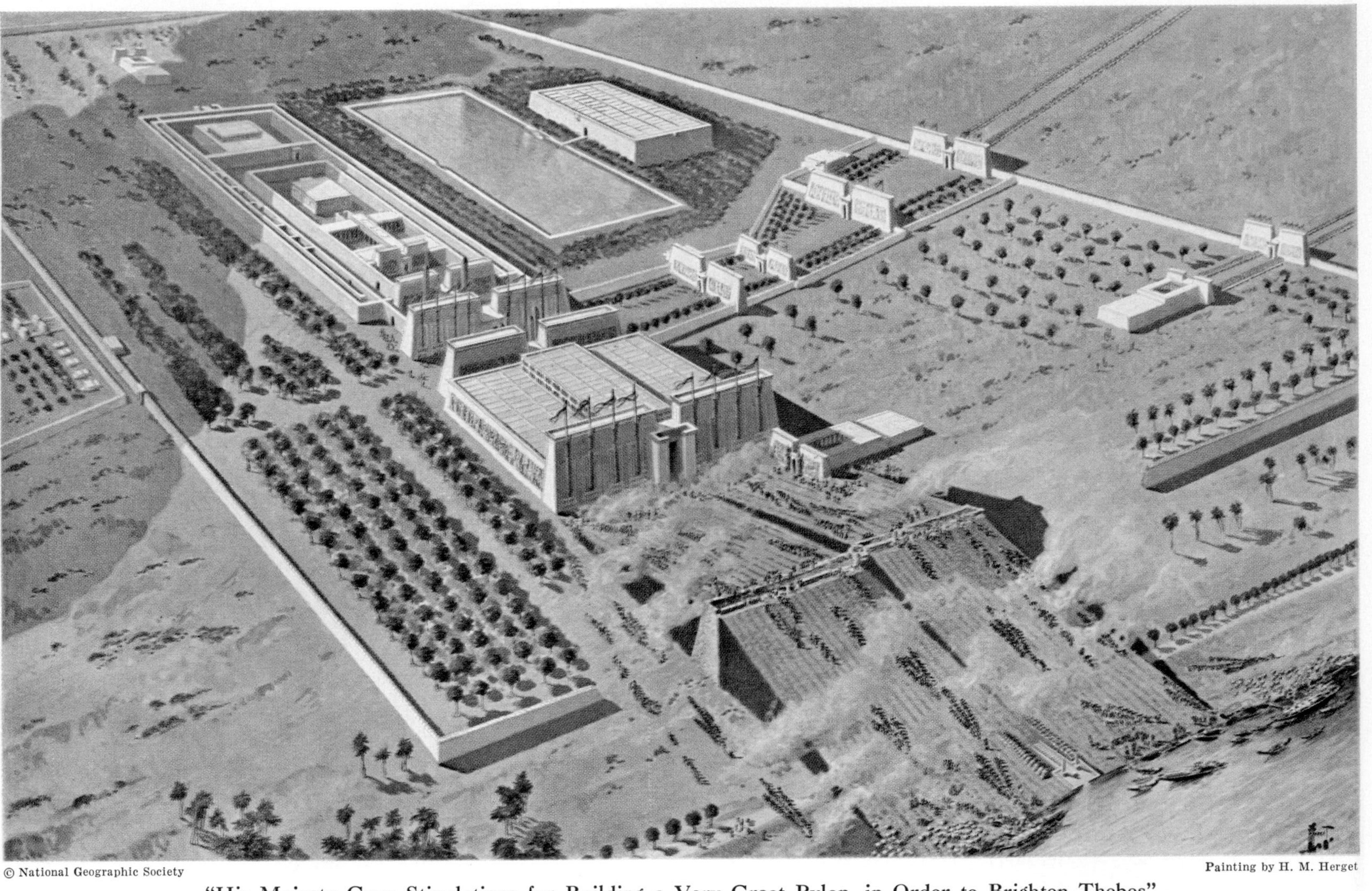

© National Geographic Society

Painting by H. M. Herget

"His Majesty Gave Stipulations for Building a Very Great Pylon, in Order to Brighten Thebes"

The never finished outermost pylon of the temple of Amūn at El Karnak, started in the 21st year of Sheshonk I of the XXIInd Dynasty (924 B. C.), is under construction. Up the temporary ramps on either side Palestinian and Nubian captives are hauling sledge loads of sandstone blocks, brought from the quarry by the stone barges (right foreground). To the right of the rear portion of the temple is the sacred lake; to the left, the enclosure of the temple of the war-god Montu. Mid-distant on the [illegible] which the pylons and avenue of sphinxes lead to the temple of the goddess Mut, Amūn's wife.

The Largest Temple Ever Erected by Man—2,000 Years Building

Few of the great Egyptian temples of dynastic times were planned and executed as single units, most of them having been built, rebuilt, and added to at irregular intervals over long periods of years. Yet, nearly all of them conform to the same basic plan, which is that of the more elaborate Egyptian dwelling house or palace.

The central, or inner, portion of the temple—always the first part built—contains the *sanctuary* and the adjoining private chambers, in other words, the living quarters of the god. In front of this is the columned audience chamber, or *hypostyle hall,* corresponding to the semi-public reception room in the ordinary Egyptian house.

This, in turn, opens on to a walled and usually colonnaded *forecourt,* approached from the front of the temple through a monumental gateway, flanked by two great rectangular towers, supporting tall flag-staffs. The whole of the last named element, the *pylon,* is repeated again and again before the earlier parts of the temple, each of these parts having at one time been the front of the building.

Far and away the largest building of this type—indeed, the largest columnar structure ever erected by man—is the temple of Amūn at El Karnak, situated in the midst of a 200-acre sacred precinct, a mile and a half north of the modern town of Luxor. Founded at least as early as the Middle Kingdom, this gigantic shrine was 2,000 years building, its latest architectural addition having been made under the Ptolemies, shortly before the dawn of the Christian Era.

More than four hundred yards in length, the temple, with the exception of the now ruined Middle Kingdom structures, was built almost entirely of sandstone, surfaced with white stucco and covered with miles of painted reliefs.

The forecourt, fronted by the colossal first pylon, covers 93,000 square feet. Both court and pylon were built under the Libyan pharaohs of the XXIInd Dynasty.

Behind the court and screened by the second pylon is one of the wonders of the ancient world, the great hypostyle hall, erected, together with the pylon, by the first three kings of the XIXth Dynasty: Ramesses I, Sethy I, and Ramesses II. The roof of this hall, into which the entire cathedral of Notre Dame in Paris could be fitted, with room to spare, is supported by 134 tremendous columns. Those of the central aisle tower 69 feet to the 7-ton stone roof beams. Six acres of painted relief sculpture decorate the interior (page 131).

Back of the hypostyle hall and surrounding the remains of the original limestone temple of the Middle Kingdom is a series of obelisks, pylons, courts, halls, and inner chambers, built by the great kings of the XVIIIth Dynasty, from Thut-mosĕ I to Amen-ḥotpe III, inclusive. Of the extant obelisks—granite monoliths, ranging in height from seventy-one to ninety-seven feet—one of Thut-mosĕ I and one of his daughter, Ḥat-shepsūt, are still standing.

The "Most Select of Places," as the temple was called, is now a huge, dingy brown ruin; but in its heyday it sparkled with color and reflected light, its brightly painted cornices standing out vividly above its pure white walls, its gigantic bronze doors, its tall pennant-tipped flag-staves, encased in electrum, and the electrum caps of its towering obelisks gleaming in the fierce Egyptian sun.

Painting by H. M. Herget

"The Stranger People from Without Are Come into Egypt"

Queen Amun-dyek-het is questioned by her captor, King Esarhaddon of Assyria. Routed by the Assyrians before Memphis, Egypt's Ethiopian pharaoh, Taharḳa, has fled southward. (XXVth Dynasty, 19th regnal year of Taharḳa, 670 B. C.)

The Assyrians (and Others) Come Down Like a Wolf on the Fold

IN 945 B. C., following 145 years' rule by the high priests of Amūn who composed the XXIst Dynasty, the throne of Egypt was seized by a Libyan soldier, named Sheshonk̦. This pharaoh, the Biblical Shishak, was responsible for the sack of Jerusalem in 930 B. C. and the building of the first pylon and forecourt at El Karnak a few years later.

His dynasty, the XXIInd, ruled a minimum of 200 years, but its later kings exercised only local authority in the north, the rest of the country having been taken over by the Ethiopian kings of Napata. The same conditions prevailed during the short, feeble XXIIIrd and XXIVth Dynasties.

The pharaohs of the Ethiopian XXVth Dynasty passed most of the years 712-663 B. C. trying vainly to defend Egypt against the Assyrians, who invaded and ravaged the northern part of the country almost at will.

In our plate an Ethiopian queen of Egypt, Amun-dyek-het, whose husband, the pharaoh Taharḳa, has abandoned her and the rest of his family, stands before her Assyrian captor. The queen's crown is surmounted by the double plume, the lunar disk, and the cow's horns of the goddess Ḥat-Ḥor. The necklace with bronze counterpoise, held in Amun-dyek-het's right hand, is her insignia as priestess of Ḥat-Ḥor.

When, at the end of this period, more important wars with Babylon and Elam had diverted the main force of the Assyrians from Egypt, Psammetik, an Egyptian prince of the Delta city of Saïs, drove out their remaining garrisons and established a new native dynasty, the XXVIth.

During the "Saïte Period," so inaugurated, Egypt took a new lease on life. Though its holdings in Syria and Palestine were lost to Nebuchadnezzar of Babylon, the country itself was not invaded, and for 138 years enjoyed some peace and prosperity.

Trade was re-established with the rest of the eastern Mediterranean world and mutually beneficial relations were entered into with the rising country of Greece. Art, using as its models the outstanding works of bygone eras, enjoyed a splendid revival, many of the artistic productions of the Saïte period ranking with the best that Egypt has to offer.

The final blow to Egyptian independence was, however, not long in coming. In 525 B. C. the XXVIth Dynasty fell before the onslaughts of King Cambyses of Persia, and Egypt became a Persian province. It remained so until, with the rest of the Near East, it was conquered by Alexander the Great of Macedon.

At Alexander's death in 323 B. C. a Macedonian general named Ptolemy was appointed governor of Egypt; and for almost 300 years the country was ruled by his descendants.

The last of the Ptolemies was Cleopatra VI. Ironically enough, this Greek woman has come to be the best known "Egyptian" queen in history.

After her the Romans ruled Egypt for nearly 500 years. Then the Moslems conquered it. Since A. D. 650, Egypt has been a key state in the Mohammedan world. From 1517 to 1919 Turkey held it almost continuously.

We leave the ancient Egyptians, well content if, in our pictures and in our story, we have portrayed them truly, not as a weird collection of mummy-making freaks, but as the very ordinary men and women they were—simple, hard working, cheerful, and, above all, thoroughly human.

National Geographic Photographer B. Anthony Stewart

School Children of Athens Gaze on Poseidon, Defeated Opponent of Athena, Their City's Namesake

Poseidon's trident brought forth salt water; Athena produced the olive tree and so won guardianship of the ancient city. This colossal figure of the "earth-shaker" and world-girdling sea god gives its name to the Room of Poseidon, in Greek, on the wall above. A recent acquisition of the National Archeological Museum at Athens is the bronze figure of Zeus Hurling the Thunderbolt (foreground), an original by Pheidias, found in the sea off the island of Euboea. Zeus (the Roman Jupiter) and Poseidon were brothers.

The Greek Way

Love of Play, Freedom of Speech, Athletic Games Built a Mighty Civilization in the Days of Homer

By Edith Hamilton *

THE GREEKS were the first people in the world to play, and they played on a great scale. All over Greece there were games, all sorts of games; athletic contests of every description: races—horse-, boat-, foot-, torch-races; contests in music, where one side outsang the other; in dancing—on greased skins sometimes to display a nice skill of foot and balance of body; games where men leaped in and out of flying chariots; games so many one grows weary with the list of them.

They are embodied in the statues familiar to all, the disc thrower, the charioteer, the wrestling boys, the dancing flute players (pages 176, 226-227).

A Truce of God Was Proclaimed for the Four Great Games

The great games—there were four that came at stated seasons—were so important, when one was held, a truce of God was proclaimed so that all Greece might come in safety without fear. There "glorious-limbed youth"—the phrase is Pindar's, the athlete's poet—strove for an honor so coveted as hardly anything else in Greece (pages 177, 178, 208-209).

An Olympic victor—triumphing generals would give place to him. His crown of wild olives was set beside the prize of the tragedian. Splendor attended him, processions, sacrifices, banquets, songs the greatest poets were glad to write. Thucydides, the brief, the severe, the historian of that bitter time, the fall of Athens, pauses, when one of his personages has conquered in the games, to give the fact full place of honor.

If we had no other knowledge of what the Greeks were like, if nothing were left of Greek art and literature, the fact that they were in love with play and played magnificently would be proof enough of how they lived and how they looked at life. Wretched people, toiling people, do not play.

Nothing like the Greek games is conceivable in Egypt or Mesopotamia. The life of the Egyptian lies spread out in the mural paintings down to the minutest detail. If fun and sport had played any real part, they would be there in some form for us to see. But the Egyptian did not play.

"Solon, Solon, you Greeks are all children," said the Egyptian priest to the great Athenian.

At any rate, children or not, they enjoyed themselves. They had physical vigor and high spirits and time, too, for fun. The witness of the games is conclusive. And when Greece died and her reading of the great enigma was buried with her statues, play, too, died out of the world.

The brutal, bloody Roman games had nothing to do with the spirit of play. They were fathered by the Orient, not by Greece. Play died when Greece died and many and many a century passed before it was resurrected.

Joy in "Little Pleasures"

To rejoice in life, to find the world beautiful and delightful to live in, was a mark of the Greek spirit which distinguished it from all that had gone before. It is a vital distinction.

The joy of life is written upon everything the Greeks left behind and they who leave it out of account fail to reckon with something that is of first importance in understanding how the Greek achievement came to pass in the world of antiquity.

Never, not in their darkest moments, do they lose their taste for life. It is always a wonder and a delight, the world a place of

* This article contains excerpts from the author's book, *The Great Age of Greek Literature*, published by W. W. Norton and Company, Inc. Copyright, 1930, 1942. The volume is a remarkably lucid account of the intellectual life of the Greeks and their influence upon modern thought, art, and literature.—Editor.

© Nellys

A Greek Mona Lisa of Mégara, Near Athens

Noted for their gayety, the people of Mégara pride themselves on the purity of their Greek descent.

beauty, and they themselves rejoicing to be alive in it.

The little pleasures, too, that daily living holds, were felt as such keen enjoyment: "Dear to us ever," says Homer, "is the banquet and the harp and the dance and changes of raiment and the warm bath and love and sleep."

Eating and drinking have never again seemed so delightful as in the early Greek lyrics, nor a meeting with friends, nor a warm fire of a winter's night—"the stormy season of winter, a soft couch after dinner by the fire, honey-sweet wine in your glass and nuts and beans at your elbow"—nor a run in the springtime "amid a fragrance of woodbine and leisure and white poplar, when the plane-tree and the elm whisper together," nor a banqueting hour, "moving among feasting and giving up the soul to be young, carrying a bright harp and touching it in peace among the wise of the citizens."

It is a matter of course that comedy should be their invention, the mad, rollicking, irresponsible fun of the Old Comedy, its verve and vitality and exuberant, overflowing energy of life.

Birth of the Idea of Freedom

Abject submission to the power on the throne which had been the rule of life in the ancient world since kings began, and was to be the rule of life in Asia for centuries to come, was cast off by the Greeks so easily, so lightly, hardly more than an echo of the contest has come down to us.

In the *Persians* of Aeschylus, a play written to celebrate the defeat of the Persians at Salamìs, there is many an allusion to the difference between the Greek way and the Oriental way. The Greeks, the Persian queen is told, fight as free men to defend what is precious to them. Have they no master? she asks. No, she is told. No man calls Greeks slaves or vassals. Herodotus in his account adds, "They obey only the law."

Something completely new is here. The idea of freedom has been born. The conception of the entire unimportance of the individual to the state, which has persisted down from earliest tribal days and was universally accepted in all the ancient world, has given place in Greece to the conception of the liberty of the individual in a state which he defends of his own free will. That is a change not worked by high spirit and abounding vigor alone. Something more was at work in Greece. Men were thinking for themselves.

One of the earlier Greek philosophic sayings is that of Anaxagoras: "All things were in chaos when Mind arose and made order."

In the ancient world ruled by the irrational, by dreadful unknown powers, where a man was utterly at the mercy of what he must not try to understand, the Greeks arose and the rule of reason began. The fundamental fact about the Greek was that he had to use his mind.

The ancient priests had said, "Thus far and no farther. We set the limits to thought."

The Greeks said, "All things are to be examined and called into question. There are no limits set to thought."

It is an extraordinary fact that by the time we have actual, documentary knowledge of the Greeks there is not a trace to be found of that domination over the mind by the priests which played such a decisive part in the ancient world.

The Right of Free Speech

The right of a man to say what he pleased was fundamental in Athens. "A slave is he who cannot speak his thought," said Euripides.

Socrates drinking the hemlock in his prison on the charge of introducing new gods and corrupting the youth is but the exception that proves the rule. He was an old man and all his life he had said what he would. Athens had just gone through a bitter time of crushing defeat, of rapid changes of government, of gross mismanagement. It is a reasonable conjecture that he was condemned in one of those sudden panics all nations know, when the people's fears for their own safety have been worked upon and they turn cruel.

Even so, he was condemned by a small majority and his pupil Plato went straight on teaching in his name, never molested but honored and sought after. Socrates was the only man in Athens who suffered death for his opinions. Three others were forced to leave the country. That is the entire list and to compare it with the endless list of those tortured and killed in Europe during even the last five hundred years is to see clearly what Athenian liberty was.

The Greek mind was free to think about the world as it pleased, to reject all traditional explanations, to disregard all the priests taught, to search unhampered by any outside authority for the truth. The Greeks had free scope for their scientific genius and they laid the foundations of our science today.

"Thoughts and ideas, the fair and immortal children of the mind," as a Greek writer calls them, were a delight to them. Never, not in the brightest days of the Renaissance, has learning appeared in such a radiant light as it did to the gay young men of imperial Athens.

Socrates has but to enter a gymnasium;

Staff Photographer Maynard Owen Williams

Greek Shepherds Watch While Whey Drips from the Cheesecloth

In near-by Dimitsána many a family has some relative in America, or one returned from the United States. On this rocky Peloponnesian hillside the sheep's milk is made into cheese as it was in Greece before butter was introduced from Scythia, thousands of years ago.

exercise, games, are forgotten. A crowd of ardent young men surround him. Tell us this. Teach us that, they clamor. What is Friendship? What is Justice? We will not let you off, Socrates. The truth—we want the truth. "What delight," they say to each other, "to hear wise men talk!"

"Egypt and Phoenicia love money," Plato remarks in a discussion on how nations differ. "The special characteristic of our part of the world is the love of knowledge.

"The Athenians," said St. Luke, "and the strangers sojourning there spend their time in nothing else but to tell or to hear some new thing." Even the foreigners caught the flame.

That intense desire to know, that burning curiosity about everything in the world—they could not come into daily contact with it and not be fired. Up and down the coast of Asia Minor St. Paul was mobbed and imprisoned and beaten. In Athens "they brought him unto the Areopagus, saying, 'May we know what this new teaching is?' "

The poet Sophocles, so the story is told, in his extreme old age was brought into court by his son who charged him with being incompetent to manage his own affairs. The aged tragedian's sole defense was to recite to the jurors passages from a play he had recently written. Those great words did not fall on deaf ears. Judge a man who could write such poetry not competent in any way? Who that called himself Greek could do that? Nay: dismiss the case; fine the complainant; let the defendant depart honored and triumphant.

Again, when Athens had fallen and her

© Nellys

Sports Photographs of Ancient Times Are the Carvings of Greek Athletes

Depicted from top to bottom are: muscular wrestlers with their coach at left; indolent spectators of a cat-and-dog fight; action in a ball game, man at left pitching; and hockey players bullying off. These eyewitness "shots" give a magic-eye image of Greeks at play.

Staff Photographer B. Anthony Stewart

Bare-legged under Summer's Sun, She Spins the Wool for Winter Warmth

Her distaff, bunched with snowy fleece, is symbol for a woman's work. Her spindle, tool of Clotho, twists and twirls at tasks she dare not shirk. The rocky Peloponnesus is no place for sloth. She needs warm stockings and good homespun cloth (pages 230-231).

Spartan conquerors held high festival on the eve of destroying the city altogether, razing to the ground the buildings, not a pillar to be left standing on the Acropolis, one of the men charged with the poetical part of the entertainment—even Spartans must have poetry to their banquet—gave a recitation from Euripides, and the banqueters, stern soldiers in the great moment of their hard-won triumph, listening to the beautiful, poignant words, forgot victory and vengeance, and declared as one man that the city such a poet had sprung from should never be destroyed.

Herodotus is the historian of the glorious fight for liberty in which the Greeks conquered the overwhelming power of Persia (Iran). They won the victory because they were free men defending their freedom against a tyrant and his army of slaves. So Herodotus saw the contest. The watchword was freedom; the stake was the independence or the enslavement of Greece; the issue made it sure that Greeks never would be slaves.

The modern reader cannot accept the proud words without a wondering question. What of the slaves these free Greeks owned? The Persian defeat did not set them free. What real idea of freedom could the conquerors at Marathon and Salamis have had, slaveowners, all of them?

The question shows up, as no other question could, the difference between the mind of today and the mind of antiquity. To all the ancient world the freeing of slaves would have been sheer nonsense. There always had been slaves. In every community the way of life depended on them.

First Movement to Abolish Slavery

From time immemorial there was never anywhere a dreamer so rash or so romantic as to imagine a life without slaves. The loftiest thinkers, idealists, and moralists never had an idea that slavery was evil. In the Old Testament it is accepted without comment exactly as in the records of Egypt and Mesopotamia.

Even the prophets of Israel did not utter a word against it, nor, for that matter, did St. Paul. What is strange is not that the Greeks took slavery for granted through hundreds of years, but that finally they began to think about it and question it.

To Euripides the glory belongs of being the first to condemn it. "Slavery," he wrote:

> That thing of evil, by its nature evil,
> Forcing submission from a man to what
> No man should yield to.

He was, as usual, far in advance of his age. Even Plato, a generation later, could not keep pace with him. He never spoke against slavery; in his old age he actually advocated it. Still, there are signs that he was troubled by it. He says, "A slave is an embarrassing possession." He had reached a point when he could not feel at ease with slaves, and he does not admit them to his ideal Republic.

Except for this mild and indirect opposition and for Euripides' open attack, we have no idea how or why the opposition to slavery spread, but by Aristotle's time, a generation after Plato, it had come out into the open.

"There are people," Aristotle writes—he does not include himself—"who consider owning slaves as violating natural law because the distinction between a slave and a free person is wholly conventional and has no place in nature, so that it rests on mere force and is devoid of justice."

That is the point Greek thought had reached more than two thousand four hundred years ago. Less than a hundred years ago America had to fight a great war before slavery was abolished.

The matter for wonder is not that Herodotus saw nothing odd in slaveowners being the champions of freedom, but that in Greece alone, through all ancient and almost all modern times, were there men great enough and courageous enough to see through the conventional coverings that disguised slavery, and to proclaim it for what it was. A few years after Aristotle, the Stoics denounced it as the most intolerable of all the wrongs man ever committed against man.

Herodotus the Humanist

Herodotus was that rare person, a lover of mankind. He liked people, all of them. But he liked them more than he admired them, and he never idealized them (page 233).

Everything everywhere in the world of men was of interest to him. He tells us how the homely girls in Illyria get husbands, how the lake dwellers keep their children from falling into the water, what Egyptian mosquito nets are like, that the King of Persia when travelling drinks only boiled water, what the Adyrmachidae do to fleas, how the Arabians cut their hair, that the Danube islanders get drunk on smells, how the Scythians milk their mares, that in Libya (Libia) the woman with the most lovers is honored, how the streets of Babylon are laid out, that physicians in Egypt specialize in diseases, and so on, and so on.

"A tyrant disturbs ancient laws," Herodotus writes, "violates women, kills men without trial. But a people ruling—first, the very name of it is so beautiful; and secondly, a people does none of these things."

Staff Photographer B. Anthony Stewart

Beyond Constitution Square, Center of Modern Greek Life, Rises the Acropolis, Crown of Periclean Athens

The Syntagma, around whose tables and chairs the life of the capital surged at the day's end, is now a scene of starvation and hastily dug graves. But above it still stands the Parthenon, perfect symbol of the Greek way, the way of freedom of thought, speech, and religion. Greek blood has been ruthlessly spilled, but the glory that was Greece lives on in the hearts of Hellas and her admirers everywhere (pages 196, 222, 223, 234-239).

Close Behind This Farmer, Cultivating His Field in Thessaly, the Early Stork Gets the Worm

Staff Photographer B. Anthony Stewart

Through This Portal at Olympia Passed the Most Famous Athletes of All Time

The modern Twelfth Olympic Games, scheduled for 1940, were canceled by war. But in ancient Greece all hostilities ceased during the Olympic games when athletes contested for the crown of wild olive.

Staff Photographer Maynard Owen Williams

Greek "Ballet Skirts," Here Festival Attire, Won Fame When Greeks Were Chasing Mussolini's Legions

On a slope of Mount Parnassus, these shepherds and Athenian citizens stood during the last Delphic Festival. Greek soldiers in heavy wool stockings and khaki skirts met and repulsed the Italians, even though Fascist warplanes dominated the Athenian sky.

Staff Photographer Maynard Owen Williams

Octopuses Dry in the October Sun at Kaválla, Famous Tobacco Port near the Field of Philippi

Since October was originally the eighth month and octopus means eight-footed, language reveals a relationship which a changed calendar has severed. While a fisherman mends his net, citizens lunch on the breakwater not far from Philippi, where Brutus and Cassius met defeat in 42 B. C. Though octopuses are eagerly sought for food around the Aegean, they sometimes endanger swimmers.

Staff Photographer B. Anthony Stewart

The Greek Staff of Life Looks More Like a Tire

Brown of crust, but snow-white inside, were the firm loaves of Greek bread before war brought starvation to Hellas. In ancient times the size and quality of the loaves were carefully inspected. Dunked in clabber, this white bread is delicious.

Only the tyrant was known throughout the East. When the Great King was on his march to Greece a very rich noble of Lydia entertained not only him and his courtiers, but his multitudinous host of soldiers as well. He set sumptuous feasts before all, Herodotus says, and in return begged humbly that one of his five sons, all in the army, might remain with him.

"You make such a request?" said the king. "You who are my slave and bound to give me all that is yours, even to your wife?"

He ordered the body of the eldest youth to be cut in two and placed on either side of the road where the army was to pass. The Persians were slaves, so called and so treated; the richest and most powerful claimed nothing as their right; they were completely at the disposal of the king.

Herodotus tells another story. A noble, who had for years enjoyed the royal favor and then had lost it, was invited to dine with the king. After he had feasted on the meat placed before him, he was presented with a covered basket. Lifting the lid, he saw the head and hands and feet of his only son.

"Do you know now," the king asked pleasantly, "the kind of animal you have been eating?" The father had learned the lesson slaves must master, self-control. He answered with perfect composure, "I do know, indeed—and whatever the king is pleased to do pleases me."

That was the spirit of the East from time immemorial, first clearly recorded for the world in Herodotus' book.

Little, poor, barren Greece was free. "You know perfectly what it is to be a slave," Herodotus reports some Greeks as saying to a Persian official who was urging them to submit to Xerxes. "Freedom you have never tried, to know how sweet it is. If you had, you would urge us to fight for it not with our spears only, but even with hatchets."

The idea of the Athenian state was a union of individuals free to develop their own powers and live in their own way, obedient only to the laws they passed themselves and could criticize and change at will. And yet underneath this apparently ephemeral view of law was the conviction, peculiarly Athenian, which dominated the thought and the art of the fifth century—that the unlimited, the unrestrained, the lawless, were barbarous, ugly, irrational.

Freedom, strictly limited by self-control—that was the idea of Athens at her greatest. Her artists embodied it; her democracy did not. Athenian art and Athenian thought survived the test of time. Athenian democracy became imperial and failed.

The Delights of Hunting

Xenophon writes a charming essay about hunting: of the delights of the early start, in winter over the snow, to track the hare with hounds as keen for the chase as their masters; in spring "when the fields are so full of wildflowers, the scent for the dogs is poor"; or a deer may be the quarry, first-rate sport; or a wild boar, dangerous, but delightfully exciting. Such rewards, too, as the hunter has: he keeps strong and young far longer than other men; he is braver, and even more trustworthy—although why that should be our author does not trouble to explain.

A hunting man just is better than one who does not hunt and that is all there is to it. Ask any fox-hunting squire in English literature. Hunting is a good, healthful, honest

Staff Photographer B. Anthony Stewart

Amid the Whitewashed Cubist Homes of Mýkonos This Green-goods Merchant Roams

Bright walls throw back the sun and blind both eye and lens to the halftones of dark cloth. This tiny island, neighbor of Dēlos (page 263), played no great part in ancient history, but in 1822, under the leadership of a woman, the people repelled a savage attack by the Turks. Now it is a place to which seamen retire.

pleasure, and a young man is lucky if he takes to it. It will save him from city vices and incline him to love virtue.

The guests at Xenophon's dinner, except for himself and Socrates, were ordinary people who would quickly have been bored by the speeches in the *Symposium* (pages 242-3). But no one could possibly have been bored at the party Xenophon describes. It was from first to last a most enjoyable occasion. There was some good talk at the table, of course—Socrates would see to that; and now and then the discourse turned to matters sober enough to have engaged even Thucydides' attention. But for the most part, it was lighthearted as befitted a good dinner.

There was a great deal of laughter when, for instance, Socrates defended his flat nose as being preferable to a straight one, and when a man newly married refused the onions. There was music, too, and Socrates obliged with a song, to the delighted amusement of the others.

A pleasant interlude was afforded by a happy boy, and Xenophon's description reveals his power of keen observation and quick sympathy. The lad had been invited to come with his father, a great honor, but he had just won the chief contest for boys at the principal Athenian festival.

He sat beside his father, regarded very kindly by the company. They tried to draw him out, but he was too shy to speak a word until someone asked him what he was most proud of, and someone else cried, "Oh, his victory, of course." At this he blushed and blurted out, "No—I'm not."

All were delighted to have him finally say something and they encouraged him. "No? Of what are you proudest, then?" "Of my father," he said, and pressed closer to him.

As was usual, entertainment had been provided for the guests. A girl did some diverting and surprising feats. The best turn was when she danced and kept twelve hoops whirling in the air, catching and throwing them in perfect time with the music. Watching her with great attention Socrates declared that he was forced to conclude, "Not only from this girl, my friends, but from other things, too, that a woman's talent is not at all inferior to a man's." A pleasant thing to know, he added, if any of them wanted to teach something to his wife.

A murmur passed around the table: "Xanthippe"; and one of the company ventured, "Why do not you, then, teach good temper to yours?" "Because," Socrates retorted, "my great aim in life is to get on well with people, and I chose Xanthippe because I knew if I could get on with her I could with anyone." The explanation was unanimously voted satisfactory.

A little desultory talk followed that finally turned upon exercise, and Socrates said, to the intense delight of all, that he danced every morning in order to reduce.

"It's true," one of the others broke in. "I found him doing it and I thought he'd gone mad. But he talked to me and I tell you he convinced me. When I went home—will you believe it? I did not dance; I don't know how; but I waved my arms about." There was a general outcry, "Oh, Socrates, let us see you, too."

By this time the dancing girl was turning somersaults and leaping headfirst into a circle formed by swords. This displeased Socrates. "No doubt it is a wonderful performance," he conceded. But pleasure? In watching a lovely young creature exposing herself to danger like that? I don't find it agreeable."

Of himself Xenophon says nothing throughout the essay except at the very beginning when he explains that he was one of the guests and decided to give an account of the dinner because he thought what honorable and virtuous men did in their hours of amusement had its importance.

No Compulsion by Church or State

Athens had no authoritarian church, or state either, to formulate what a man should believe and to regulate the details of how he should live. There was no agency or institution to oppose his thinking in any way he chose on anything whatsoever. As for the state, it never entered an Athenian's head that it could interfere with his private life: that it could see, for instance, that his children were taught to be patriotic, or limit the amount of liquor he could buy, or compel him to save for his old age. Everything like that a citizen of Athens had to decide himself and take full responsibility for.

The basis of the Athenian democracy was the conviction of all democracies—that the average man can be depended upon to do his duty and to use good sense in doing it. *Trust the individual* was the avowed doctrine in Athens, and expressed or unexpressed it was common to Greece.

Sparta we know as the exception, and there must have been other backwaters; nevertheless, the most reactionary Greek might at any time revert to type. It is on record that Spartan soldiers abroad shouted down an unpopular officer; threw stones at a general whose orders they did not approve; in an

Staff Photographer B. Anthony Stewart

Who, Seeing This, Can Doubt the Story of the Baby-bearing Stork

In the yard of a country school at Halmyrós, near Vólos, children come running while storks preen themselves over a job well done.

emergency, put down incompetent leaders and acted for themselves. Even the iron discipline of Sparta could not completely eradicate the primary Greek passion for independence. "A people ruling," says Herodotus, "—the very name of it is so beautiful."

Socrates and Plato

Together Socrates and his pupil, Plato, shaped the idea of the excellent which the classical world lived by for hundreds of years and which the modern world has never forgotten.

Socrates believed that goodness and truth were the fundamental realities, and that they were attainable. Every man would strive to attain them if he could be shown them. No one would pursue evil except through ignorance. Once let him see what evil was and he would fly from it. His own mission, Socrates believed, was to open men's eyes to their ignorance and to lead them on to where they could catch a glimpse of the eternal truth and goodness beneath life's confusions and futilities, when they would inevitably, irresistibly, seek for a fuller and fuller vision of it.

In the prison cell when the time had come to drink the hemlock, he had a kind word for the jailor who brought him the cup, and he broke off his discourse with his friends when he was telling them that nothing was surer than that beauty and goodness have a most real and actual existence, by exclaiming: "But I really had better go bathe so that the women may not have the trouble of washing my body when I am dead."

One of those present, suddenly recalled from the charm of his talk to the stark facts, cried: "How shall we bury you?" "Anyway you like," was the amused answer. "Only be sure you get hold of me and see that I do not run away."

And turning to the rest of the company: "I cannot make this fellow believe that the dead body will not be me. Don't let him talk about burying Socrates, for false words infect the soul. Dear Crito, say only that you are burying my body."

© Nellys

A Homely Task Adds Life to the Old-fashioned Statue of the Calf-bearer

When Pheidias and Praxiteles touched perfection in Greek sculpture (pages 235-252), this stiff figure, with its enigmatic smile, was already called archaic—the Greek word for old-fashioned. Originally the drapery, hair, and beard were painted, and the eye sockets were set with colored stones. The statue, representing a man carrying a calf to sacrifice, charmed visitors to the Acropolis Museum at Athens.

Greece—the Birthplace of Science and Free Speech

Explorations on the Mainland and in Crete and the Aegean Isles Reveal Ancient Life Similar to That of the Present

By Richard Stillwell

Formerly Director of the American School of Classical Studies at Athens

ONCE, soon after I had gone to Greece for the first time, a friend and I were picking an uncomfortable way down from the top of Mount Ithōme. The mountains of the Peloponnesus threw long shadows across the Messenian plain, but the late afternoon sun was still hot (map, pages 192-3).

A small, deserted monastery on the very summit had been our goal during a long afternoon's climb. We had inspected it thoroughly for remains of a sanctuary of Zeus, not much in evidence, but none the less a legitimate objective for archeological travelers.

Now we were thinking of the possibility of a good dinner and a night's rest at the seaport town of Kalamata—a town toward which, some years later, several thousand British soldiers were to struggle in the vain hope of being evacuated to Crete or Egypt before the Germans could cut off their retreat.

Presently we met a young man. "Chairete" (rejoice), he cried. "Where are you going?"

Ever since the first marathon runner gasped his life out with "Chairete, we have conquered," as he raced into the anxiously crowded market place of Athens with news of the great victory over the Persians, the word has been a salutation among the Greeks.

On learning where we were bound, our new acquaintance took us to his home, where his sister brought us a pitcher of resinated wine. He then went with us down the road until we could no longer mistake our way, and when we would have paid him he gracefully avoided any reward save our spoken thanks.

Such was the hospitality of which Homer wrote time and again in the *Odyssey*. After many centuries it remains the same.

A thirteen hours' tramp next day through the wild Langada Gorge, across Mount Taygetus, from Kalamata to Sparta, ended with a couple of hours' walk through fragrant, moonlit orange groves and gave our first impression of Sparta a quality all its own. We felt like travelers of ancient days.

To lie out on a rocky, sunlit slope overlooking the dark sea, and hear sheep bells and a shepherd's pipe; to pass near a village and see women drawing water from a fountain, or washing clothes in great stone troughs near by; to ride through dense olive groves down to a little harbor—all these things are a part of knowing both modern and ancient Greece.

At harvest time the cutting of the grain with hand sickles, rows of donkeys' feet twinkling along as if part of animated haystacks, and finally the threshing on great, round, cobbled threshing floors—all take one back to the pictures on ancient vases.

The excavator at an ancient site uncovers the past in pieces, but unless the place is too remote he may relive the past in many customs of the village whence his workmen come.

One winter two friends and I enjoyed Christmas on the little island of Skýros. If we had needed an archeological excuse to go there, we could have said that it was the island where Achilles, to avoid having to go to the Trojan War, put on a girl's dress and successfully avoided the draft until he betrayed himself by showing a most unmaidenly interest in some weapons the sly fox Odysseus put around where he could see them.

While we were there, we were invited to attend a wedding, and our host insisted that we wear native island costume.

Thus I found myself in a pair of full blue pantaloons which resembled nothing so much as a large bag, with holes for the legs in two corners, and the mouth of the bag held, I hoped, around my waist by a sash. Also there were a richly embroidered shirt, goatskin leggings, and strangely laced sandals.

The women's costumes were voluminous and elaborate, and I never did learn how many layers went to make them up.

We danced, after a fashion, and feasted, and went back to our house to fall into bed, but the wedding festivities went on for three days and nights. The celebrants were still making

Minoan Snake Goddess in Ivory and Gold

Slender as a modern movie queen in tight bodice and flounced skirt was the Cretan maiden who posed for this chryselephantine statue, which is now in the Boston Museum of Fine Arts. The great statue of Athena in the Parthenon was also of ivory and gold (pages 191 and 235).

merry, though a bit wearily, when we took the little steamer back to the mainland. Many of the details of such festivities can be paralleled in what we know of ancient Greek weddings (page 241).

Funerals also follow old traditions. The wailing women, the procession bearing the body, usually exposed in its coffin, the breaking of symbolic vessels—today a bottle, but once a beautifully shaped vase—and the placing of a sack of nuts or fruit with the body—all find parallels in ancient days.

Many of the graves of the ancient Greeks contained rich collections of vases and jewelry. Bronze pins, mirrors, and other articles were buried with the dead. An interesting custom was the habit of placing a bronze *strigil,* or scraper, in the grave of a youth, while a woman's grave was always indicated by the inclusion of a *pyxis,* or jar for cosmetics.

Children's graves often contain toys, and a warrior's grave a helmet. One such grave I saw opened at Corinth. In it was a beautiful bronze helmet, too small for a man, and the size of the stone sarcophagus showed that it probably belonged to a boy who did not live to fulfill his parents' hopes of a brilliant military career.

It brought to my mind the epitaph by Callimachus: "Philip his father laid here the twelve-year-old child, his high hope, Nikoteles."

Eggshells have also been found in graves, as a symbol of the awaiting of a new life.

When I was living in Corinth, I often examined the citadel of Acrocorinthus, which towers steeply behind the old city (page 197). I looked for the cliff from which, according to the story, Leon Sgourós, who was defending the citadel, is said to have leaped on horseback when he could no longer hold out against the enemy.

Workmen Can Climb Like Goats

It was one pleasantly recurring problem to try to make out just what route Aratus of Sicyon took up the crags of the fortress when he scaled the walls by night and recaptured the citadel from the occupying Macedonian garrison, 243 B. C. I often pitied the attackers fighting at the summit after they had climbed the steep slope. My pity was not just vicarious; for we ran an excavation up there all one spring, and every morning the climb took us about 40 minutes of very stiff uphill work.

Possibly, however, the pity was misplaced, for we had some workmen from Mycenae who camped up there, save when they went away for week ends. They would show up on Monday morning after walking from a little station several miles away and climbing the steep south slope, where ordinarily only goats can go.

Some years later I saw a race among shepherds at Aráchova, a few miles east of Delphi. The prize was a sheep. The course was about one hundred yards up a 30-degree slope. Since there was no timekeeper, I cannot say what the record was; but those men literally sprinted up the hill. After that the performance of our Mycenaean workmen did not seem so remarkable to me.

Once on an unforgettable nine-day cruise through the Aegean islands on a 60-foot

Gilbert Grosvenor

Around Threshing Floors, Transformed into Song-and-dance Arenas, Greek Drama Grew

In this 2,400-year-old theater at Epidaurus, twenty thousand spectators took their recreation seriously. The first orchestra—or dancing place—was marked out by circling cattle, threshing grain. The dancers sang lyrical interludes, against which formal drama made slow headway. Now the stage has retired behind curtain and footlights, and only musical comedy and the opera continue the song-and-dance tradition of early Greece. No loudspeaker is needed here, for the acoustics of the theater are so good that the words of the man in the white trousers can be heard to the top row without his raising his voice (page 261).

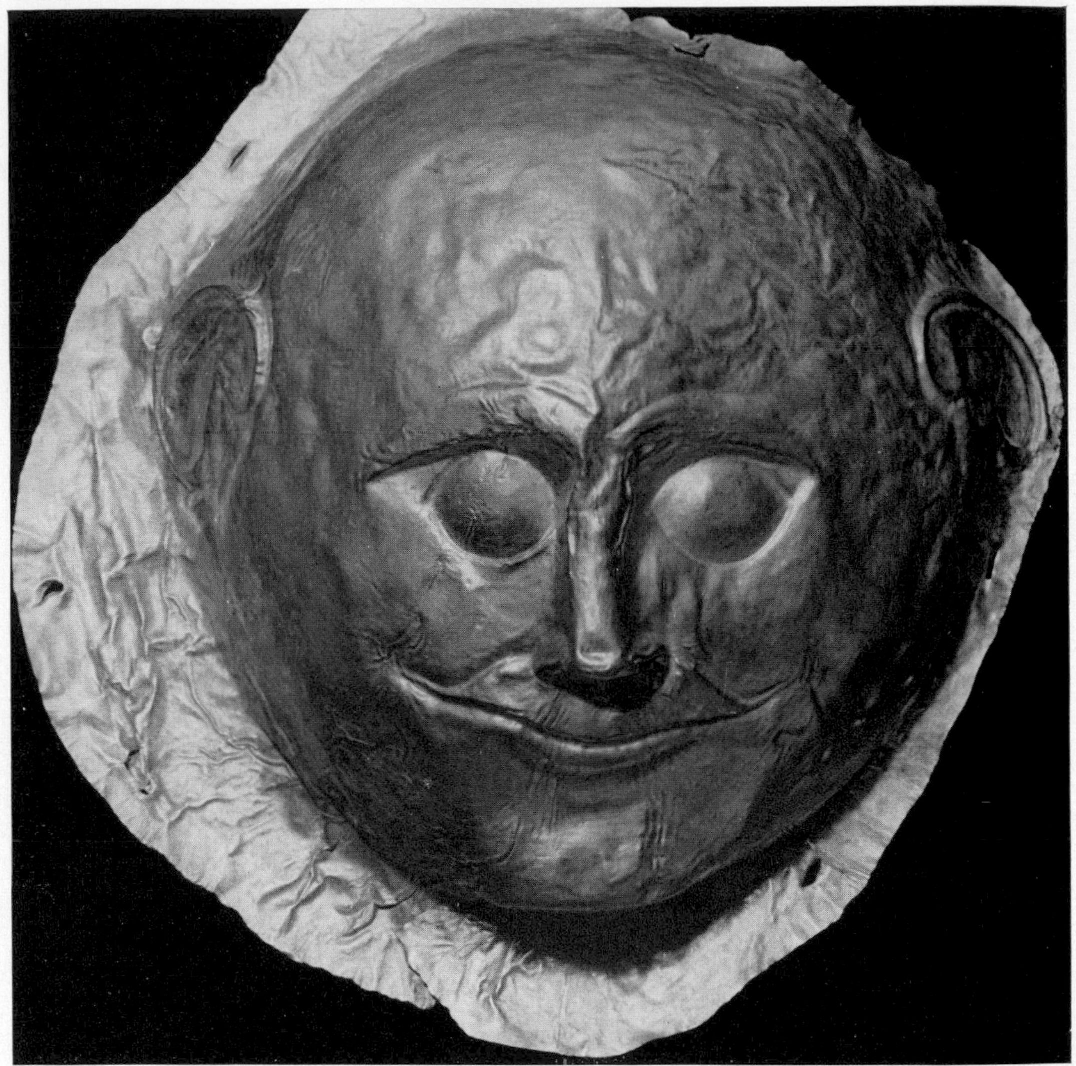

© Nellys

Following Homer's Tip in the "Iliad" about Mycenae "Abounding in Gold," Schliemann Found This Golden Mask

From royal tombs sunk upright in the rock, Heinrich Schliemann in 1876 recovered priceless Mycenaean treasures which had been almost forgotten even in Homer's day. Thus fame returned to the city of Agamemnon. Beaten out of a thin sheet of gold, this funerary mask once covered the face of a prince as he lay surrounded by ornaments and weapons. So pure is the gold, it bends to the touch (pages 189, 191, 204-5).

caïque (fortunately provided with a Diesel engine) some of us went ashore at Tēnos, where there is a famous church of healing.

It is surrounded by an arcaded portico where the pilgrims sleep when they come to the Feast of the Annunciation, just as the ancient Greek visitors to a sanctuary of Asklepios used to sleep in porticoes connected with the temple.

Inside the church were many votive objects in tin, silver, or occasionally gold—parts of bodies, ships, small replicas of automobiles—probably put there by people who had escaped serious injury in accidents. There were even one or two models of airplanes.

I was interested by one offering in particular, although I did not learn anything about it. It was a small replica of part of a man's skeleton beautifully executed in silver. Only the backbone and ribs were shown, and through the cavity of the chest was a small golden arrow!

Our cruise was leisurely, since we followed the custom of the ancient sailors and put into a harbor each night. The chief difference was that we did not beach our ship. Our farthest point out was the volcanic island of Santorin, where the harbor is the old crater and too deep for anchorage.

We made fast to some bitts which had been set on the edge of a little lava cone that was forming in the center of the bay, and in the morning went for a swim. The water ran in layers: cool, warm, cool, and suddenly uncomfortably hot. No one tried swimming through the hot water for fear of being suddenly parboiled.

There was nothing archeological in that particular spot, but the fact that it lay in a region of continuous ancient tradition gave the savage prehuman aspect of the place an unusual significance.

Two days later we anchored in a cove under the columns of the Temple of Poseidon at Cape Soúnion. I had seen them first, tantalizingly, from the porthole of a steamer on the way from İstanbul. This time I could enjoy them at leisure. Many of the column drums had been rolled down to the sea to be taken away for Venetian marble cutters, and doubtless some of that material, now unrecognizable, is built into the walls of Venice.

The surviving columns are much weatherbeaten, but they show the unmistakable character of Greek architecture in the middle of the fifth century. Then the Doric style reached its peak and culminated in the buildings of Periclean Athens.

Greece Nurtured the Spirit of Freedom

Greece is a rugged, mountainous country. The coastline is so deeply indented that the sea is never very far from any part of the interior.

In ancient times, as now, the country was divided into two parts: the Peloponnesus, and northern Greece, reaching up as far as Macedonia, which was not a part of Greece until the time of Philip.

The mountain spurs run down to the sea and divide the land into many small communities. From earliest times these districts were independent, save when some of them were brought together under a strong ruler or under one of the larger and richer cities.

This individualism, so marked in ancient times, is equally noticeable today.

The astonishing thing is that the ancient Greeks as a whole, no matter how much they fought and disagreed among themselves, were able to forge a civilization which has left its imprint so strongly marked on our own that we are indebted to them in almost every phase of our daily lives.

The idea of a community in which every citizen had an equal vote in the business of the state is one of the greatest of Greek contributions, although their ideas of democracy were limited to the citizens proper and by no means included the large body of slaves and foreign residents of the state, Greek though they might be. The democratic idea flourished especially in Athens (pages 171, 194).

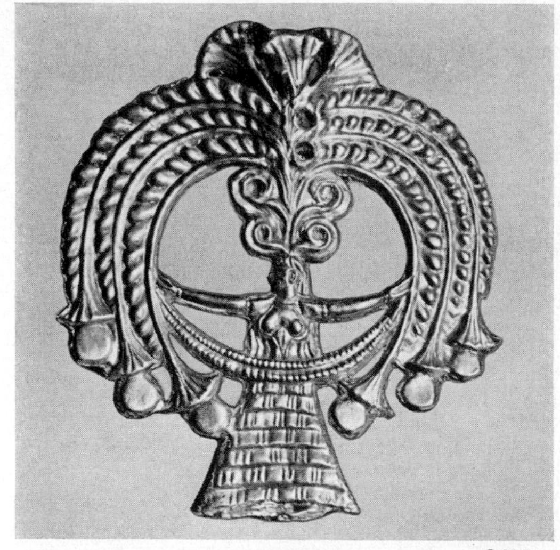

© Nellys

Goldsmith's Art of 3,500 Years Ago Furnished Details for Herget's Paintings

Bare breasts and many-flounced skirt were the fashion in Crete. But this golden pin, found at Mycenae, proves the style was copied on the Greek mainland (pages 204-5).

Science owes a great debt to the Greeks. Geometry was developed by their scholars; they studied astronomy, and geography, and mechanics, and on their work we base an incalculable amount of our present-day knowledge (pages 228-9, 264-5).

Their philosophers led the way along nearly every path of speculative thought which has been followed since.

In the arts the Greek imprint was so strong that it has affected sculpture and architecture ever since. The Lincoln Memorial in Washington, D. C., famed art galleries in the heart of America, and many buildings of our great cities attest the enduring art and architecture of classic Greece (pages 176, 196).

The outstanding characteristic of the ancient Greeks which has survived most strongly is their fierce love of freedom.

The guerrilla bands which wrecked the railroad line near Lamía in World War II recall the long struggle the Greek states put up against the overwhelming power of the Roman Empire and the centuries of resistance to Turkish domination.

Sir Alan Cobham from Galloway

Planned by the Ancients, but Only Fifty Years Old, the Corinth Canal Makes the Peloponnesus What Its Name Implies—Island of Pelops

This four-mile waterway shortens the voyage from Piraeus to Patras by more than 200 miles. Along the right edge led the roadway over which small ships were hauled (pages 201, 214-215). Near the dark spot (upper right) lay the stadium where in 336 B. C. Alexander the Great became leader of all Greeks against the Persians.

As we go about among the Greek people in city and country; as we read and understand what the ancient Greeks themselves wrote, their history and philosophy, their plays and their poetry; as we see the remains of their buildings, and, with the aid of our ever-growing knowledge, restore them in our mind's eye, we can begin to form some idea of the race which glorified the heroes of the Trojan War, defied and successfully withstood the great Persian Empire, the world power of the day, and, 150 years later, led by Alexander, humbled her and spread Greek culture through the Near East (pages 195, 259).

Who were these gifted people and whence did they come? The question is as hard to determine as any other involving migrations and fusings of peoples. Although one may speak glibly of Pelasgians, Mediterranean stock, Minyans, Achaeans, and Dorians, it is difficult to trace them down to their original homes.

Briefly, before the dawn of written history strange tribes came down out of the north into Greece through the Balkans, and mingled with the earliest inhabitants. Some of the invaders were long-haired and blond. Homer's warlike Achaeans were among these.

The archeologist can distinguish different periods before historic times by their distinctive pottery or architecture, or modes of burial.

Modern Scholars Unearth Forgotten Lore

Our knowledge of ancient Greece has been greatly extended during the last fifty years. In some ways we know much more about the early prehistoric times than did the Greeks of the great period of Athens. The ancients had their legends. The *Iliad* and the *Odyssey* were known to nearly every Greek; the playwrights—Aeschylus, Sophocles, Euripides—built their plays around well-known stories and thus saved them for us.

It was reserved, however, for the modern archeologist to discover the great shaft graves at Mycenae, the golden treasure at Troy, and the labyrinthine palace at Cnossus in Crete where legend says Theseus killed the Minotaur (pages 202, 205).*

Heinrich Schliemann, who started life as a grocer's apprentice in a small German town, firmly believed that the *Iliad* was more than a mere legend. He set out to make a fortune, became an American citizen in California in 1850, and later went out and dug up Troy.

To his surprise he found the remains of no fewer than nine separate cities, built one above the other. Lacking proper control material, he named the second city from the bottom Troy, the city of Priam, the one sacked by Agamemnon and the Greeks. Later explorations have identified this city with the sixth layer from the bottom, or really a subdivision now known as 7A.

He worked with his wife, a Greek girl who knew Homer by heart and used to recite the *Iliad* to him by the hour.

When his workmen began to unearth a rich treasure of gold jewelry, Schliemann with great presence of mind made an excuse to get rid of them. As the men quit work, his wife rushed out and gathered up the treasure in her red shawl.

She lost her own gold thimble there. Almost fifty years later, another archeologist, working over the site, found it and returned it to the owner!

Schliemann also excavated at Mycenae, the home of Agamemnon and that leader's treacherous wife Clytemnestra. He opened five great shaftlike graves full of gold ornaments, masks, bronze weapons inlaid with silver and gold, ivories, etc. These treasures have since been shown to be much earlier than the period of the Trojan War (pages 188, 189).

The picture of those remote times, however, is still far from complete. The people of the second millennium B. C. knew writing, but no such quantity of material has been preserved as in Egypt or Mesopotamia. And, furthermore, only a start has been made in interpreting what has been found.

Schliemann's discoveries were presently complemented by the work of an English archeologist, the late Sir Arthur Evans, who uncovered the great Cretan palace and city of Cnossus, capital of King Minos.

It soon appeared that in Crete there had lived a rich seafaring people, highly cultured and possessed of much artistic and architectural skill.

Crete traded with Greece, Egypt, Syria, and the coast of Asia Minor. It had a profound influence on the art of pre-Hellenic Greece.

The rulers of Mycenae, on the Greek mainland, who may have been responsible for the overthrow of the Cretans, were a northern race. They brought with them many of their own traditions, such as buildings with pitched roofs, instead of the traditional Mediterranean flat-terrace type. Their rulers, to judge from the gold burial masks found at Mycenae, were stern, bearded men.

But constantly on the northern horizon, from beyond the mountains, more peoples were continually pressing down into Greece. They overran the tremendous fortifications

* This legend is best told by Nathaniel Hawthorne in "The Minotaur."

From Cyrus to Hitler, Tiny Greece Fought the Barbarian; Kept Freedom Alight

Aegean trade and art forms jumped from island to island. From the Caucasus to Spain, Greek colonies spread. A necklace of Hellenic cities adorned the coast of Asia Minor from Troy past Ephesus and Miletus—home of maps—to and beyond the Halicarnassus of Herodotus, Father of History (pages 232-3). When Asiatic despotism struck, mainland Greece bore the brunt at Marathon and Salamis (pages 224-5).

Chirpan
Elkhovo
Tzarevo
Malko Tarnovo
Akhtopol
Maritsa
İğneada
Black Sea
Edirne
Kırklareli
Zonguldak
Momtchilovgrad
Vize
Midye
Ivailovgrad
Thrace
Lüleburgaz
Karacaköy
Bosporus
Ereğli
Didymoteikhon
Terkos
Uzunköprü
Şile
Kandıra
Akçakoca
Souphlí
Çorlu
Silivri
Çatalca
İncirli
Komotinē
Scutari
Düzce
Tekirdağ
İstanbul
Gebze
İzmit
Hendek
Bolu
Phérai
Keşan
Sea of Marmara
Adapazarı
Alexandroúpolis
2096
Karamürsel
Enez
Sarkoy
Marmara
Mudurnu
Greece
Gemlik
İznik
Geyve
Avşa
+2635
Gallipoli
Erdek
Bandırma
Mudanya
Yenişehir
Nallıhan
5905
Karabiga
Karacabey
Bursa
Bilecik
Sakarya
İmroz
Biga
Dardanelles
Ulu Daği
[Olympus]
+8180
İnegöl
Söğüt
Mihalıççık
Çanakkale
Gönan
Mustafa Kemal Paşa
Bozüyük
Tavşan
Troy
Bozcaada
Balya
Domaniç
Eskisehir
+5810
Balıkesir
Kepsut
Edremit
Tavşanlı
Sivrihisar
Ayvacık
Seyitgazi
Burhaniye
Hagios Eystratios
Bigadiç
Kütahya
Giresun
Mólyvos
Ayvalık
Sindırgı
Altıntaş
Emirdağ
Soma
Mytilēnē
[Lesbos]
Bergama
Simav
Kırkağaç
Gediz
Dikili
Kınık
Demirci
Afyon Karahisar
3084
Potamós
TURKEY
+7645
Akhisar
Çandarlı
Lydia
Uşak
Bolvadin
Manisa
Foça
Gediz
Kula
Sandıklı
Akşehir
Karaburun
Psarà
Menemen
Esme
Antípsara
4157
3905
Turgutlu
Salihli
Chios
Sardis
Alaşehir
Yalvaç
İzmir
Çivril
Urla
Seferihisar
Günay
Çeşme
Bayındır
Torbalı
Ödemiş
Çal
Dinar
Uluborlu
Cape Phánai
Tire
Boldan
Eğridir
Greece
Kuşadası
Ephesus
Nazilli
Sarayköy
Isparta
Asia Minor
Aydın
Menderes
Denizli
Söke
Burdur
Samos
Vathy
Bozdoğan
+8250
Ikária
Priene
Çine
Tavas
Tēnos
Phoûrnoi
Acıpayam
Bucak
Miletus
Tefenni
Mýkonos
Gaidaro
Archi
Milas
Dēlos
Patmo
Lisso
Rhenea
Küllük
Muğla
Aegean Sea
Lero
+7525
Halicarnassus
(Bodrum)
Perga
Serik
Donousa
Ula
Levita
Korkudeli
Naxos
Calino
Marmaris
Antalya
Kàros
Dodecanese
Cos
Elmalı
Datça
Amorgòs
Cnidus
+8995
Kemer
Gulf of Adalia
Ios
Fethiye
Stampalia
Nisiro
Tekirova
Simi
Santorin
Rhodes
Ofidusa
[Thēra]
Piscopi
Kaş
Finike
Anáphē
Sirina
Alinnia
Kalkan
Andifli
Malona
Calchi
4068
Attairo
Rhodes
Castelrosso
Candia
Zafrana
Cape Prasso
Saria
Camiloni
Italian Islands of the Aegean
Greece
Scarpanto
Día
Crete
Mallia
Cape St. John
Hagios Nikólaos
Mediterranean
Caso
Cape Sidero
Cnossus
Sēteía
Hierápetra
0
50
100
STATUTE MILES
Drawn by H.E. Eastwood and Irwin E. Alleman

Staff Photographer B. Anthony Stewart

Hygeia, the Doctor's Daughter, Was the Personification of Health

Here in the National Museum at Athens, the hair-do of a modern Greek girl can be compared with that on the sculptured head of Hygeia, daughter of the god of healing whose shrine is at Epidaurus (pages 187, 250).

around the palaces of Mycenae and Tiryns until the glories of the Mycenaean period merged into the traditions of the Dorian invaders. Finally all came out together as a part of the social legend of the ancient Greeks.

Four Hundred Years Following the Trojan War Lost to History

The Trojan War is usually dated about 1100 B. C. We have no historical record between that time and some four hundred years later, in the eighth century before our era, when men began to record time for literary purposes by the celebrations of the quadrennial Olympian games.

It is evident from study of the comparatively scanty remains from these four centuries that this was a formative period for the burst of civilization which followed in the many small city-states which were growing up independent of one another.

Athens was, of course, always the chief center of Greek culture, but simultaneously, or in turn, other towns played an important part in Greek history, and hence in the development of Greek civilization. Thebes, in Boeotia; Mégara, 20 miles west of Athens; Corinth; and Sparta—these were the principal cities whose varying fortunes run like a magnificent pattern through the web of Greek history.

Sparta Throve on Arts of War

Sparta was a military state; her army was the body of her citizens. These were supported by the larger *Helot*, or serf class, who had no rights at all. Physical fitness and aptitude for war were stressed, and anything which tended toward softening of body or character was sternly forbidden (pages 198, 218-9).

Athens was quite different. There the spirit of a true democracy soon asserted itself.

Athens built many merchant ships and a strong navy and thus won the leading position among the Greek states. This roused the dangerous jealousy of Sparta and other Greek cities.

But the Persian menace, which had absorbed the Greek colonies of the Asia Minor coast, united Athens and Sparta for a time. In 490 B. C. the Athenians turned back the Persian hordes of Darius the Great at Marathon (page 200).

Ten years later, Darius' son, Xerxes, burned

From T. Leslie Shear

This Bit of Potsherd Helped Ostracize Aristides, Athenian Hero of the Persian Wars

When it was thought a person had become too powerful and dangerous to the state, he could be banished temporarily by popular vote. This *ostrakon,* unearthed in the ancient market place, was a ballot against Aristides the Just, classic example of virtue in public life. In hastily scratched Greek letters is the inscription "Aristeides (son) of Lysimachos" (pages 246-7).

Athens and soon afterward watched the destruction of his great armada by the little Greek fleet at Salamìs. Reluctantly the Persians withdrew, never to return (pages 220-225).

Athens, Center of Culture and Power

Athens was now the mistress of the seas. Her great prosperity and power released all that was best in Greek art and thought. The 60 years from 460 B. C. to the close of the century saw the great period of Greek drama, the rise of philosophic thinking in Socrates and Protagoras, an unparalleled blossoming in the arts of sculpture, painting, architecture, and the minor arts, and, toward the end, the biting satire and broad comedies of Aristophanes.

The Athenian commercial empire stretched mainly from the Kerch Peninsula, on the northern coast of the Black Sea, through many of the Greek islands westward to Sicily.

But Persia (Iran) still threatened, and the Greek cities of Asia Minor were still for the most part under Persian rule. Soon Persian gold incited Sparta to attack the Athenians.

The war between Athens and Sparta lasted about thirty years (432-404 B. C.), with intervals of truce. It left the rivals weak and exhausted and Athens temporarily defeated. Athens received a further bitter blow in the disaster to her expedition against Syracuse in Sicily.

Sparta fought a ruinous war against Thebes. Persian gold still animated the political marionettes of the Greek states, but in the north, in semi-Hellenized, semibarbarous Macedonia, a new power was growing up.

The Delphic oracle, the Pythian games, and Olympia's festival every four years brought together people from all parts of the Greek world and established a temporary truce among warring states (pages 177, 208-9, 216-7).

All this, however, failed to amalgamate the Greek states, and no real federation ever took place. There were leagues and alliances, but temporary expediency was their only bond, and they generally dissolved almost as quickly as they were formed.

Alexander's Conquests Spread Greek Culture

In 338 B. C., Philip, king of Macedonia, ably seconded by his brilliant son Alexander, defeated the Athenians and the Thebans in a critical battle at Chaeronea.

Staff Photographer B. Anthony Stewart

Blown Up by Venetian Artillery Only 257 Years Ago, the Parthenon, Peerless Temple of All Time, Has Had Its Columns Restored

Built as unemployment relief, the Parthenon, crown jewel of the Acropolis, was the abode of Athena, skilled in the arts of peace and war. The United States WACS wear her head as lapel and collar insignia. The colonnade was restored with American aid. Since the columns were fluted by the builders after the drums were set up, [illegible] Tested by piano-wire measurements, the fallen columns were carefully restored to their original places.

Staff Photographer Maynard Owen Williams

From the Acropolis of Corinth One Looks Down on the City of St. Paul's "Corinthians" and New Corinth (right)

Far below are seven tiny columns of the Temple of Apollo (left) in the luxury-loving city whose merchants commanded transisthmian trade and whose priestesses made Aphrodite famous in every port (pages 186 and 214). Dark areas are fields of currants (seedless raisins), which take their name from Corinth. On the hill are Greek, Byzantine, Venetian, and Turkish ruins.

Staff Photographer Maynard Owen Williams

Every Soldier Was a Tower of Defense for Unwalled Sparta, Situated in a Plain and Dominated by Mountains

"I had expected to find Sparta an uninteresting city," wrote Dr. Williams, "for Thucydides said that her ruins would give no measure of her greatness. Yet few Greek cities have as fine a site. The walls of Sparta may have been the breasts of her sons, but the surrounding mountains may have had something to do with her ... Mount Taygetus by afternoon light on a rainy day" (pages 194-5 and 218).

Staff Photographer B. Anthony Stewart

The Fortress of Methónē Is an Abandoned History Book, with Crumpled Leaves of Stone

From the underlying Greek walls which resisted the Athenians in 431 B. C., to the final crenelations of the French, more than a century ago, this commanding site has endured a colorful career. Spartan and Nauplian, Venetian Crusader and Byzantine corsair, Turk and Frenchman defended its history-stratified walls, which face a stormy coast beyond the harbor of Navarino.

Staff Photographer B. Anthony Stewart

Under This Mound at Marathon Lie 192 Soldiers Who Swept Back the Persian Tide

While their Spartan allies awaited a full moon, Miltiades' men caught Darius' army in the most famous pincers movement of ancient times. When the Spartans arrived, the battle was won, and the original Marathon runner had brought the good news to Athens. Arrows of Ethiopian archers, described by Herodotus, have been picked up on this historic site (page 194). The steps are not relics of ancient times.

Upon Philip's untimely assassination—untimely because as a statesman he was probably far more able than his son—Alexander at only 20 years of age became the foremost personage in the Greek world.

His victorious campaigns against Persia ended with the Hellenizing of almost the entire Near East, including Egypt. Although after his early death his empire was divided among his generals and ultimately was engulfed by Rome, the three hundred years from 330 to 30 B. C. saw a tremendous spread of Greek thought and culture.

Many Ancient Findings Accurate

Eratosthenes of Cyrene computed the circumference of the earth to within about two hundred miles of what we now know it to be. Aristarchus of Samos (*ca.* 310-230 B. C.) propounded the theory that the earth revolved about the sun. Physics and mathematics and geometry took on the forms given by Euclid, Apollonius of Perga, and others.

The modern excavator who attempts to fill in the picture of ancient Greece is indebted especially to a traveler who wrote an excellent guidebook of that country in the second century after Christ.

If it were not for the careful descriptions which Pausanias left of a long list of sites in Greece, it would be difficult, if not impossible, to identify many of the monuments of Athens, Delphi, Olympia, and dozens of smaller places.

For example, in the early years of this century the excavators at Corinth were looking for the fountain of Peirene. It would give a key to the location of many other monuments (pages 197, 207).

The director of the excavations lost his glasses down a well in the courtyard of the house he was occupying. His foreman, who volunteered to go down after them, found himself in about two feet of water, with a narrow tunnel just big enough for him to squeeze through leading off in two directions.

He returned for a light and continued his explorations. At length he reported that he had come to a succession of "caves" partly filled with mud and water.

Pausanias' description of Peirene included the mention of a series of "caves" behind the façade of the fountain, and the excavators immediately set about clearing away the 30-foot deposit of earth that lay over the place. When it was all cleared out, Peirene lay open to the sky. It corresponded very closely with the account of the traveler of some eighteen hundred years before.

The country which Pausanias saw was the Greece of the Roman Empire, about the period of the Emperor Hadrian. Many buildings of earlier times, however, were still in use.

I once sat on a hillside near Lebadeia, on the way to Delphi, and read Pausanias' account of a visit to the oracle of Trophonius.

The elaborate preliminaries culminated in a sort of initiation ceremony wherein the consultant had to crawl feet first through a small hole in the rock. As he began to back through, he was seized and drawn swiftly inside. When he came out, it was apparent that he had had a terrible experience, for the description says, "After a time the power of laughter returns to him."

Pausanias' interest in Greece was typical of the attitude of people of his time, for although the country had been subjugated politically, Greek culture still remained supreme in all matters of art, literature, and philosophy.

Conquered, Greece Still Ruled the World of Letters

Corinth had been entirely destroyed by Lucius Mummius in 146 B. C. for heading a league of Greek states against the Roman power, and Athens had been burnt and sacked in 80 B. C. by Sulla, who carried off, among other souvenirs, some of the columns of the temple of Zeus Olympios to adorn the Temple of Jupiter Capitolinus at Rome. But it was not long before Greece achieved a complete cultural victory.

Julius Caesar refounded Corinth almost exactly one hundred years after Mummius had driven a symbolic plow over the site and strewn salt on the fields. After him, Roman emperors vied with one another in their eagerness to adorn Greece with new monuments. Nero made a tour through the country and ordered the building of a canal across the Isthmus of Corinth.

The project lapsed at his death, but the 19th-century engineers who cut the present canal found the Roman trial borings almost exactly on the line which they themselves followed (page 190).

Athens, Eleusis, Olympia, Delphi—all are full of Roman dedications and important buildings. They cannot compare with Greek work, either in precision or in artistic merit, but the very fact that they imitate it so often is tangible proof of the spiritual domination which the Greeks had established over their temporary conquerors.

Greece Has Suffered Many Invasions

The Slavs overran Greece in the sixth century of the Christian Era, and the great Byzantine emperor, Justinian, from his capital at Constantinople (İstanbul), rebuilt a wall across the Isthmus of Corinth to defend that part of the country, at least, from the invaders.

From Sicily, the Normans, men of the same stock as William the Conqueror, invaded and pillaged parts of Greece in their time. Crusaders, bound ostensibly for the Holy Land, were diverted to Constantinople and set up for a time a Latin emperor. Greece itself fell into their power, and many ancient fortresses of the classical period have the upper parts of their walls remodeled into the appearance of medieval castles.

It was the fashion for younger sons of feudal barons to come out from France or Germany or England to look for their fortunes in the Morea, as the Peloponnesus was then called. The Prince of the Morea, Geoffroy de Villehardouin, held a celebrated court of chivalry in the Middle Ages.

The Turks conquered Greece in the middle of the 15th century and held it for nearly 400 years.

The legacy of Greek culture to our modern world is tremendous, and its stream throughout the course of history is unbroken, though at times it ran through difficult and obscure periods. But the tenacious spirit of the Greek peoples ultimately triumphed over every oppressor.*

* See NATIONAL GEOGRAPHIC MAGAZINE articles: "The Aegean Isles: Poseidon's Playground," by Gilbert M. Grosvenor, December, 1958; "Athens to İstanbul," by Jean and Franc Shor, January, 1956; "Crete, Cradle of Western Civilization," November, 1953, "War-torn Greece Looks Ahead," December, 1949, "Modern Odyssey in Classic Lands," March, 1940, "New Greece, the Centenarian, Forges Ahead," December, 1930, and "Seeing 3,000 Years of History in Four Hours," December, 1928, all five by Maynard Owen Williams; "Mediterranean Checkerboard," by Frederick Simpich, April, 1942; "'Glory That Was Greece,'" by Alexander Wilbourne Weddell, December, 1922; "Crete, Where Sea-Kings Reigned," by Agnes N. Stillwell, November, 1943; and others listed in the NATIONAL GEOGRAPHIC Cumulative Index.

© National Geographic Society

Painting by H. M. Herget

"Seized a Loud-roaring Bull That Bellowed Mightily . . . A Dancing Place Like unto That . . . in Wide Cnossus Daedalus Wrought"—Iliad

Boy and Girl Grappling Bulls at Cnossus: Crete

EXCAVATIONS during the last 50 years in the great Palace of Cnossus, near modern Candia in Crete, have gradually revealed the remains of a remarkable ancient civilization. Relics give a picture of a seafaring people who flourished more than a thousand years before the Parthenon at Athens was built.

As the work of uncovering the Minoan palace went on, it became apparent that bulls had occupied a place of honor in the customs of the ancient Cretans. Fresco paintings, bronzes, and carved gems illustrate one of the favorite sports—that of bull grappling, or *taurokathapsia*. It was not a bullfight in the usually accepted sense, but resembled more a spectacular performance still found in southern France, where the object is not the death of the bull, but rather the display of agility and daring on the part of the men who skillfully avoid the charging animal.

The Minoans, vase pictures prove, brought the sport to a high degree of acrobatic skill. They would seize the bull by the horns and vault, or turn a sort of handspring, over its back, landing adroitly behind it as it passed. Apparently several athletes might do this in turn.

What is more surprising is that girls took part in this dangerous sport, and from the manner in which they are depicted by the Cretan artists, Sir Arthur Evans suggests that they were selected from among the best families of the country, and were not necessarily professionals. For these games they wore a costume similar to that of the men.

Occasionally there were accidents, as we know by depictions on Cretan objects which have been found, and such a mishap is illustrated here. The youth has missed his hold and is being thrown, while the girl who was about to vault in her turn has already begun her leap.

The games were held in front of a specially built grandstand. Sometimes they may have taken place in the great court of the Palace, as is shown here. Near the edge of the arena stand some of the "black guard," Ethiopians, officered by Cretans.

On the balcony of the Palace are groups of fashionably dressed ladies. At the left is a pillar shrine with a central column instead of a human or animal figure to represent deity.

Horned altars are used as a decorative as well as a religious motif above the cornice, and the stucco covering the rubble stone walls, which were strengthened with half-timbering to withstand earthquake shocks, is painted in such a way as to indicate the underlying construction.

There also appears the characteristic Cretan double ax, called *labrys,* from which the Labyrinth may have got its name. Anyone who has tried to find his way about the maze of rooms and zigzag passages in Cnossus has no difficulty in crediting the suggestion that the Palace of King Minos was indeed the Labyrinth where Theseus slew the Minotaur.

The exploits of Theseus were carved on the metopes of the Athenian temple known by his name.

On one of those metopes is a representation of Theseus struggling with the Minotaur, the mythical monster, half man, half bull, whom he was said to have sought out in the Labyrinth of the Cretan king, Minos, when he went to deliver Athens from the yearly tribute of youths and maidens sent to be the victims of the monster.

Painting by H. M. Herget

"Cherish the Stranger in the House, and Speed Him as Soon as He Has the Mind"—Odyssey

Travelers at a Mycenaean Palace

ABOUT 1400 B.C. the great Palace at Cnossus was destroyed by fire, and although part of it was rebuilt, Cretan civilization had passed its peak and never recovered. For a long time before that date, however, the people of Crete had traded with the people inhabiting the mainland of Greece. Many Cretan motifs and architectural ideas had been brought to the Peloponnesus, where, from about 1600 to 1200 B.C., flourished a civilization called Mycenaean, from the name of one of its principal cities, Mycenae.

There were many other rich centers as well, such as Pylos, Sparta, Tiryns, and Orchomenus in Boeotia, to the northwest of Athens. All these had added the graces of Cretan culture to their own basic northern ideas, for the lords of Mycenae and Tiryns in those days were probably northerners whose ancestors had come down into Greece in successive waves during the earlier centuries.

Cretan dress, slightly modified, was worn by the women. The characteristic Cretan column, tapering downward instead of up, was common; decorations patterned after shields which resembled a figure eight and are found in Crete also appear in Greece. Certain basic northern ideas, however, are found in Mycenaean architecture, especially the *megaron* type of house. The Mycenaean house, which stood isolated under its own gabled roof, was entered from the end through a porch with columns which stood between the projecting side walls of the building.

In the picture a youthful traveler is receiving from his Mycenaean host and hostess rich gifts—a golden cup and a woven garment. His companion is busy with the chariot in which they are to drive away, and in the courtyard at the left a servant is roasting a kid for a farewell breakfast.

Two great hounds, such as appear on a fresco painting of a boar hunt found at Tiryns, stand near by, and a cat rubs its back against one of the pillars of the porch.

The cat is not supposed to have been domesticated in Greece before the sixth century, but relics of the period prove that the Cretan and Mycenaean artists knew and represented cats. The commercial relations which existed between Egypt and Crete, and extended through Crete to the mainland, make it not impossible for a tame Egyptian cat to have found its way to the hearth of a Mycenaean palace.

Although the period of the Trojan War and Homer's *Iliad* and *Odyssey* is later than the height of the Mycenaean civilization, many of its glories remained in the memory of the later people, to be written ultimately into these great epic poems. Some startling parallels are to be found in Homer's description of certain objects, such as the famous silver cup of Nestor with two doves wrought on the handle, and works of art actually found in Mycenaean graves.

Our picture, though of the pre-Homeric period, illustrates such an incident as occurs in the Odyssey when the young Telemachus, in search of news of his father, Odysseus, drove from Pylos to Sparta and was welcomed and entertained by Menelaus and his fair wife Helen. On this journey Telemachus was accompanied by his friend Peisistratus.

The King of Mycenae, Agamemnon, was leader of all the Greeks in the Trojan War. His fleet of one hundred ships was the largest of the Greek contingents.

Painting by H. M. Herget

"Water Nymphs . . . May Your Lovely Feet Tread on This Watery House . . . . While You Fill It with a Pure Draught"—Greek Anthology

A Fountain House of 2,500 Years Ago

In Greece, just as in any other land which is baked by the summer sun, water has always been precious. Today the fountain in the square of any small Greek town which does not have a modern piping system is a meeting place for most of the women of the village, who now fill empty gasoline tins, instead of beautiful clay jars, and carry them away on their heads.

In ancient times, as now, the carrying of water was woman's work, and in the picture we see a group of girls who have come to a fountain house to perform their daily chore. The period represented is what is generally known as the Archaic; that is, it comes somewhere between the seventh century and the end of the sixth century B.C.

Many of the fountains were provided with draw basins, from which water could be dipped up, and the parapet wall was sometimes cut away behind so as to make it easier to let a water jar, or *hydria,* down into the water. In front of the parapet runs a little channel to carry off the overflow. It is provided with a catch basin to collect silt, so that the channel can be kept clear.

The water basins and draw basins were waterproofed with a very hard, fine stucco, and the architectural features, walls, and columns were also stuccoed, unless they were actually of marble. Marble was never used as a building material before the sixth century. The stucco, however, was exceedingly hard and white and gave an almost marblelike appearance to the stone.

Bronze or marble spouts usually took the form of lions' heads and might be used to supply the draw basin; or sometimes they were arranged so that a jar could be placed directly beneath them. The rear wall of the chamber conceals a large storage basin, or basins, where a great quantity of water could be collected to take care of a rush hour.

The wide, bell-shaped echinus of the capital, below the square abacus block, is characteristic of the early period, as is the row of leaves painted around the top of the shaft just below the spread of the capital. They recall the deep gorge which often occurs on capitals of the Mycenaean period.

Frequently the original spring from which the water came was at some distance from the fountain, and required a long underground channel. In other cases, as the fountain of Peirene at Corinth, the fountain house was cut in a stratum of stiff clay which underlay a formation of conglomerate rock. Collecting channels were driven through the clay, and the water which seeped through the rock drained into them and thus was supplied to the reservoirs.

The fountain, especially if it had been the chief source of water from the times of the early settlement, naturally established the location of the *agora,* or meeting and market place, and might also dictate the location of certain industries. The waters of Peirene had the reputation of being peculiarly suited to the tempering of bronze, for which Corinth was famous, and there is evidence that at one time a bronze foundry was set up close to this fountain.

The women in the picture wear the Doric *peplos,* of wool, with brightly decorated borders, and two of them also carry a cloak, or *himation.* Felt caps, much like some worn today, acted as cushions for the water jars carried on the head.

Painting by H. M. Herget

"They Called Every Man to His Horses as They Flew amid Their Dust across the Plain"—Iliad

Chariot Race at Olympia

Homer describes a chariot race in connection with the funeral games celebrated in honor of Patroclus, and it is certain that the sport existed in Greece in very early times. Enormous sums were spent on the training of teams and the maintenance of racing stables. Although women were not allowed to compete in the games, and were, moreover, excluded from watching them, we hear of chariot teams owned by women being driven in the races and winning prizes.

The chariot race probably was introduced to Olympia in the early part of the seventh century B.C. (*ca.* 680) and in its earliest form was for two-horse teams. Later, but still quite early, the four-horse team was introduced.

The sculptures on the east pediment of the great Temple of Zeus at Olympia represent the moment before the legendary race between Pelops and Oenomaus, the prize being the hand of Oenomaus' daughter, Hippodameia. More than a dozen luckless suitors had been beaten in similar races and slain, their heads being hung up by the jealous father. Pelops, however, is said to have bribed his rival's charioteer to remove the linchpin from the wheel, and won the race when Oenomaus' chariot upset.

Pindar tells us that the games at Olympia were established by Heracles in honor of Pelops.

Nothing remains of the Olympic hippodrome, which was, after all, a simple affair. Any flat, sandy stretch of land would do, and Pausanias tells us that at Olympia it lay between the stadium and the river. It was necessary merely to set up pillars at the turns, and occasionally there seem to have been wooden grandstands. The circuit of the course was about six stades, a little less than three-quarters of a mile. The total distance varied for different types of race, but was usually about twelve circuits of the course, or between eight and nine miles.

We hear of as many as forty entries in a race. A complicated system of starting gates to insure fair alignment was developed. One of the hazards of the course was an altar along the circuit called *Taraxippos*—terror of horses. Around this grew up a mass of superstition and legend. What frightened horses at that point and caused so many accidents is not known, but the ancients believed that it was some unfriendly demon.

The charioteers who drove were, for the most part, professionals, like our own jockeys, but occasionally an owner drove. As in races of our own time, the prize went to the owner, or trainer. A Spartan, Damonon, records that he and his son won 68 victories in eight festivals. They could hardly have done all the driving.

The charioteers always wore a long, white, sleeveless dress, called *chiton*. Their chariots were light, two-wheeled affairs with open backs, modeled after the earlier war chariots. In a race the starting signal was given by a trumpet blast; the turn was always to the left.

In the picture the chariots are seen passing in front of three judges, or *Hellanodikai,* who are seated on thrones of honor, and beside them are bronze tripods such as were given as prizes, or sometimes set up as dedications in the precinct at Olympia. Two chariots have come to grief rounding one of the columns set up at a turn.

Athena's Gift to Greece Was the Precious Olive

Besides decorating their vases with scenes from mythology, Greek artists delighted in showing events of everyday life. On some of the vases which have survived, especially those from the latter part of the sixth century B. C., are scenes having to do with one of the major industries of ancient Greece—the picking and pressing of olives and the marketing of olive oil.

To the ancient Greek, olive oil was really indispensable. He served it in many ways as food and used it to rub himself down. All athletes massaged their bodies with olive oil before entering the contests of the gymnasium. Whenever an ancient site is excavated in Greece, diggers find scores of the shallow clay lamps for which the fuel was olive oil poured from a specially shaped clay cup.

We are told that oil was even used for preserving fabrics, and read that Alexander, when he visited the Persian capital, Susa, in 331 B. C., saw some textiles, nearly two centuries old, which had been kept supple by being dipped in a mixture of olive oil and honey.

Attica was especially renowned for its olives. Solon, the Athenian lawgiver, who forbade the exportation of other crops, allowed oil to be exported freely. Athenian oil in clay jars found its way all over the Mediterranean.

Quite properly, Athens, as the center of oil cultivation, attributed the invention of the olive to her patron goddess, Athena, and a special enclosure was built on the Acropolis to protect the supposedly first, sacred olive tree.

The olives were usually picked in the winter months, and in the picture we can see men beating the branches with pliant rods to shake down the fruit. The olives are then collected in baskets and bruised in a mill. Next they are placed in woven containers and piled up on a marble or stone press block with a groove around it and a spout at one side.

Numerous presses have been found in excavations. Some early paintings and reliefs show different types, but the simplest, and probably the first, was a long beam, wedged into some rocks and weighted with a net full of stones. The man in the foreground is pulling down on the lever, and his assistant has added his own weight.

The mash was often pressed several times over, but the quality of the oil became poorer at each pressing. Occasionally "summer oil" was made from green olives, but since this called for hand picking, the quantity was limited and the price correspondingly high. Aristotle says that a measure of ordinary oil, equaling about three and a half quarts, sold for three *drachmai,* about 32 cents a quart.

At the left of the picture are customers sampling oil or haggling over the price. A man with hunting boots is smelling some which he has rubbed on the back of his hand. Farther off another pours some into a little vase through a pottery funnel. Near the small storage shed is a cart loaded with oil jars to be taken into town.

The curious type of wheel appears on early vases and in terra-cotta models of wagons. One vase shows two men, seated, sampling olive oil, with the prayer inscribed on the scene: "O Zeus, would that I might become rich." On the other side is the fulfillment of this pious wish.

Painting by H. M. Herget

"Amyntichos . . . Planted in Thee the Olive Stock . . . and Made Thee Plenteous in Fruit"—Greek Anthology

Fishermen in the Gulf of Corinth

Fish was a popular item in the diet of the Greeks, especially for the poorer classes. The Homeric Heroes seemed not to regard it highly but preferred great roasts of oxen, sheep, and goats. In this it is likely that they reflect their northern origins, for they came from inland countries where sea food was not obtainable.

In the fifth century, however, an Athenian banquet almost invariably included a fish course, and all sorts of rarer fish and mollusks were found at a well-set table.

The Athenian gourmets were especially fond of the great eels which were brought from Lake Kopaïs in Boeotia, and the ringing of the fish bell to announce the arrival in the market of a fresh catch of fish was the signal for a rush of householders to get there in time to obtain the best. For a long time it was the Athenian custom for the master of the house, accompanied by a slave, to do the marketing, and it was not until relatively late times that the women were allowed to have any part in it.

An old story relates that at a recital by a lyre player his entire audience, with the exception of one deaf old man, departed without ceremony when the fish bell rang. When the musician thanked him for his courtesy in remaining in spite of the ringing of the bell, the man said, "What! Did the fish bell ring?" and rushed off as fast as he could go.

Large quantities of sardines were caught in Phaleron Bay at Piraeus and, being plentiful and cheap, formed a major part of the diet of the poorer classes. Tunny also were plentiful. We hear of salt and smoked fish being brought from the Black Sea ports and the Spanish coast.

In fishing, the ancient Greeks used nets mainly, but they also angled with hooks and lines. Bronze hooks have been found in excavations. There is little to show, however, that fishing was ever regarded as a sport; it was always a serious business. Octopuses were caught then as now with tridents, which could also be used in spearing fish, especially at night by the light of torches.

Our picture shows a fishing scene on the shore of the Gulf of Corinth, beyond which rises Mount Helicon. A fishing boat has just put in, and baskets of herring and some tunny are being carried up to be taken to the fish market in the city, two miles or more away from the shore.

One old man has come down to the source of supply and is bargaining with the fisherman. Possibly he is convinced of the truth of the epithets found in the comedies, that fishermen were assassins and robbers.

Near by, on some rocks, a boy is fishing with rod and line. In one hand he holds a sort of landing basket, and in the water near him is another basket in which he probably puts the fish he catches so as to keep them fresh until it is time to go home.

Out beyond the young angler a warship is headed westward, her mast stepped and sail set to catch the breeze. The high latticed forecastle, single animal's head ram, and one bank of oars are characteristic of sixth-century ships.

In the tree above the man who is engaged in cleaning fish sits a small owl, such as still may be seen flitting about, even in broad daylight, although they usually come out at dusk and pass the greater part of the day in small burrows.

Painting by H. M. Herget

"When a Man Sits on a Jutting Rock and Drags a Fish Forth from the Sea"—Iliad

Hauling a Ship over the Isthmus

BETWEEN the Greek mainland and the Peloponnesus is a narrow neck of land about four miles wide. Today it is cut by a canal through which fairly large ships pass between the Gulf of Aegina and the Gulf of Corinth. The passage saves a long trip around the storm-beaten southern extremity of the Peloponnesus.

The picture shows a Greek merchant ship being moved on rollers across the Isthmus along the roadway called the *diolkos*. Vessels may have been cradled on wheels—a possibility indicated by two parallel grooves along part of a mile length of the road excavated in 1957.

Such vessels were usually propelled by a single sail, of a square pattern, stretched on a great yardarm. The masts could be easily unstepped, since it was customary to beach ships frequently. There were also a limited number of oars on the merchantmen for use in case of unfavorable winds or in warping out of a harbor, but the great banks of oars and large number of rowers were found only on the warships. It was customary to raise woven mats above the bulwarks to help protect the cargo.

A ship was steered by means of a large oar suspended in a socket over the quarter; sometimes there were steering oars on either side, connected by a beam so that they would turn together. Because of the sharp stern construction, rudders were not used. The high curving sternpost found on all Greek ships, as well as on later Roman ones, was sometimes decorated with a swan's head.

Bows of merchant ships were rather bluff, and the stem projected forward as it rose from the water line. In the warships, however, the bow was drawn forward into a long beak fitted with a bronze ram. The planking was butt joined and smooth, and seams were calked with oakum and pitch. In fact, the entire hull might be pitched.

Although they must have been fairly seaworthy, the ships of ancient Greece were unable, on account of their rig, to sail against the wind, and consequently depended on favorable breezes to reach their destination. Usually the crew put ashore at night, which was not difficult where the distances were so small. It was only rarely that a ship kept the open sea for more than a few days at a time.

The city of Corinth grew rich in Greek times with the trade which passed by the Isthmus, and many goods were doubtless transshipped there, being carried across on muleback from the eastern ports of Cenchreae and Isthmía. There was another port, Lechaion, on the shore of the Gulf of Corinth, connected in classic times with Corinth by long walls built down to it from the ring of the fortifications.

Little is known of the actual harbor in Greek times, but the Romans, when they refounded Corinth, dredged several capacious basins where shipping would lie safely sheltered from heavy westerly winds that often raged down the gulf.

Behind the city, which appears dimly on the terraced plateau halfway up from the shore line, rises Acrocorinthus, strongly fortified by walls. Some of these walls, dating from early days, recall the scenes of many a siege through the course of Greek history. Near the shore, in line with Acrocorinthus, is a low bluff where in pre-Mycenaean times there was a prosperous settlement, known today as Korakou.

Painting by H. M. Herget

"Come, Let Us Draw down a Black Ship to the Fair Salt Sea"—Odyssey

The Famous Oracle at Delphi

Of all the oracles of the ancient world the most important by far was that at Delphi. Here were the richest offerings and dedications. The Greek states from all over the Mediterranean sent their embassies to consult the Pythian Apollo, who spoke through his priestess and prophetess, the Pythia.

Like all ancient mysteries, the secrets of the oracle were well guarded; so much so that when the temple where the oracle stood was excavated, every part of the *adyton,* the holy of holies inside the *cella* of the temple, was found to have been ripped out. From various literary sources, from a few stones, and from sculptures and vase paintings, however, we may reconstruct the scene to some degree.

Within the temple was a small stone chamber, partly or wholly below the floor level. Here stood a huge bronze tripod with the *omphalos,* which marked the navel or center of the world, in front of it. By the omphalos stood two golden eagles representing the birds which Zeus had released, one on the east, the other on the west, in order to determine by their meeting place the center of the earth. On this omphalos were laid sacred fillets or bands of wool.

By the tripod stood bronze laurel branches which the Pythia is said sometimes to have shaken in her prophetic frenzy. No one could understand her incoherent ravings, but the priests professed to do so and provided for the ambassadors who came to consult the oracle a written form of the prophecy.

There was always, however, enough doubt as to the exact meaning of the prophecy so that the oracle could never be called wrong.

The suggestion has been made that the Pythia, chosen at first from among the young women of Delphi, would go down into a chamber under the adyton, light a fire of herbs whose smoke had a narcotic effect on her, and then reappear and mount the tripod. In the omphalos was a hole through which smoke or vapor could rise into the room and increase the mystic effect.

Somewhere in the temple, very possibly in the adyton, was a golden statue of Apollo, holding in one hand a flat bowl for libations and in the other a bow. Helmets were hung on the walls as votive offerings.

The influence of the oracle was tremendous, and its pronouncements are legion. Sometimes it seems that the oracle was influenced, as in the case of the Spartan delegation which was sent to inquire as to the legitimacy of Demaratus in connection with his kingship.

Cleomenes, to be revenged on Demaratus, gained the help of a certain Cobon who persuaded the prophetess Perialla to say what they desired, and she gave judgment that Demaratus was not the son of his supposed father. As a result, he was deposed from his kingship. Herodotus goes on to say, however, that at a later day these doings were discovered, Cobon was banished from Delphi, and Perialla was deprived of her honorable office.

After the Persian Wars, a scandalous attempt to kidnap the priestess resulted in her always being selected from among the older women. In general, the woman who served as the Pythia was not required to have any training or education, but acted entirely on the instructions of the priests who managed the oracle.

© National Geographic Society

Painting by H. M. Herget

"The Delphian Priestess Sits on the Holy Tripod Chanting to the Greeks Whatever Apollo Bids Her"—Euripides

Young Spartans Were Tough

After the age of seven, Spartan boys no longer lived at home, but were brought up by the state in barracks, under the charge of a *paidonomos,* or governor. Their schooling was slight so far as reading and writing were concerned.

On the other hand, their physical training was of a severe order. From the time they were twelve they were allowed only a single garment, winter or summer, and for bedding they used rushes which they gathered for themselves on the banks of the Eurotas River.

Quarrels were encouraged among them and fights promoted, so that it went hard with any who were not able to take punishment. Military exercises were preferred to purely athletic sports, and all training was calculated toward strengthening the youth for bearing arms and enduring the rigors of a long campaign. On the feast of Artemis Orthia, some of the older youths were flogged at her altar so as to give an example of fortitude to the rest.

The young men were not allowed to marry until they were about 30 years of age. During all that time they continued to live with their units and to eat in the common mess. In fact, all citizens were required to take one meal a day at an eating club and had to provide, in grain and wine, their share of the provender, on penalty of losing their status as citizens.

The girls were also given rigorous physical training so that they might become the mothers of healthy children. When a man married, he continued to live in barracks for some time and used to visit his wife secretly at night. Newborn children were reared only if perfectly formed; the weaklings were thrown from a cliff of Mount Taygetus.

Although the old story of the Spartan boy who concealed a stolen fox under his *chlamys* (stealing was encouraged as long as the offender escaped detection) may not be true, it is typical of the code under which the youths were trained. As every schoolboy knows, the boy, rather than be caught carrying stolen goods, allowed the fox to tear at his body.

No Spartan could engage in trade. That was reserved for the *Perioeci,* who lived in Lacedaemon but were not citizens, and for the servant class, the *Helots,* who were in much the same condition as the medieval serf and were bound to the soil. They usually accompanied their masters on military expeditions, acting as armor bearers and camp servants. When the Spartans went to war, they allowed their hair to grow, as an indication that to them war was a luxury.

The economic difficulties which arose in the later period of Sparta's history when women could and did inherit property, and in fact controlled a great deal of it, led ultimately to the downfall of the state. Many of the Spartan citizens became so impoverished that they could not supply their share of rations at the common mess and accordingly were deprived of their rights as citizens.

As a result, when the political power of Sparta reached its height in the fourth century B. C., the supply of Spartiates had diminished to such an extent that they were no longer able to fill all the necessary posts and supply the garrisons which were needed. Their code had been admirably adapted for a small state, but it lacked the elasticity needful to adapt itself to changing conditions.

Painting by H. M. Herget

"Superiority Lies with Him Who Is Reared in the Severest School"—Thucydides

Leonidas' Immortal Sacrifice at Thermopylae

In the summer of 480 B.C. the Persian king, Xerxes, was moving down with a vast army against Greece. Most of the Greek states forgot their differences in the face of the common peril. Athens, fortunately, possessed a well-equipped navy, and, aided by contingents from other cities, was leader in the defense against the danger by sea.

Sparta, the other chief military state of Greece, advanced a shortsighted plan of campaign, which was to defend the narrow Isthmus of Corinth, hold only the Peloponnesus, and abandon the remainder of the country to the invader. But this was not approved by the majority of the Greeks.

For a time the Greek allies, led by Themistocles, an Athenian general, contemplated a defense of Thessaly near Mount Olympus. But the position was untenable, and the forces withdrew, leaving part of the army to block the Persian advance at Thermopylae, where the narrow pass between the mountains and the sea offered some hope of success.

This defense was led by Leonidas, the Spartan king, with some three hundred Spartans and their followers, and nearly five thousand other fighters from Tegea, Orchomenus, Corinth, Thespiae, Thebes, Locris, Phocis, and elsewhere.

For a time the resistance was highly successful, and the Persian numbers were of no advantage in the narrow defile. But a certain Epialtes from Malis betrayed to the Persians a secret way around the position, and in the night word came to Leonidas that his forces were being cut off from behind.

At daybreak, therefore, he dismissed his allies save for a thousand Phocians, 700 Thespians, and the Thebans, and with his three hundred fought an immortal delaying action at the pass. He himself and all but two of the Spartans perished, but the glorious memory of his devotion forms one of the brightest pages of Greek history.

The Spartan dead were buried under a mound near where they fell, and a stone lion was set up over it. Simonides wrote their epitaph: "O passer-by, tell the Lacedaemonians that we lie here obeying their orders."

In the picture Leonidas is seen bidding farewell to the departing allies. In the distance, watched by sentries, rises smoke from the Persian campfires, and in the middle distance appears part of a rough stone fortification erected by the people of Phocis as a defense in an earlier war.

The Greek warrior of that period wore a corselet of bronze and leather over a shirt. Lappets of leather hung from the cuirass to protect the abdomen, and the lower legs were protected by bronze greaves. On the head was a high-crested bronze helmet lined with leather or worn over a leather cap.

The shields were usually round, although the Thebans carried oval shields with indentations on either side. Swords were short and double-edged, and a spear completed the warrior's offensive armament.

Troops from the noncitizen class were equipped with a simple helmet or cap and carried bows, spears, or slings.

In World War II Thermopylae was held again, this time by men from Britain—an island that was unknown in Greek times except to some Phoenician tin traders. Again the pass was taken, and the defenders had to fall back, leaving some of their number behind to hold off the enemy as long as possible, because they, too, had been outflanked.

© National Geographic Society

Painting by H. M. Herget

"O Passer-by, Tell the Lacedaemonians That We Lie Here Obeying Their Orders"—Simonides

The Persians Storm the Acropolis

After the Persians had passed Thermopylae, there remained no effective natural barrier between them and Athens. Themistocles, one of the most influential of the Athenian generals, persuaded the people to withdraw to the island of Salamis, which would provide a secure refuge as long as the fleet held out. Some Athenians, however, were reluctant to leave, and decided to defend the Acropolis. The Delphic oracle had pronounced, cryptically, that their safety lay in wooden walls.

The exact nature of the Acropolis walls at this period is somewhat uncertain, but it is fairly safe to say, on the grounds of later evidence, that above the massive stone foundations the walls were built of unburnt brick, strengthened with wood, and that there was considerable wood in the upper portions of the walls where they were crowned by covered galleries.

At first the Persian assault was successfully repulsed, but flaming arrows were shot against the defenders, and the old gateway, or Propylaea, was soon in flames. So, too, was the scaffolding around a great new building which was being erected at that time. Herodotus tells us that the Persians finally broke in by climbing up a path on the north side of the Acropolis, where no one thought it was possible to go. They probably made their way through the unguarded battlements and took the defenders from behind.

In those days, the principal temple was not, as later on, the Parthenon, but an earlier and smaller building called the Hecatompedon, or the Old Temple, which lay farther north. Not many decades before the sack, the Peisistratid rulers of Athens had remodeled and adorned this temple with a surrounding colonnade, and had also given it a roof of marble tiles and fine sculptured pediments.

Early in the fifth century a new and greater temple was planned. It was to be of Pentelic marble throughout, and to stand on a massive stone platform near the south edge of the Acropolis. Work on this temple, which was to have had a peristyle with six columns across each end, had been begun, and the steps and first few drums of the columns were already set up when the Persians came. Possibly the building had been begun as a thank offering for the defeat of Xerxes' father, Darius the Great, at Marathon in 490 B.C.

The marble work which had already been erected was badly calcined by the fire which raged through the scaffolding, and many of the damaged column drums were built later into the north wall of the Acropolis when it was hastily refortified after the Persians had gone. The foundation remained, however, and was enlarged somewhat to take the Parthenon, the great new temple which Pericles ordered built a little more than thirty years later.

We know that there were a number of other smaller buildings on the Acropolis at the time of the invasion, but only a few architectural fragments of them remain, and we have no good indication as to where they stood.

Practically all the old statues and monuments were destroyed by the Persians. Excavators have found large quantities of the fragments in the fill which was made at the south side of the Parthenon when in Periclean times the Acropolis was remodeled and widened toward the south.

Painting by H. M. Herget

"Yet Shall a Wood-built Wall by Zeus All-seeing Be Granted"—Herodotus

Painting by H. M. Herget

"Divine Salamis, Thou Shalt Destroy the Children of Women"—Herodotus

Xerxes Watching the Battle of Salamìs, 480 B.C.

ABANDONING their homes, most of the Athenians escaped to the near-by island of Salamìs, and the Greek fleet, well equipped and resolutely manned, although numerically inferior to the Persian, lay between the invader and the future of the civilized world.

Various schemes of defense were proposed, but the obvious tactical maneuver was to take advantage of the narrow waters between Salamìs and the mainland, where the Persian numbers would not count so heavily. On the other hand, this would probably expose the Greeks to a long blockade, and there was every reason to attempt some operation which would result in a quick decision.

Themistocles resourcefully contrived to send off a message which would be sure to fall into the Persians' hands and indicate to them that the Greek fleet was on the point of slipping away. Xerxes, confident in the size of his fleet, and also, probably, impelled by the difficulty of supplying his forces for a long time, determined to join battle at once.

Accordingly, the Persian fleet was sent in to force the narrow waters between the mainland and the narrow peninsula of Salamìs called Cynosura, "dog's tail." A small island, Psyttalea, split the Persian fleet into two parts and, so far as it is possible to reconstruct the battle from varying accounts, it appears that the great number of the Persian galleys, lacking sea room to deploy, were helplessly and hopelessly crowded together. The Greek squadrons swung into and rammed their enemies before they had any chance to open out in the broader reaches of the bay.

Xerxes watched the fight from a throne set up on a spur of Mount Aegaleos. Herodotus tells how, when the galley of Queen Artemisia, one of Xerxes' allies, ran down a friendly ship in a successful effort to escape, the monarch thought she was actually ramming a Greek vessel and exclaimed, "My men fight like women, but my women fight like men!"

Warships in those days were propelled by oars. A trireme had usually as many as two hundred rowers, and three banks of oars on each side, arranged thus: ·:·:·:·:· It carried a single large mast and sail which was unshipped and sent ashore if possible before going into action, but there was often a jigger mast which was retained to help in maneuvering or in escaping.

The bronze beaks on the bows were used for ramming, which was the favorite form of attack, but when a group of vessels became locked the fighting men boarded the opposing ship and fought hand to hand. Blazing arrows, bearing bundles of tow and pitch, were used as incendiaries. Most actions were fought near shore, and we frequently hear of crews "bailing out" and swimming to safety on the beach.

The disaster to his fleet and the impossibility of maintaining his land forces once they were cut off from sea-borne supplies forced Xerxes to return to Persia, leaving an army to winter in Thessaly. His plans to send reinforcements were delayed, however, and when his general, Mardonius, was defeated at Plataea the next year he made no further attempt to conquer Greece.

Thus the Battle of Salamìs made Athens the mistress of the seas for many years and cleared the way for her notable political, commercial, and cultural expansion.

Painting by H. M. Herget

"There Is No Greater Glory for a Man . . . Than That Which He Achieves by Hand and Foot"—Odyssey

To Greeks We Owe Our Love of Athletics

From the earliest times of which we have any record the Greeks were passionately fond of athletic games. To them we owe a large measure of our interest in track and gymnastic sports. In the Homeric Age we hear of jumping, discus throwing, running, wrestling, and boxing. Both high and distance jumping were popular, although only the latter was included in the Olympic contests.

We are told that it was customary to use weights, called *halteres,* to aid the jumper in getting greater momentum for his leap; some of these objects made of stone or bronze have been found, and many representations of them may be seen on Greek vase paintings. Probably the weights were used also to exercise the hands and arms just as dumbbells are used today.

The foot races were of varying lengths, the short straightaway being one *stadion,* or about 600 feet. In several of the old stadia there are still rows of stone blocks at either end, with grooves cut in them to give the sprinters' feet a firm hold for the take-off. There are also sometimes holes for posts which may have held ropes to divide the running lanes.

There was, as well, a distance race, which at Olympia was about three miles. Racing in full armor was also popular.

Throwing the discus and the javelin formed part of the standard pentathlon contest. Javelins were equipped with a thong wound around the shaft. This gave the missile a rotary motion.

Two types of wrestling were in favor. In one the object was to throw the opponent so that his shoulder touched the ground, while the adversary remained on his feet. The other was more rough and tumble, and the match continued until one wrestler declared himself beaten.

Boxing, considered a separate sport, was practiced more generally by the athlete who wished to win special prizes in the games. In earlier times skill counted more than brute force, and the hands were bound for protection, with soft leather thongs only. These later gave way to hard oxhide wrappings, often weighted with lead.

In Hellenistic and Roman times it was considered sport to watch two powerful boxers maul each other. This form of the sport would have been considered far too brutal for the high period of Greek civilization.

Training diet for contestants in the games consisted at first of fresh cheese, dried figs, and wheaten porridge. Sweets were forbidden and wine was used very sparingly. In later times there was a change in diet to beef, pork, and kid.

The youth in the foreground of the picture is using a *strigil* to scrape off the sweat and dust which have mingled with the olive oil rubbed on his body before the contest. By no ordinary bath could such a coating be removed. It had to be scraped off before the athlete went to the shower with which all the *palaistrai* were provided.

Great distinction attended an athletic victor. He might set up a statue of himself (at his own or his friends' expense) in the sacred precinct of Olympia.

At Athens after the time of Solon, an Olympic victor received a reward of 500 *drachmai,* and had the privilege of eating at the public expense in the Prytaneum. He might also be accorded a front-row seat of honor at the theater.

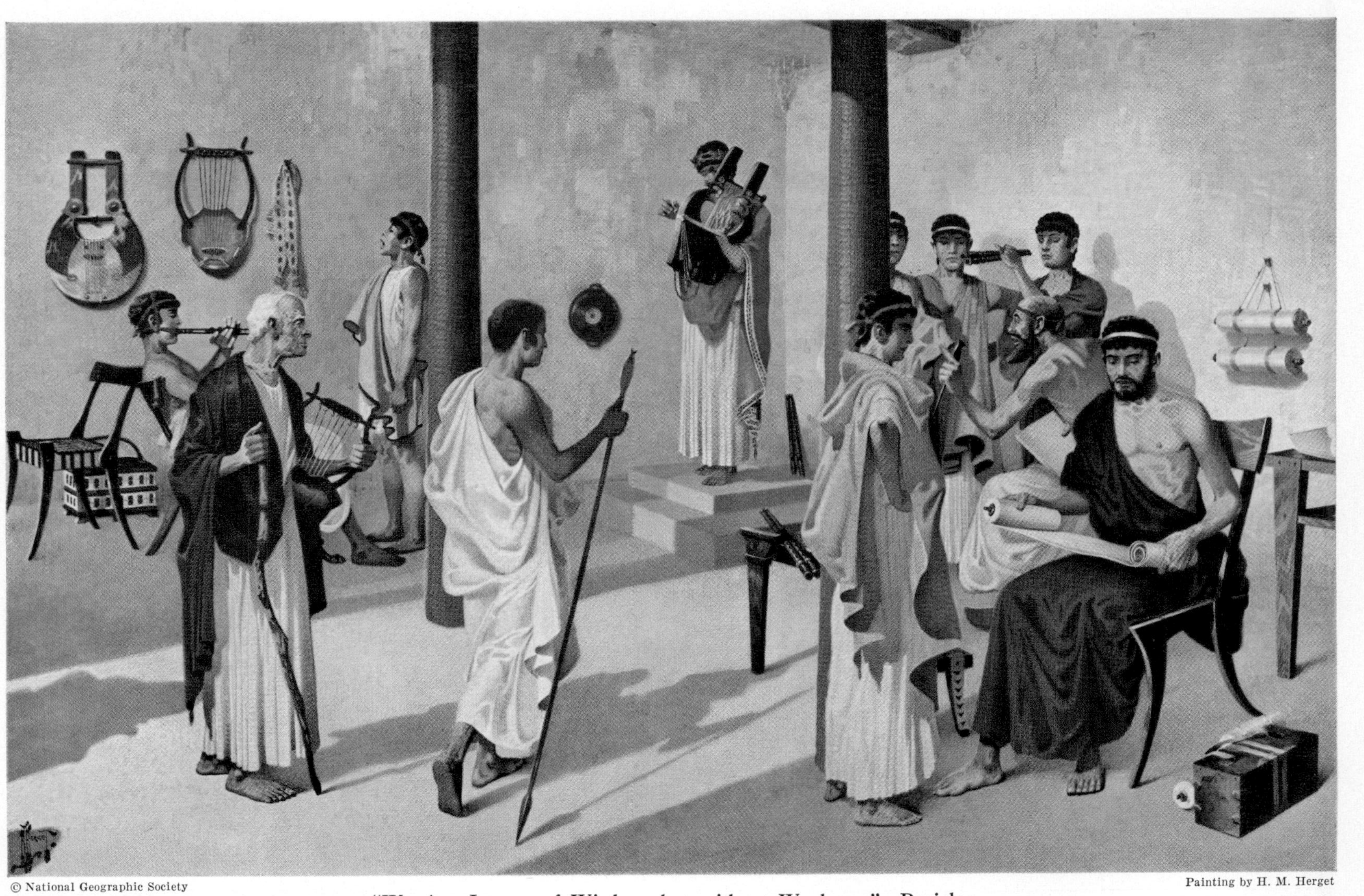

Painting by H. M. Herget

"We Are Lovers of Wisdom, but without Weakness"—Pericles

An Athenian School

EXCEPT for the supervision of certain boards which were appointed by the state, education in Athens was left entirely to individual enterprise. After their sixth year the boys were put in charge of a *paidagogos,* who was usually an old slave. He had no responsibility for their education; his function was to accompany them to school and generally to keep watch over them. On a familiar Greek vase painting is a representation of one of these old men carrying the lyre of his master's son as the latter makes his way to school.

The school buildings were simple and had little in the way of furniture save some benches and chairs, with possibly a platform on which performing students might stand. On the walls hung various implements: lyres, citharas (a sort of lyre with a larger sounding board), flutes, goatskin flute cases, and sometimes a drinking vessel or so.

We also see scrolls of papyrus, which was the only paper the Greeks knew, and sometimes there are boxes in which such scrolls might be stored. Generally, however, papyrus was used sparingly, since it was expensive. Nearly all the work was done on waxed tablets, which corresponded to the slates generally used in American schools not long ago.

Reading and writing were taught first. With them came some work in numbers, but the Greeks used letters of the alphabet for their numeral system, and most simple mathematical calculations were performed on an abacus.

By the time a boy was 12 or 13 years old he took up music, not with the intention of becoming a professional performer, but because it was highly essential for an educated man to be able to accompany himself in singing or declaiming lyrics; hence singing also formed part of the curriculum. Flute playing was popular for a time in Athens, but later became less so; and flute players tended to be more of a professional entertainer class.

Languages, save native Greek, were not taught. The principal textbook from earliest times was Homer, and all young Greeks knew their *Iliad* and *Odyssey,* many of them by heart. Such subjects as natural science, geography, and history formed part of a higher stage of education and were generally taught in the philosophical surroundings of the academies.

As early as the fifth century some geometry was added to the usual curriculum, although Socrates thought it should be limited to what was strictly necessary. In the fourth century, however, the philosophers recommended geometry as an excellent subject for developing the intellect.

As stated elsewhere, gymnastic training was a prime requirement in education and continued for much longer than the purely scholastic training.

When the youth reached the age of 18 he was enrolled as a citizen of the state, received a warrior's shield and spear, and took the oath of allegiance: "Never to disgrace his holy arms, never to forsake his comrade in the ranks, but to fight for the holy temples and the common welfare, alone or with others; to leave his country not in a worse, but in a better state than he found it; to obey the magistrates and the laws, and defend them against attacks; finally, to hold in honor the religion of his country."

Painting by H. M. Herget

"Go to Thy Chamber and See to Thine Own Tasks, the Loom and the Distaff"—Odyssey

Weaving and Spinning

MOST SCHOOL children have read about the famous web that Penelope was weaving during the long courtship of the suitors who came to win her hand while she was waiting for her lord, Odysseus, to return from the long Trojan War. She undid each night what she had woven during the day, thus postponing the time for choosing a wooer.

The story describes one of the occupations of women throughout Greece in the old days. Even today small looms often form part of a household, and the women work on them as they did 2,000 to 3,000 years ago.

The pattern of the modern looms has changed somewhat, but we have several representations of ancient Greek looms. They have been carefully studied in an attempt to restore the system on which they were worked. Though restoration is not easy from vase paintings, study proves that the looms were upright, that the cloth was wound up in a roll at the top as the work progressed, and that the threads of the warp were weighted at the ends with small clay weights.

Hundreds of these weights have been found in excavations all over Greece. They are usually of clay and take the form of small cones or sometimes pyramids, each with a hole in the top through which threads of the warp were strung.

Spinning wheels were unknown, but the distaff and spindle whorl were used, just as they are today in Greece, where it is a common sight to see women walking up and down in the courtyard spinning as they go. Spinning baskets are often represented on vases.

The girl seated on the stool is rubbing wool over a roughened clay semicylinder which fits over her knee. This device was called *epinetron.* Farther off another girl is weighing wool on a scale.

Pet birds frequently appear on vases. In the courtyard may be seen a tame crane.

In Athens, which was always strongly influenced by Ionian styles and ideas from the Asia Minor coast, women's dress usually consisted of the thin, clinging Ionic *chiton.* This graceful garment was frequently draped so as to form short sleeves which were clipped together along the upper edge by studs or sometimes by elaborate gold pins. Occasionally the fasteners were fashioned in the likeness of grasshoppers.

There were various ways of catching the falling drapery up under a girdle, or sometimes two girdles, so as to obtain different effects.

In later days the intricate arrangement of the draperies is hard to explain unless one assumes that extra pieces were sewn to the basic garment.

Wool and linen were the most common materials. Cotton, muslin, and silk, introduced from abroad, were rare and costly and could be worn only by the rich.

The girl at the right wears a *peplos* over her chiton, rather an unusual combination but apparently one which was sometimes used.

For outdoor use, an *himation,* a cloaklike garment, was also worn. It is sometimes shown as draped over the head to form a sort of hood.

The styles of headdresses in the picture are all of types commonly found on fifth-century vases.

 Painting by H. M. Herget

"They Dedicated a Tithe of the Ransom, Making of It a Four-horse Chariot"—Herodotus

Herodotus—Geographer and Historian

HERODOTUS is the first Greek geographer and historian whose works have survived. Born in Halicarnassus (Bodrum), a Greek colony in Asia Minor, about 484 B. C., he is often called the Father of History. Without him we should lack the knowledge of a highly important part of it.

He was the greatest traveler of his day. He visited Egypt, and went as far up the Nile as Elephantine. He went westward to Cyrene, and east to Babylon and as far as Susa, the capital of Persia. Northward his wanderings took him to the Greek cities on the shores of the Black Sea.

About 447 B. C. he came to Athens, where he settled down to write of his travels. The Athenians enjoyed his public readings and voted him a good sum of money. He gives us a history of the entire ancient eastern Mediterranean from earliest times to the close of the Persian Wars. Naturally, the record is far from complete or accurate, in many cases, since he depended for his information on many sources which it was impossible to verify. He heard and recorded many "tall stories" about some of the more remote peoples of whom he wrote.

However, he was not so gullible as is sometimes thought, for he says, "I am under obligation to tell what is reported, but I am not obliged to believe it; and let this hold for every narrative in this history."

When Herodotus depends on his own observation, he is fairly reliable, and although his patriotism leads him to exaggerate the numbers of the Persian army, and probably to minimize the numbers and the losses of the Greeks who withstood them, he gives us a sound basis for historical research in those times.

In Athens during the great period of Pericles' leadership, he visited the Acropolis many times while the work on the Parthenon was going on. He tells of a four-horse chariot group of bronze that was set up on the Acropolis to commemorate a victory of the Athenians over the Boeotians and the people of Chalcis about sixty years before (506 B.C.).

The Athenians, by the sound tactical maneuver of defeating one enemy before the other's ally could come to their aid, took prisoner some 700 of each. Later the prisoners were ransomed, but the chains in which they had been bound were hung on a wall on the Acropolis and the chariot group was made from a tithe of the ransom money.

On the base was inscribed:

Athens' bold sons, what time in glorious fight
They quelled Boeotian and Chalcidian might,
In chains and darkness did its pride enslave;
As ransom's tithe these steeds to Pallas gave.

The dedication was made before the Persians had sacked the Acropolis (480 B.C.); hence the group appears in an earlier picture. (Page 223.)

A small surviving portion of the inscription gives us the forms of the letters. For the text we are dependent on Herodotus, who is seen here, on a rainy day in autumn, studying the inscription which he is to record later in his history.

The site chosen for this group is at the foot of a terrace wall that ran across a part of the Acropolis west of the site of the Old Temple of Athena. Near by is the base of the bronze statue of Athena Promachos.

Painting by H. M. Herget

"Pheidias . . . Gave His Orders to All the Workmen . . . Because of His Friendship with Pericles"—Plutarch

Pericles and Pheidias in the Parthenon

THERE can be no doubt that the architectural magnificence of the Athenian Acropolis is due as much to Pericles as to any other. He came of a fine family and his father had fought at Salamis, but he owed his greatness to his own ability as a statesman. Although he soon abandoned the conservative oligarchic party for the more liberal people's party, he believed in the restriction of the franchise.

He knew the importance of keeping the mass of the people gainfully employed, and, to quote Plutarch, "It was his desire and design that the undisciplined mechanic multitude should not go without their share of the public funds, and yet should not have these given him for sitting still and doing nothing."

Funds for constructing the massive buildings that still adorn the Acropolis were obtained by transfer of the treasury of the Delian League to Athens. The Parthenon itself was built to hold the heroic-sized gold and ivory statue of the goddess Athena.

We are told that 44 talents (2,545 lbs.) of gold went into this figure. It is difficult to draw comparative values of money across so many years, but the amount has been computed as the equivalent of about $6,000,000, an enormous sum for those days, and relatively far greater in purchasing power than it would be now.

The artist who was responsible for the building and for its sculpture was Pheidias, already an elderly man. With him as architects worked Callicrates and Ictinus.

The Parthenos, as the statue was called, stood some 45 feet high. All the flesh parts were of ivory. The rest was of gold so attached, as Pericles carefully pointed out to the people, that it could be removed and borrowed for the treasury in case of need. Presumably there was a carved wooden core to which the plates were attached, since we hear of the statue's being regilded many years later, after its gold had been taken away.

We have from Pausanias a full description of the figure, and a few small-scale copies, all rather poor in workmanship, survive—sufficient to give us some idea of the statue, but contradictory in a number of details. It appears, however, that the goddess stood on a pedestal of marble which was carved across the front with a scene representing the birth of Pandora. Beside her was a great shield with reliefs showing combats of Greeks and Amazons.

One of the figures was said to resemble Pheidias, and this was held against him as an act of impiety when he was accused of withholding some of the gold.

The only light for the interior of the temple came through the east doorway, but in the brilliantly clear air of Greece, and especially at the time of year when, on Athena's feast, the rising sun shone directly through the opening, the illumination must have been entirely adequate.

Pheidias worked on the building for nine years, from 447 to 438. After his accusation, he was released on bail by his friends and went to Olympia, where he made the colossal gold and ivory figure of Zeus, and where his descendants for many generations remained as the special technicians in charge of its upkeep. This great work, which has also disappeared entirely, and is known to us only by Pausanias' description and by coins of Elis, was rated as one of the Seven Wonders of the Ancient World.

Painting by H. M. Herget

"The Bright Land of Athena . . . Where There Are . . . Most Holy Processions of the Blessed Gods"—Aristophanes

The Panathenaic Procession Brings a New Robe to Athena

AFTER the defeat of Mardonius at Plataea (479 B. C.) had removed the Persian threat, the oligarchic landholders of Sparta viewed the rising power of Athens and her economic stranglehold on other Greek states as a menace to themselves. Athens had it practically all her own way, however, until the fatal thirty years' war broke out in 432 B.C.

During the heyday of Athenian power, one of the famous institutions was the great Panathenaic procession, which every four years brought a new *peplos,* or robe, to the goddess Athena. The robe, woven by the women and girls of the city, represented the battle of the gods and giants.

At early dawn on the feast of the goddess, the procession assembled at the Pompeion, near the Dipylon Gate at the north side of the city, and made its way through the streets to the foot of the west slope of the Acropolis. The chief place in the procession was occupied by a ship on wheels bearing a mast and yardarm on which the peplos was spread. Priests, archons (chief executive magistrates), and dignitaries came first. After them came maidens bearing sacrificial vessels; then foreign residents carrying flat dishes filled with honey cakes, fruit, and other offerings.

The sacrificial animals were led in the procession, and there were also youths carrying on their heads large jars possibly filled with tribute money. Finally came the flower of the Athenian army, the cavalry, splendidly mounted.

At the foot of the Acropolis the procession halted while the robe was removed from the yardarm and folded, to be carried the rest of the way. Then the procession passed through the great Propylaea, and shortly after turned to the right through a smaller gateway which led to a plaza opposite the west end of the temple.

The sacrificial animals, however, probably followed along a different path outside the precinct, while the greater part of the procession passed directly alongside the north colonnade of the building to the main entrance at the east end. There the priest of Athena was waiting to receive the offering to the goddess.

The whole procession has been preserved for us in the splendid carved frieze which Pheidias contrived around the top of the *cella,* or sanctuary proper.

In the background of the picture is the Propylaea, through the wide central opening of which comes the procession. It is not certain whether the cavalry rode up on horseback, although this would have been entirely possible, since it is known that sacrificial animals were led up, and the usual steps were omitted at the center of the building.

To the left, just inside the Propylaea, was a statue of Athena Hygeia. Next in order was a sanctuary of Artemis Brauronia, in which stood a bronze copy of the Trojan Horse, faithfully reproduced, even to the wheels on which it was said to have been mounted, and having two small windows on either side through which the hidden Greeks could be seen peeping out.

On the right, behind the group of elders who are watching the procession, stands the bronze statue of Athena Promachos, the goddess who fights in the forefront of battle. Her gilded helmet and twinkling spear point could be seen by homecoming sailors soon after rounding Cape Soúnion.

Painting by H. M. Herget

"Mighty Monuments Which Shall Make Us the Wonder of Succeeding Ages"—Pericles

Setting a Capital on the Erechtheum

THE Erechtheum, only a few hundred feet north of the Parthenon, is one outstanding example of departure from the usual style of Greek architecture.

This remarkable building, in the Ionic style, was built on two different levels to house spots sacred to Athenian tradition and religion. Chief of these was the Temple of Athena Polias, the guardian of the city. Her image, carved from olive wood, was lighted by a perpetually burning golden lamp. Beside several altars to other divinities, there was the spot where a thunderbolt from Zeus had split the rock of the Acropolis.

Also, near by, was the Pandroseion where grew the miraculous olive tree which Athena had produced in her contest with Poseidon for the right of being the patron of the city. Since the olive was adjudged to be a greater gift to man than the horse, Poseidon's contribution, the contest went to the goddess and she gave her name to the city.

The picture shows a part of the northeast corner of the building. Two workmen are setting one of the carved marble Ionic capitals. The upper drum of the column has a round wooden peg set in a square block of wood sunk into the center of the shaft to aid in centering the capital and to serve as a dowel.

The columns when first set up were unfluted, save at the top and bottom, and the fluting was then cut on afterward, thus assuring perfect jointing and avoiding any breaks or spalls at the edges.

Since no mortar was used in these buildings, the greatest care had to be taken not to chip the edges of the stones at the joints; therefore a protecting surface was left to be worked off after the blocks had been set in place. This explains the narrow sunken band around the edges of the block in the foreground. The moldings were, for the most part, cut as simple profiles, and further carving was done later.

Another device to insure tight joints was that of cutting back the end surface of a block over all its area save for a band called *anathyrosis* around the edge. Adjacent blocks in a course were secured with bronze clamps, leaded in.

The small cutting between the two H-shaped clamps is a pry hole, to allow the right-hand block to be shifted slightly from side to side when it was forced up against its neighbor. Bronze dowels fastened the blocks of one course to the course below, and at the corners of the building, where there might be a shift in two directions from earthquakes, T-shaped dowels were frequently employed. One of these lies in front of the workman at the left.

In the distance appears the irregular cone of Mount Lycabettus and farther off are the slopes of Mount Pentelicus, site of the marble quarries from which came much of the material for the fifth-century buildings on the Acropolis.

It is usual to think of Greek buildings in terms of the symmetrical temple, oblong in plan, with a row of columns, or peristyle, surrounding it on all four sides. This, however, is not a complete picture. Although the temple had to follow a traditional form which had developed from the pre-Greek *megaron* type of house, identified with the house of the ruler and hence of the god, the Greek architect was capable of solving new problems in an unorthodox way.

Painting by H. M. Herget

"Beneath the Blaze of Torches They Were Leading the Brides from Their Chambers"—Iliad

An Athenian Wedding Party

THE NARROW streets of ancient Athens, where the houses clustered against the north slope of the Acropolis, must often have witnessed scenes such as this—a wedding party come from the banquet at the house of the bride's parents and on the threshold of the new home the parents of the bridegroom standing to welcome the newly married pair.

Almost invariably marriages were arranged by the parents, sometimes with the aid of an intermediary. Close attention was paid to the marriage settlement and to the arrangements for the dowry, or its return in case of the death or divorce of the wife.

The old Homeric custom of obtaining a wife by means of rich gifts was no longer in use during the historic period. Marriages were contracted strictly between citizens' families, and almost always between families of the same station of importance. Occasionally, however, the state provided dowries for the daughters of impoverished citizens who had rendered signal service to the city.

The legal part of a marriage consisted actually in the betrothal. The wedding ceremonies, although they had a religious significance, were not actually religious in the sense that the presence of a priest was necessary. The marriage gods were invoked at the wedding banquet, and libations poured and sacrifices made to them.

The flesh from the sacrificed animals probably furnished a goodly part of the feast. In the hope that the marriage should be marred by no bitterness, the gall of the animals was discarded and not burnt with the other entrails.

It was customary for the bride, and for the bridegroom as well, to bathe on the morning of the ceremony in water specially brought for the purpose from certain particularly sacred fountains.

The legal part of the ceremony, or the sacrifices, probably took place in the morning, and the feast followed. This occasion was one of the few on which men and women outside of the intimate circle of the family ate together.

By the time the feast was ended, darkness was falling, and the procession started off for the house which the couple were to occupy. Except in the poorest class of wedding, the bride rode in a chariot drawn by oxen or horses. She was seated between her husband and his best man. She was attended by a bridesmaid, and her mother followed bearing torches symbolic of the marriage rite.

Others of the party followed, singing and playing on flutes and lyres. In Athens it was a peculiar custom for a young boy, whose parents must be alive, to go around bearing a basket of cakes and singing, "I fled from misfortune, I found a better lot."

At the door of the new home stood the father and mother of the bridegroom, the mother also carrying torches. All sorts of sweetmeats were showered on the nuptial pair, and the youths and maidens sang an epithalamium. There was much laughing and joking before the well-wishers finally went away and left the newly married couple in peace. On the following day they returned with the couple's relatives, who came to pay visits and offer congratulations to the new husband and his wife.

The festivities ended with a banquet given by the bridegroom, or by his father, but this time the women were not included.

Socrates Enjoys a Banquet

EXCEPT in the intimacy of the family circle, it was invariably the custom for men to be the only guests at a banquet. Any women present were either professional entertainers, or members of the special class of the *hetairai*. Many of the latter were highly educated and cultivated women who were employed as companions of an evening. No respectable Athenian woman ever went out at night, nor did she even venture forth by day unless properly accompanied, and usually veiled.

When guests had assembled, they removed their footwear and were presented with basins and towels, while a boy poured water over their hands. Then they reclined, usually in pairs, on couches in front of which were tables arranged around the room on three sides of a square. The center of the room was left open for the servants and for whatever entertainment the host might provide.

The variety of Epicurean delicacies of later times was virtually unknown at Athens in the fifth century. The meals were generally plain and wholesome. The first course consisted of meats, including game; fish; bread; and some green vegetables, among them the onion and garlic that are still favorites in the Mediterranean. For dessert there were cheeses and all kinds of fruits and cakes.

After the meal the tables were cleared, and the symposium, or drinking part of the evening, began. Wreaths of flowers were given the guests, and dainties were set about on the tables, on which also were placed drinking cups. It was not usual to drink unmixed wine, and large *craters,* or mixing bowls, were furnished.

Three libations were offered at the beginning of the symposium: to the Olympian deities, to the Heroes, and to Zeus Soter. A *symposiarch* was chosen by lot to determine what proportion of water to wine should be drunk.

If the company was inclined to serious discourse, as in Plato's symposium, the flute girl might be dismissed. Sometimes not only a flute girl, but other entertainers, such as jugglers, dancers, or acrobats, might be brought in.

Socrates, who is shown near the center of the picture, was most certainly present at many symposia besides the two known to us from Plato and Xenophon. There is no evidence that he drank any less than the rest of the company. The records, however, seem to show that he was able to imbibe freely without being in any way affected.

In an account of a symposium, Xenophon mentions that the dancing girl, after swords had been fixed in a circle with the points upward, immediately leaped headforemost into it through the midst of the points, and then out again with marvelous agility. A similar feat shown on a vase painting has been reproduced here.

Socrates is quoted as saying: "If I am not mistaken, nobody will deny but courage may be learned, and that there are masters for this virtue in particular; since a girl, you see, has the courage to throw herself through the midst of naked swords, which none of us dare venture upon."

The long evening ended with a delightful pantomime representing the story of Bacchus and Ariadne. The company then departed for their homes, but Socrates and some others, we are told, went walking in the early morning.

© National Geographic Society

Painting by H. M. Herget

"The Girl Leaped Headforemost . . . through the Midst of the Points . . . Then out Again"—Xenophon

Greek Women Used Mascara and Beauty Lotions

Thucydides, the Greek historian, says, "The name of a decent woman, like her person, should be shut up in her house."

This somewhat harsh dictum of a masculine observer reflects, for fifth-century Athens, the general attitude toward women, and also indicates the strong oriental influence that appears so often in Athenian art, as opposed to the more rugged Dorian ideals of the Peloponnesus.

Save among a certain class of women, known as the *Hetairai,* or companions, education and intellectual pursuits were not encouraged among the Athenian women. It was not until after the fifth century that women began to escape from a sort of intellectual bondage.

Aristophanes in his comedies makes fun of them, but indicates a trend toward their emancipation in a play in which the women go in disguise to the assembly, to take over the government of Athens on the ground that the men are incapable of handling affairs properly.

Normally, a woman's life was concentrated on home tasks—weaving, spinning, the care of small children, and a host of domestic duties. Marketing was usually done by the master of the house, and it was only under cover of a veil that the wife of a respectable citizen appeared on the street.

Ladies of less reputable character, however, went about quite freely, and special places were often reserved for them in the theaters. We hear of many courtesans, famous either for their beauty or, more rarely, their wit.

Prominent among these was Aspasia, who for many years was Pericles' companion, and who must have been a woman of remarkable talent. Socrates credited her with composing the funeral oration which Pericles delivered on the first men to be killed in the Peloponnesian War, and said that he himself had learned the art of eloquence from her.

The *chiton* was the normal indoor dress. On going out, a woman wore an *himation,* or cloak, as well. This rectangular piece of cloth, heavier than the chiton, could be draped about the body or pulled partly over the head.

Sometimes a scarf which could be drawn over the face was worn.

The young woman in the foreground of the picture is inspecting her coiffure by means of a polished bronze mirror. A servant girl is holding a casket with a necklace for her mistress to put on if she approves.

Beside her stands a *thymiaterion,* or incense burner, and on the low table at the right are a couple of small *pyxides,* in which were the cosmetics women used as freely in ancient days as later. Many exquisitely decorated examples of these little covered jars have been found, some even with remains of powder or rouge still inside them.

Eyes were darkened with mascara, and creams and beauty lotions were popular.

It is questionable, however, that the wife of an Athenian citizen would have bedizened herself with cosmetics in such a bold manner as to deserve the scornful ridicule of a reproach given woman in an Athenian comedy: "If you go out in summer, two streaks of black run from your eyes; perspiration makes a red furrow from your cheeks to your neck; and when your hair touches your face it is blanched with white lead."

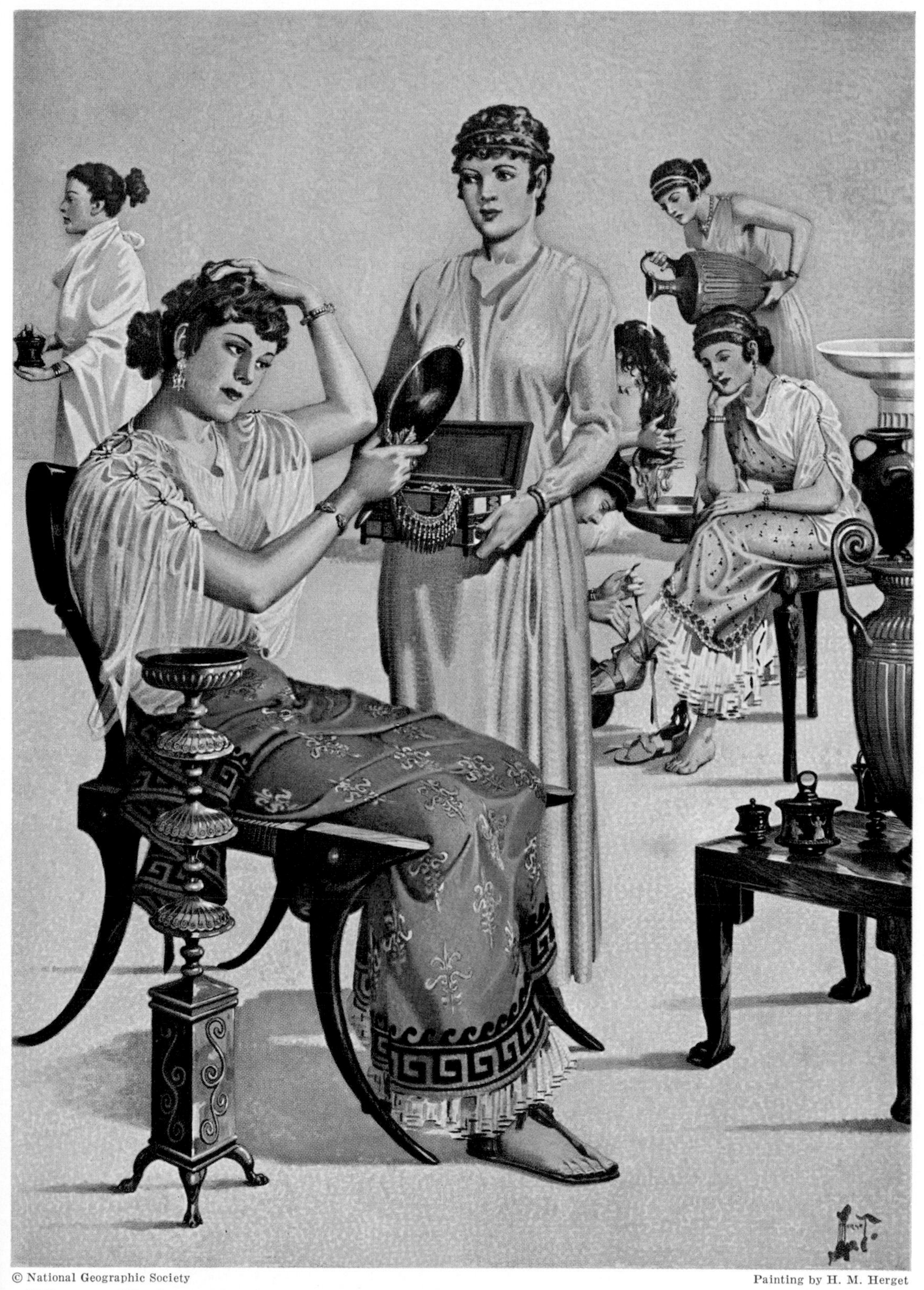

© National Geographic Society

Painting by H. M. Herget

"We . . . Sit Around with Our Paint and Lipstick and Transparent Gowns"—Aristophanes

Voting in the Market Place at Athens

EXCEPT in the earliest period of its history, when there was a palace of the Mycenaean period on the Acropolis, the civic center of Athens was in the Agora, or market place, to the north, and beneath the steep slope of a small rise of ground, the Kolonos Agoraios.

Although there were other meeting places, such as the Pnyx, farther to the southwest, hardly a day went by without most of the citizens passing through the Agora.

Every citizen belonged to a *deme,* and on the basis of this division were chosen the lawmakers, the *Boule,* or Council, the *archons* and other magistrates, and the *prytanes.* By no means the entire population, however, enjoyed the rights of citizenship. In Pericles' time there were little more than 40,000 citizens out of a population of possibly 300,000.

Only a man born of two free Athenian parents could be a citizen after he had reached the age of 21. The remainder were slaves, *metics* (resident aliens), or women, none of whom enjoyed any franchise.

Every voter was a member of the governing body, the Assembly; there was no representative government at this level. The Boule was a legislative committee of the Assembly chosen by lot from among the register of citizens, and served with pay for a year. The Council was divided into ten committees, called *prytanes,* each of which presided in turn over the Council and Assembly for a month of 36 days.

One of the peculiar customs at Athens was the practice of ostracism, whereby any man could, by the majority of a quorum vote of the Assembly, be banished from the city for ten years. A way of eliminating any individual who began to play too prominent a part in affairs, it was intended as a safeguard against anyone's setting himself up as a tyrant.

It was customary to inscribe on a potsherd the name of the person whom one wished to have banished. Such a fragment was called an *ostrakon;* hence the word ostracism. Great numbers of these fragments have been found in the excavations carried on in the market place. It is evident that sometimes the ostracizing pieces were prepared in advance, with names painted on them. They could then be distributed to anyone who needed to have his mind made up for him. Some ostraka have been found on which a name has been scratched in one hand, obviously rather illiterate, and then obligingly corrected in another, much better hand.

Although no large number of citizens was banished in this way, the abuses and futility of the system finally brought about its abandonment.

The scene in the picture attempts to show an ostracism going on. The buildings on the west side of the Agora are the background. At one side on a boundary stone is inscribed *Horos eimi tes agoras*—I am the boundary of the Agora.

Pausanias, visiting the Agora in the second century of our era, mentions first the Stoa Basilike, where the king *archon,* an elected magistrate, transacted affairs. Farther on was a temple of Apollo Patroos. Then came the Bouleuterion, or council house. In the fifth century it became necessary to erect a new one behind the old to take care of the greater number of *bouleutai* representing the people in council. Next came the *tholos,* a circular building with conical roof. Here foreign ambassadors were entertained.

 Painting by H. M. Herget

"The Fragrant and Much-trodden Center of the City . . . and the Richly Adorned and Famous Agora"—Pindar

Potter Making Clay Figurines

MAKING figurines was a flourishing branch of the potter's art from earliest times, and although, generally speaking, the best known are from Tanagra in the fourth and third centuries, there were other centers of manufacture as well.

A few years ago, at Corinth, was discovered a potters' quarter that yielded an amazing quantity and variety of figurines of all periods, from the seventh century down through the fourth.

Many were hand-made. Many, also, were turned out in quantities from baked clay molds.

Figures of horses and dogs were particularly abundant. Some horses have riders, and some of the riders are unmistakably meant to represent monkeys.

Grotesque heads are found, as well as the delicately modeled features of female deities or priestesses. Plaques in relief might represent a warrior, with sword, helmet, and shield, and occasionally small circular votive shields were decorated with the figure of a warrior leaping down from his horse.

In this Corinthian factory, molds were found for the bodies and legs and arms of jointed dolls, and the actual impresses from the molds which also came to light fitted them exactly, if one made allowance for the shrinkage of the clay in the baking process. The heads of these dolls were molded separately and then attached to the torsos.

Small models were made of household furniture, such as tables, chairs, and couches. Models of boats, mirrors, tools, roof tiles, articles of food, and even miniature pots were turned out. These probably delighted the children of that time. Carts with curiously constructed, primitive wheels were found, pierced with holes in which small pieces of wood could be inserted to suspend the axle and to form the body of the cart. These may have been woven in grass to imitate a wicker-basket construction in the real ones.

Even a covered buggy came to light, with two women seated inside it. One had her *himation* drawn over her head, completely veiling her features; the other, seated beside her, wore no headdress. Perhaps they represented a lady and her slave. Near the buggy were found two clay horses yoked together and of the proper scale to belong to the group.

The establishment was a modest one, simply built. On one side of a small courtyard four plain rectangular stone piers apparently supported a projecting roof which sheltered a series of shelves on which the objects could be stored. Large quantities of them were found piled up at that spot.

Clay was brought from a deep ravine just below the city wall.

The old potter in our picture is pressing clay into a mold. Immediately alongside his hands is the mold for the dolls' bodies, some of which are arranged on the edge of the bench. A boy is carrying a tray of finished figurines which have come out of the kiln, and a few more may be seen on the table in the courtyard.

Many of the figurines were painted, at least in part, in reds, reddish brown, and black. Pink and yellow were also used. Occasionally a faint trace of blue appears, but this color was used sparingly, at least at Corinth, and in any case usually fails to resist weather as well as the earth and iron oxide colors.

© National Geographic Society

Painting by H. M. Herget

"Another Earns a Living Fashioning with His Hands the Works of Hephaestus of Many Crafts"—Solon

Hippocrates, Father of Medicine

Born on the Aegean island of Cos, Hippocrates, the son of a physician, became the best-known physician of his time and laid the foundations of modern medicine. His early years were passed on his native island, where there was a famous sanctuary of healing, or *Asklepieion,* to which came great numbers of invalids and tourists. The school which he founded there was still the finest school of medicine under the Ptolemies.

About 430 B.C. he went to Athens, by invitation, to help combat a plague that was raging there. He thus forms part of the picture of the last half of the fifth century—a period of growing culture, science, and philosophy which blossomed in the Periclean Age.

There is a tremendous amount of Hippocratic literature, much of which was written after Hippocrates' time, but by general consent four works may be ascribed directly to him: the *Aphorisms,* the *Prognostics,* the *Regimen in Acute Diseases,* and the monograph on *Wounds in the Head.*

Hippocrates' principal contribution was, like that of his followers, the separation of practical medicine from religion and philosophy, and the expression of the conviction that all diseases are due to natural causes and not to the interference of the gods. Preventive medicine plays a large part in his writings. Hippocrates believed that a good doctor could, from a careful study of bodily conditions, learn to foresee the course a disease would follow. His practice made relatively little use of drugs, but included emetics, enemas, blood-letting, massage, and hydrotherapy.

According to Hippocrates, the best way to avoid disease was to lead a wholesome life, and the best way to cure disease was to observe a proper diet and way of life.

Anatomy and surgery made rather slow progress in Greece, although the action of the heart was known, and the brain was recognized as the seat of consciousness and thought. Trephining operations for head wounds were performed, and reductions for dislocations, closely resembling modern methods, were known. Anaesthetics, however, were not in general use. A late manuscript of Apollonius of Citium is illustrated with drawings showing the tortures undergone by patients when dislocations of joints were reduced.

Throughout the Greek world there were centers of healing known as *asklepieia.* Here, doubtless, many simple and rational cures were effected by therapeutic means, and the presence of a big theater at one of the largest (Epidaurus) indicates plainly that relaxation and entertainment, combined with proper diet, fresh air, and a certain amount of mental suggestion, were recognized as an effective way of curing numerous ills.

Naturally, at such places the credit for the cure was given to the god Asklepios, and innumerable dedications have been found at the sanctuaries belonging to him. These dedications, in the form of affected parts of the body, might be made of marble, bronze, or terra cotta.

Inscriptions also testify to the miraculous nature of many of the cures, and we must assume that some of these were advertisements. Nevertheless, Hippocrates and his fellows of the fifth century set the high standard of professional ethics still observed by physicians who take the Hippocratic Oath.

Painting by H. M. Herget

"I Will Use Treatment to Help the Sick According to My Ability and Judgment"— Hippocrates

Phryne Poses for Praxiteles

The citizens of the island of Cos, we are told, commissioned Praxiteles to carve them a statue of Aphrodite, and according to the story he did so with the aid of Phryne, a courtesan famous for her beauty.

The story, however, goes on to say that, when the work was finished, the good people of Cos were shocked to find the goddess quite nude. The sculptor thereupon did them another which was fully draped.

Meantime, the first statue was bought by the Cnidians, and it became one of the principal attractions of their town. It probably inspired the epigram by an unknown author: "The Cyprian (Aphrodite) said when she saw the Cyprian of Cnidus, 'Alas, where did Praxiteles see me naked?' "

The original statue has been lost, but several copies exist, and from them we may gain some idea of the original work. Phryne was so celebrated that some of her admirers, and, according to some reports, Phryne herself, dedicated a statue of her at Delphi.

She was indicted once on a charge of impiety, but was ably defended by the orator Hypereides. Athenaeus tells us that the case was really won, however, when she allowed her tunic to slip off her shoulder slightly. At that the judges immediately gave a verdict in her favor.

We have few works today that are certainly from the hand of any of the Greek sculptors known to us through the accounts of ancient writers; but, thanks to the Roman's passion for copying Greek statuary, we have a wealth of second-hand material.

Some of the fine pediment groups from Olympia, from the Temple of Aphaia on Aegina, and from the Parthenon give us an idea of what Greek sculpture was like, but of the works which were celebrated by the Greeks themselves, scarcely one remains.

Until recently, however, one work from the hand of Praxiteles seemed sure. Pausanias speaks of a statue of Hermes in the Temple of Hera at Olympia, and during the excavations in the ruins of the temple in 1877 there was found a statue of Hermes, holding the infant Dionysus on one arm. It had been preserved by being buried in the ruins of the unbaked brick walls of the building.

Volumes have been written about it, and although archeologists are now divided as to whether it really is an original, or a most excellent Roman copy, the balance of opinion is still in favor of calling it an original Greek work.

It is characteristic of Praxiteles' style, as we know it from copies of his other works, and shows a softness and sensuality of form which is a definite stepping stone from the sterner, more idealized sculpture of the Periclean Age to the realism, or sometimes the bravura, which appears in a great deal of the sculpture of the Hellenistic period.

The interior of a sculptor's studio was probably very plain. The tools he worked with resemble those used by marble and stone cutters ever since. Although the drill was known rather early, it came to be used much more frequently in later periods. Flat chisels, pointed chisels, and surfacing hammers were used.

Since even the early sculptors worked in bronze, the use of clay for modeling is certain, and even if a statue was planned to be executed in marble, it is likely that by the fourth century, at least, a clay maquette, or study, would first be made.

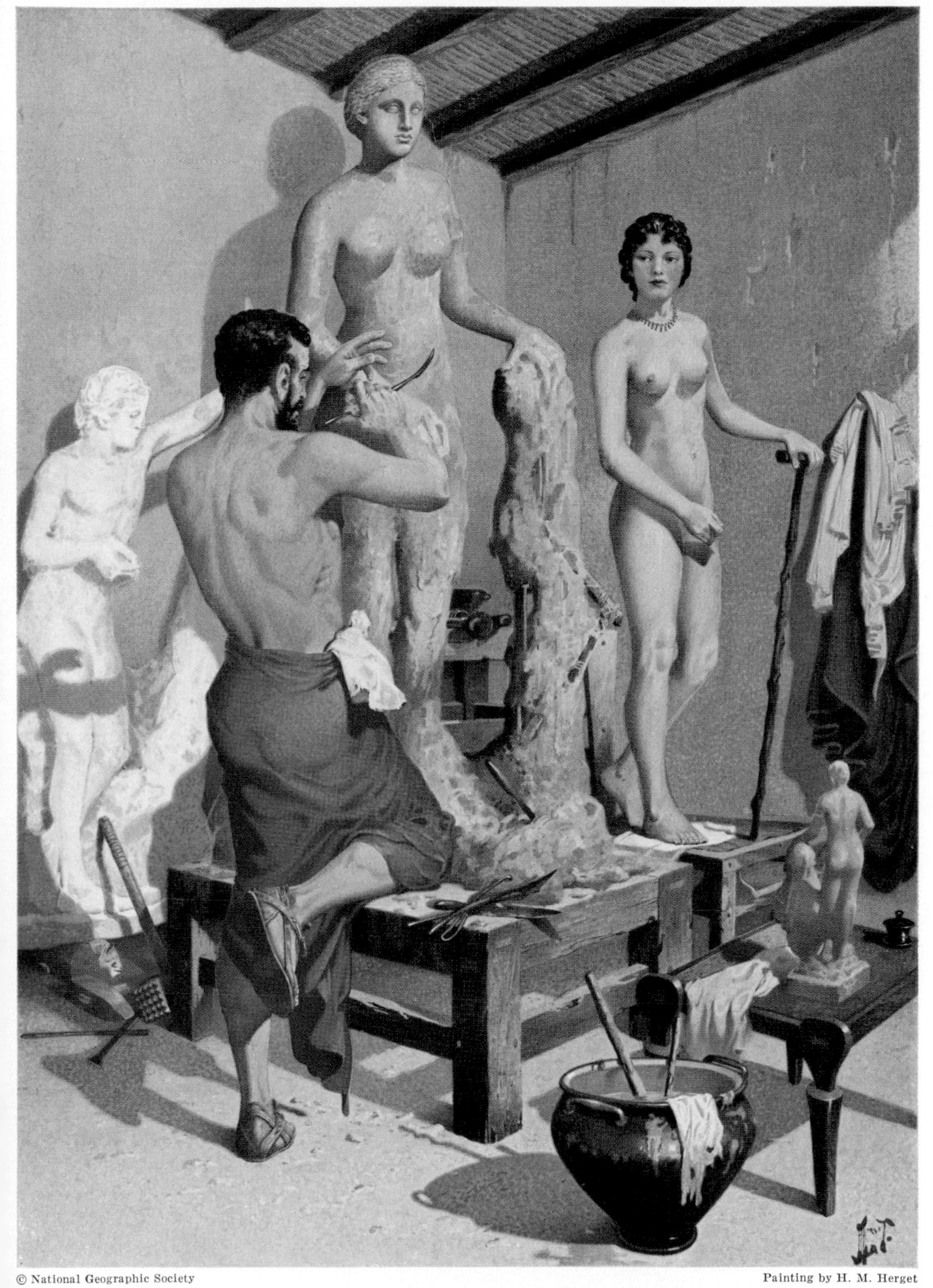

Painting by H. M. Herget

"Said the Cyprian . . . 'Alas, Where Did Praxiteles See Me Naked?'"—Greek Anthology

The Countryside Is Smiling; "Therefore, Ye Soft Pipes, Play On"

Except in the earliest times, the land available for cultivation in Greece was insufficient to supply enough grain. In Attica, for instance, barely two-thirds of the area was suitable for cultivation, and a large part of this was taken up by the olive groves which furnished one important part of Greek diet and, as noted elsewhere, sufficient surplus to allow export in exchange for other necessaries.

In many other parts of Greece, available land was even more scarce and, just as today, in ancient times there were many small fields tucked in among the hills. Each year the lands were carefully tilled, but the rocky soil must have been a perpetual discouragement to the farmer.

Cereals and vegetables, such as lentils, peas, beans, cabbages, asparagus, and garlic, were stables of diet. Fish was plentiful but meat was scarce, even as it is for the majority of the population in modern Greece. Sugar was unknown, but honey was an adequate substitute, and the flocks of goats and sheep furnished milk and cheese, just as they do now. Figs, and of course grapes, were the principal fruits. Citrus fruits were unknown, but mention is made of apples, pears, pomegranates, and quinces.

Hesiod, a resident of the little town of Askra, in Boeotia, wrote in *Works and Days* about the hard work of the farmer who elected by honest toil to wring a living from the land.

He tells of the hard winters of the country, the "piercing wind that flays the steers"; how one should dress warmly in winter and avoid drinking heavily in summer. He lays down precepts for plowing, planting, and reaping. The little hill town where he lived he calls "wretched in winter, insufferable in summer, and never good."

Primitive wooden plows may still be seen in the more remote parts of Greece, though the modern steel plowshare is generally used. It is only in the northern part of the country, where there are wide, flat, tillable areas, that any tractor plowing can be found. Oxen were generally used for plowing in ancient times, and some can still be seen today, although other draft animals are more common.

In our picture, near the walls of a small fortified town not too far from Athens, is a plowing scene, and in the foreground another pastoral scene, as common today as in antiquity. A shepherd sits piping to his flock, which rests or grazes near him. His dogs rush off to attack a couple of strangers passing by on the road, and the foremost traveler is about to pick up a stone to fling at the dogs.

If the traveler were to follow the modern custom, he would throw the stone over and beyond the dogs; and they would turn and rush after the stone, and then return to the attack. This procedure, if kept up for a time, usually results in keeping the dogs away until the traveler is beyond the area which they feel it their duty to protect.

The idyllic piping of the shepherd, which can be heard today on almost any Greek mountainside much as in olden times, recalls another writer who lived long after Hesiod. Theocritus, in the third century B.C., perfected pastoral poetry to a degree which left little or nothing for others, and showed a feeling such as no other Greek poet possessed for the sweetness and beauty of Nature.

Painting by H. M. Herget

"The Shepherd on the Mountains, Piping at Noon, under a Copse of Leafy Plane"—Greek Anthology

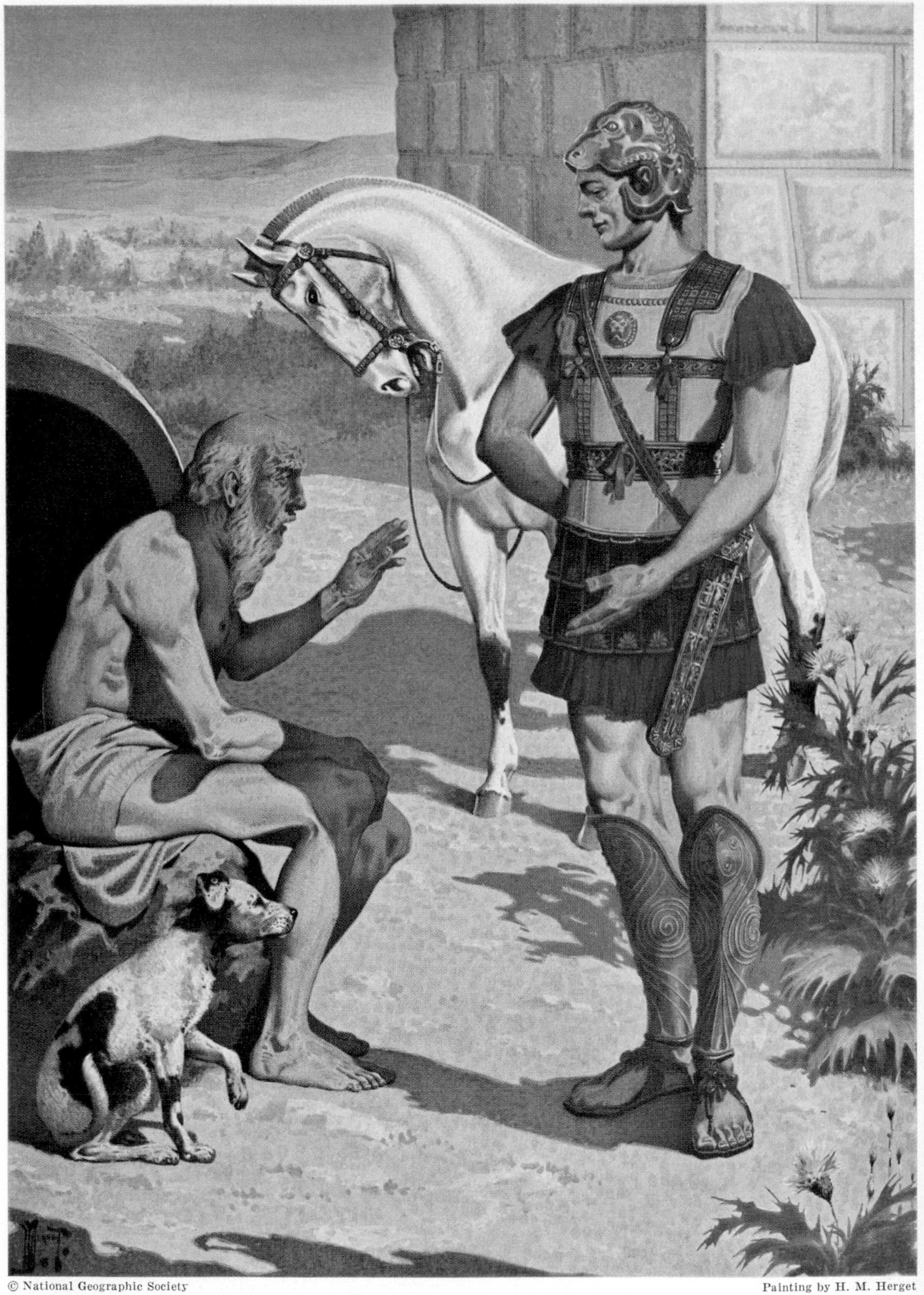

Painting by H. M. Herget

"If I Were Not Alexander, I Would Be Diogenes"—Plutarch

Alexander Calls on Diogenes the Cynic

To the cultured Athenian, the Macedonians of the north were barbarians. They produced no writers, artists, or philosophers of note.

From Macedonia, however, came one of the most successful military leaders of all time. The conquests of Alexander changed the cultural history of the world.

Alexander's father was Philip, king of Macedon. After passing a part of his youth as a hostage at Thebes, where he learned much of Greece and its people, Philip returned to his kingdom with the ambition of welding all the Greek states into a united nation. After reorganizing his army and training it in the Theban phalanx formation, he set out to make conquests.

The people of Chalcidice, east of modern Salonika, had been in alliance with Philip, but they realized that his interests were diametrically opposed to those of Athens, the city with which they had closer cultural relationships.

They broke with their dangerous ally, and paid the penalty for their defection. Several of their cities, among them Olynthus, were mercilessly destroyed, and it was not long before Philip appeared in Greece ostensibly as the arbiter of a dispute regarding the trusteeship of the Delphic oracle and its very considerable treasury.

The orator Demosthenes finally aroused the Athenians to form a Hellenic League against the rising power of the Macedonian; but the forces of the League, which Thebes had joined, were defeated at the Battle of Chaeronea, 338 B.C. Although the Greek cities, with the exception of pillaged Thebes, were allowed to retain their own constitutions, the power passed to the conqueror.

Philip then prepared to move over to Asia and destroy the only remaining great power which could oppose him—Persia. Before he could do so, however, he was assassinated. He was succeeded by his son, Alexander, at that time only 20 years old.

Contemporary with Alexander, but much older, was the philosopher Diogenes, known as the Cynic. The school of which he was the principal exponent took its name from the gymnasium called Cynosarges where its members were accustomed to meet.

The essence of their philosophy was to reduce the things of the flesh to the barest necessities so as to leave the mind as free as possible. Diogenes is reported to have lived for a time in a tub, outside the city walls.

There is a Neo-Attic marble relief which depicts the famous meeting between him and Alexander as described by Plutarch. The Cynic sits in the mouth of a huge clay jar, or *pithos*—many of these jars were large enough to accommodate a man—and on the top of it, as an allusion to the occupant, is carved a dog. The genitive form *kynós* of the word for dog suggests *cynic;* and probably the marble dog set over the philosopher's tomb at Corinth was a punning reference to his sect.

The famous conversation between the soldier and the philosopher probably took place at Corinth at a time when we have no evidence to show that a tub was still a part of Diogenes' domestic arrangements; but our picture is an attempt to bring the elements of the story together. When Alexander rather patronizingly offered to grant the philosopher any favor he might choose, Diogenes answered, "Yes, you can stand a little to one side and not keep the sun off me."

Painting by H. M. Herget

"He Himself Fought among the Foremost . . . and Was Wounded in the Thigh . . ."—Plutarch

Alexander Defeats Darius the Persian at Issus, 333 B.C.

After his accession to power, Alexander wasted no time in restoring his father's kingdom to order and in stamping out rebellion in Greece. Thebes was destroyed, with the exception of the temples and Pindar's house. This terrible example put a speedy end to Greek resistance, but the rest of Greece Alexander treated leniently and continued all the rights which had been granted by Philip.

The destruction of Persia was now Alexander's chief aim. In spring of 334 B.C. he crossed the Hellespont, or, as it is now called, the Dardanelles, with an army of about 40,000.

It was clear that in order to carry out a successful campaign against the immense Persian Empire, he would have to control the seacoast. Accordingly, he devoted the first part of his campaign to securing the principal Greek cities on the Asia Minor coast and posting Macedonian garrisons in them so as to secure his communications with Macedon and to prevent any assistance from disaffected Greek states from reaching the enemy. He was careful, however, to grant each city a democratic government, although this had certain strings attached to it.

Near the entrance to Syria, just a little north of the present Turkish boundary, Darius III attempted to prevent Alexander's further advance to the southward.

Although the Macedonians were outnumbered nearly 20 to one, Alexander, by superior tactics which rendered the mass of his opponent's force ineffective, routed the enemy at the Battle of Issus.

Darius fled and left behind him an immense quantity of booty, as well as his mother, his wife, and his children. The booty was immensely welcome; and the captives were treated with great consideration.

Alexander rushed into the thick of the fight with his cavalry, as was his custom, and was wounded by a sword thrust through the thigh. A famous ancient painting, of which a magnificent version in mosaic was found at Pompeii, represented Alexander attempting to reach the person of his fleeing enemy. This scene is the basis for our picture.

After the battle the Syrian cities surrendered peaceably, but Tyre, where there was a strong Phoenician fleet in Darius' pay, held out. Alexander took it after a bitter siege. Tyre was left in ruins, and its defenders were massacred or sold into slavery.

Next, Alexander went down to Egypt, visited the sanctuary of Zeus Ammon in the Libian Desert, and received assurance that he was indeed the son of Zeus—hence a god.

While in Egypt, he founded the city of Alexandria near one of the mouths of the Nile, and it became one of the centers of Hellenistic culture and learning. Alexander then turned north and met Darius in a final battle at Arbela, 250 miles north of Babylon. Darius was murdered not long afterward by one of his satraps.

His last words to Polystratos, who found him dying and gave him a drink of water, were: "This is the worst of my misfortunes, that I am unable to recompense you for your kindness to me. But Alexander will reward you, and the gods will reward Alexander for his courteous treatment of my mother and wife and daughters. Wherefore, I pray you, embrace him as I embrace you."

Painting by H. M. Herget

"All Life Is a Stage and a Play"—Palladas

In Such a Theater Orestes and Electra Played Their Tragic Roles

THE THEATERS of the Greeks were always open to the sky, and almost invariably took advantage of the slope of a hill on which to support the rows of stone seats of the *koilon,* where the audience sat.

The auditorium formed slightly more than a semicircle. At either side was a passageway, known as the *parodos,* through which the Dionysiac procession made its entrance, and which could also be used by actors. The *parodoi* led directly to the circular orchestra, of hard-packed earth, surrounded by a stone curb and a gutter, deep or shallow, which collected the rain water funneled down from the seats. Flights of steps divided the *koilon* into a series of wedge-shaped sections, known as *kerkides,* and, if the theater were large, there might be a level aisle, called a *diazoma,* partway up the slope.

The front row of seats, facing on the orchestra, was reserved for the dignitaries and persons of greatest importance. These seats often were provided with backs, or even took the shape of individual thrones.

The stage was never connected into an architectural whole with the *koilon,* or auditorium, until Roman times. The stage, or *skene,* shown in the picture is typical of about the third century B.C. or slightly later. Only foundations remain of the stage buildings which saw the initial performances of the great plays of Aeschylus, Sophocles, and Euripides in the fifth century.

There was a shallow *proskenion,* consisting of a row of half columns backed against stone piers, between which were painted screens, called *periakta,* which in some cases could be turned in their sockets to afford a change of scenery. Realism or naturalism in scenery was unknown.

Above the *proskenion* is the *logeion,* a narrow platform where, according to some authorities, virtually all the action of the play occurred.

Access to the *logeion* was either by stair at the back of the scene building, or by ramps at either end of the *proskenion.* Some theaters show a sort of trapdoor on the highest roof, from which a god could be made to appear.

Masks designed for the type of play were invariably worn by the actors. Women never appeared on the stage, all parts being taken by men or boys.

The Greek theater gave us several theatrical words. Scene comes, of course, from *skene,* which originally meant a tent, once made of skins, to which the actors retired. Our proscenium arch gets its name from the *proskenion,* which was in front of the *skene. Tragedy* and *comedy* both come from Greek words. Chorus derives from *choros,* the group which danced and sang in the early plays. The very word "drama" comes directly from the Greek.

The occasional revival of one of the political and social satires of Aristophanes shows the vital quality of Greek humor. The plays of Menander, in the fourth century B.C., set comedy in a path from which it has departed very little. The dramas of Aeschylus, Sophocles, and Euripides are among our greatest literary heritages. Among recent successes on the American stage was an English version of Aristophanes' *Lysistrata,* presented on Broadway in 1930 and taken later on a triumphal tour of this country.

Painting by H. M. Herget

"Now Is the Season of Sailing . . . Weigh Thine Anchors and Unloose Thine Hawsers, O Mariner"—Greek Anthology

A Key to the Classic Sea Was the Port of Dēlos

The island of Dēlos, the legendary birthplace of Apollo and his twin sister Artemis, was a sacred site. Its strategic location at a crossing of sea routes through the eastern Mediterranean gave it great power.

After the Persian Wars, the Greek cities of Asia and the Aegean organized a league to protect themselves against further Persian aggression, and all contributed to a fund which they placed under the protection of the Temple of Apollo at Dēlos. This fund later was transferred to Athens, since Athens was the dominant sea power, and went to build the Parthenon.

The advantages of its location, which was favorable as regards winds and passages between the islands, assured it a continued prosperity that lasted down into Roman times. In the Hellenistic period—that is, from the early part of the third century B.C.—it was adorned by many elaborate houses of the rich merchants and many fine public buildings.

Here came grain ships from Egypt and Syria. Merchants brought and exchanged their wares from the Black Sea ports; rich argosies came over from the Asia Minor coast, and as a free port Dēlos prospered in much the same way that other free ports have done in later times. The good natural harbor was improved by large moles. There were extensive quays to which vessels could be moored, and a few of the old mooring bitts of stone or marble have been found, although the harbor has for the most part become silted up.

Across the narrow bay was another island, Rhenea, where there were also dwellings. To that island all women had to withdraw to give birth to children, for it was sacrilege for anyone to be born or to die on Dēlos.

The picture is drawn as if from the deck of a merchantman putting out from the port, laden with dried figs, melons, and other fruits, and amphoras of oil or wine. The steersman is guiding the steering oar with a sort of whipstaff.

Near him, the ladder which was always carried instead of a gangplank has not yet been properly stowed. These ladders were always carried near the stern of the ship, since it was customary to moor the vessel with her stern to the shore, just as small caïques are handled now.

Near by is a warship, with three banks of oars. Her single mast is stepped, her yard squared off, and she is running out of the harbor with a favorable breeze, assisted by her oarsmen. The three-pronged bronze beak shows clearly, and just above and behind it one of the painted eyes of the ship, always included so that it might see its way.

On a raised walk between the banks of oars is the station of the "oar masters" (*toicharchoi*) and the *trieraules* who gave time to the rowers by playing on a flute. The captain, or governor, of the ship had a cabin at the stern, and immediately in front of the cabin are two steersmen, one to each of the large steering oars.

The sails could be brailed up if need be, and the yards either sent down completely or "cockbilled." A ship usually carried two anchors, similar to the old wooden stock anchor generally used until the last part of the nineteenth century.

Nearly all the ships seen in the background are merchant vessels with characteristic bows and pronounced sheer.

© National Geographic Society

Painting by H. M. Herget

"Eureka! I Have Found It"—Vitruvius

Archimedes and His Principle of Buoyant Force

FROM THE seventh century B. C. on, Greek culture had taken a firm root in Sicily and southern Italy, and even while Rome was a small provincial city, just making its way in the world, Greek art and Greek artisans had been pouring into the Etruscan cities of central and northern Italy.

Carthaginians from the region of Tunis and Bizerte had swept into Sicily in the fifth century and withdrawn again, with the varying fortunes of war; Pyrrhus of Epirus had come and gone; Greek had fought Greek at Syracuse, and thousands of Athenians had starved to death in the quarries of that city.

The impact of Alexander on the Greek world and the eastern kingdoms had not, however, been felt so strongly in the west, and Syracuse continued serenely as one of the great centers of Greek life, although its social life had had its ups and downs between radical revolution and a despotic, oligarchic oppression.

Fortunately, in the third century B. C., Syracuse came under the power of a comparatively enlightened ruler, Hieron II, who reigned for 54 years according to Polybius "without killing, exiling, or injuring a single citizen."

Under Hieron worked one of the foremost of the Greek men of science. Archimedes, observing that water ran out of his bath as he himself got in, evolved the physical principle for which he is best known: *A body immersed in a fluid is buoyed up by a force equal to the weight of the displaced fluid.* Applying this principle to establish specific gravities enabled him to determine for his patron whether all the gold supplied for a crown had been used, or whether some silver had been substituted.

The picture shows him immersing the crown, or wreath, as it probably was, in a basin of water and preparing to measure the amount of water displaced. Scales of a pattern not unknown today were used then, and numerous leaden and bronze weights have been found, many of them carefully marked with their value.

Besides weighing Hieron's crown, Archimedes experimented with many mechanical devices. He was one of the foremost mathematicians of antiquity, and wrote extensively. Although he was keenly interested in theory, his chief interest seems to have been in applied science.

He made a planetarium to represent the movements of the heavenly bodies; he invented the compound pulley and the endless screw used to pump out ships. Hieron, in reply to Archimedes' alleged statement that he could move the earth if given a place whereon to stand, challenged him to beach a large galley with which his men were having difficulty, and Archimedes arranged a mechanism in such a way that he himself, working at one end of it, was able to draw the vessel up to dry land.

When Syracuse was besieged by the Romans a few years after the death of Hieron, he invented all sorts of engines of war: grapnels that drew enemy ships up out of water by one end and then allowed them to fall back and sink; great engines for hurling stones; and mirrors that concentrated the sun's rays and set the ships afire.

Although the Roman general Marcellus had given strict orders to spare his life, he was killed by an impetuous Roman soldier whom he declined to accompany until he had finished a mathematical problem.

National Geographic Photographer B. Anthony Stewart

His Bow Lost, Apollo the Archer Seems to Be Lighting Vesuvius

At Pompeii, 14 miles southeast of Naples, a copy of the original statue of the Greek god stands in the Temple of Apollo. Recent excavations have revealed a new section of the handsome Roman city which will be left just as uncovered to show customs and life at the very hour when Pompeii was buried in pumice stone and ashes, A. D. 79. Twice a week in summer the ruins are illuminated by colored floodlights. At the same time concerts are held in the original theater.

The Roman Way

Stern Warriors Drilled in Military Discipline Came Home from the Wars to Find Relaxation in Comedies of Family Life

By Edith Hamilton *

WHAT do the words Republican Rome call to mind?

Discipline, first and foremost; then frugality, hardihood; white-togaed figures of an incomparable dignity; ranks of fighting men drilled to the last degree of military precision; an aura of the simple life lived, not quite on heroic heights, but at any rate on perpetual battlefields; Cincinnatus at the plough; the death of a son decreed by a father for disobedience of orders even though a victory resulted.

That is the sort of thing we think of as early Rome.

This edifying picture is considerably enlarged and diversified by Roman comedy.

In Plautus we get the reverse of the shield, the senator not in his toga but in the Roman equivalent of dressing gown and slippers; the soldier dispensing alike with armor and discipline; dignity, iron resolution, the stern compulsion of duty, the entire arsenal of the antique Roman virtues, completely in the discard.

Thus, when the curtain rings up for the stupendous drama which we know as Ancient Rome, it is raised surprisingly on two comic writers (Plautus and Terence, authors of plays from which Shakespeare borrowed). The oldest substantial piece of Roman literature we have is a collection of comedies.

Comedy, Not Martial Ballads, Started Roman Literature

Our notion of the proper beginning for the literature of the mistress of the world would be something martial and stirring, old ballads of valiant men and warlike deeds with spirited bards to sing them, culminating in a great epic, a Latin *Iliad*.

But it actually begins as far away from that as the wide realm of letters allows, in a series of comedies which are avowedly founded upon the popular Greek comedy of the day.†

No other great national literature goes back to an origin borrowed in all respects.

That brief flowering of genius, the golden age, not of Greece alone but of all our western world, had been brought about by a lofty and exultant spirit, conscious of heroic deeds done and full of joyous courage for great enterprises to come.‡

It had lived in the audiences who shouted at Aristophanes' riotous nonsense, who delighted in every brilliant bit of his satire, appreciated each delicate parody, with minds keen to follow his master mind.

Aristophanes founded no school. He had no followers, ancient or modern. Menander has lived only as a shadow in Roman plays. Plautus and Terence were the founders of the drama as we know it today.

Peoples Are Known by the Plays They See

We may perhaps account ourselves fortunate that comedy was the survivor. There is no better indication of what the people of any period are like than the plays they go to see (page 349). Popular drama shows the public quality as nothing else can.

But comedy does more. It must present the audience, as tragedy need not, with a picture of life lived as they know it.

The domestic drama, which is essentially

* This article contains excerpts from the author's book, *The Roman Way,* published by W. W. Norton and Company, Inc. Copyright 1932.

† Latin plays taken from the Greek were called *contaminationes.* Often they were combinations of two or more Greek plays. The scenes, names, and costumes were Greek, but the ideas, the action, the real meaning of the plays were definitely Roman.

‡ See articles on Greece by Edith Hamilton and Richard Stillwell with 32 color reproductions of Herget paintings, pages 168 to 265; from the National Geographic Magazine, March, 1944.

Staff Photographer B. Anthony Stewart

One Name Links Two Majestic Symbols of the Wealth and Power That Were Rome

The Arch of Titus was built in A. D. 81 to commemorate that Emperor's capture of Jerusalem (page 308). Its realistic reliefs form a picture story of the epic siege. The famous Colosseum was completed by Titus in A. D. 80 and inaugurated by 100 days of gladiatorial combats (page 351). Lightning, earthquake, war, and use as a quarry have reduced the amphitheater by two-thirds.

© P. A.—Reuter

A Teutonic Blitz Uncovered These Roman Mosaics in Exeter, England

Big aerial bombs of modern warfare sometimes penetrated to the physical level of Roman civilization. Bomb-shattered Exeter divulged the plan and extent of its Roman precursor. Battered St. Catherine's Almshouses, near busy High Street, produced these provincial mosaics. An Italian expert sifted thousands of pieces from the rubble and patiently put together the work of his forefathers (page 284).

the drama as we know it today, has its direct origin in these Latin plays. The intimate domesticity of family life in one of its most impressive manifestations, the Roman family, is the pivot they all turn on, and character after character is shown which the theater has never let go of since.

Stern Mothers and Henpecked Husbands

Here is the very first appearance upon the world's stage of the figure so dear to audiences everywhere, the Mother, essentially what she is to be through all the centuries down to our own with the white carnation and Mother's Day. Greece never knew her. The Mother, capitalized, was foreign to Greek ideas.

The father has a place even more prominent. What they called in Rome the *Patria Potestas,* the Father's Authority, was clearly an awful matter. There was no rebelling against it.

But the authority of the master of the house had its limits. Plautus' Rome was the Rome of the Mother of the Gracchi and it is not difficult to understand that the Roman *Pater Familias,* though weightily endowed by law and edict and tradition, might meet his match in the determined virtues of the Roman matron.

Indeed that resolute lady seems to be responsible for the creation of one of the most popular characters in literature, the henpecked husband.* He makes his very first bow upon the stage in these plays.

Perhaps the most familiar passage in Virgil† is the one in which he bids the men of Rome remember that to them belongs the rule of the earth (page 309). They are to "spare the submissive and war down the proud." It would seem that this high charge was subject to modifications within the home.

But there is one notable difference between what an audience would accept from women in Plautus' day and in later times.

The deceived husband, so familiar for so many centuries to the European stage, never appears in Roman comedy. There is no indication of any other bar to the activity of the Roman wife, but she could not put horns upon her husband's head. No Puritan morality could be more unyielding on this point.

* The luckless old man with the "unlovely dowered wife" was a stock figure to deride.

† See "Perennial Geographer (Virgil)," National Geographic Magazine, October, 1930, by Dr. W. Coleman Nevils, S. J.

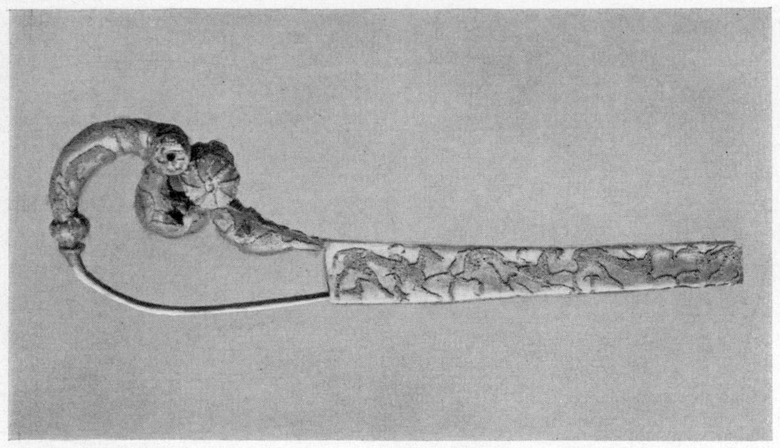

Metropolitan Museum of Art

Gold Safety Pins Were Used by the Etruscans in the 7th Century B. C.

Although much of the treasure unearthed from the burial chambers of these early overlords of Rome was of Greek workmanship (page 297), motifs such as the decoration on this were definitely Etruscan.

ful education of their women in the idea that their supreme duty was to be chaste.

The popular story of Lucretia who killed herself when she was violated by force, completely innocent though she was in reality, and the story, even more popular of the father acclaimed a hero because he killed his daughter with his own hand rather than have her live as the tyrant's mistress, testify eloquently to the thoroughness of the women's training.

Thus disciplined they were safe to go abroad and enjoyed a degree of freedom civilized women had never known before.

Another point new to the student of Greek literature is the exaltation of woman and her purity. That, too, began in Rome.

Greek tragedy, indeed, shows women of a greatness unsurpassed anywhere. The greatest figures are women, but the fact that it is so is never directly brought to mind. We are never made to feel how wonderful that a woman should be like that, any more than how wonderful that a man should be.

In Roman literature, as in our own, a woman is always a woman. Her sex is never in the background of the picture.

That audience of more than two thousand one hundred years ago looks oddly familiar. The reflection shown in the mirror of Plautus and Terence has "nothing alien" to us as we watch it. The close family life and the masterful lady of the house and the elderly-man-in-search-of-a-mistress and the nice young lovers—we know them all only too well and we cannot feel ourselves strangers to the theater crowd that flocked to see them in Rome of the Republic.

But an enormous change has taken place when next we have a contemporary's account of the city; the government is corrupt through and through and the people completely indifferent.

Only a hundred years—less than that—changed Polybius' great Republic into one of

The fact is thrown into high relief by the complete absence of any sex morality in other directions. The courtesans are important characters in nearly every play and Terence's most estimable youths have affairs with them which their mothers on occasion hotly defend.

The Romans were franker than our grandfathers were, but their basic notions of what could and could not be done were the same. Strict virtue within the house for everyone. Outside, all the pleasant vices for the men.*

A hard and fast division of ethics into male and female received its final consummation in Rome. The double standard, which has been the world's standard for all these centuries since, is formulated, complete to the last detail, in Roman comedy.

In this respect the men of Greece were dull of wit compared with the men of Rome. Their astuteness did not rise beyond the four walls of the house for their womenfolk, with occasional assistance from bolts and bars, most futile of defenses, as storytellers the world over have shown.

Woman's Supreme Asset—Chastity

Aristophanes has many a joke about the way Athenian women eluded them and the husbands they deceived. Nothing of the kind passed with a Roman audience of the Republic.

The men saw to it that they were not deceived, and the way they did it was a triumph of Roman intelligence as well as of Roman determination.

One of Rome's greatest achievements, which has passed almost unnoticed, was the success-

* Plautus in the *Mostellaria* makes the country slave say, "Out-Greek the Greeks; be drunk both day and night; buy mistresses and set young slave girls free."

Acme

Peace Removes Wartime Protection of a Column Commemorating Roman Triumphs

The Column of Marcus Aurelius, in Rome, is patterned after that of Emperor Trajan. Spiral relief bands show the pictorial history of the philosopher-emperor's vital Danubian campaigns against the Germans (page 310). While fighting barbarians, Aurelius wrote his famous *Meditations*, by which chiefly he is remembered.

© Donald McLeish

Stately, Tri-tiered Pont du Gard, Queen of Roman Aqueducts, Spans the Gard in Southern France

The sun-tanned blocks of all the arches have stood uncemented since 19 B. C., but the canal on top was waterproofed with cement. Fifty-two golden arches support the water channel, still mostly covered, which served ancient Nemausus (Nîmes). A modern road crosses the "bridge" on the main tier.

Air Transport Command, Official

To Ancient Romans Their Great Capital Was "First Among Cities, Home of the Gods, Golden Rome"

As mistress of the European West, Rome ruled from Irish Sea to Persian Gulf, from the Atlantic to the Caspian. Spiritual authority replaced temporal power as "the Eternal City" lived on as capital of Christendom. Here is the more modern section of the city, with St. Peter's and part of Vatican City at the upper right.

1 Tin from Cornwall was floated on rude barges to Brittany and southern France

2 Poor-class timber dwellings, now uncovered by aerial bombings, were the slums of Roman London

3 Flocks of geese were driven from Belgium to provide livers for Roman tables—page 318

4 Amber from East Prussia was imported and prized by the Romans

5 Crossing the Pyrenees and Alps in his march on Rome from Spain, Hannibal's elephant-borne Carthaginian army lost 50,000 men

6 Vienna was the home port of the Roman Danube fleet

7 More than 1,800 years old, the Roman bridge at Alcántara is still used—page 305

8 Roman conquerors of Spain found it curious that "the women dance promiscuously with men, taking hold of their hands"

9 From the Balearic Islands were recruited the best professional soldiers of antiquity. For pay they fought for Greeks, Carthaginians, or Romans

10 Price and wage ceilings to check inflation were tried by Emperor Diocletian. His palace at Spalato still stands

11 No present-day road in Albania surpasses the old Roman one

12 Because Morocco was unmanageable, Diocletian withdrew Roman forces from all but a narrow strip commanding the Strait of Gibraltar

13 The Roman library at Timgad contained 23,000 volumes

14 Irrigation by the Romans made Tunisia's soil fertile

15 Ancient Romans and modern Fascists exiled political offenders to Pantelleria

16 Rome never made an organized effort to invade and conquer Russia
17 Trajan's 20-arch Danube River bridge was three-quarters of a mile long. Its ruins are visible at low water—page 299
18 Under Roman rule Athens became a university town, the Oxford of antiquity
19 The Romans tried four times to build a Corinth Canal; the project was not accomplished until 1,800 years later
20 Wars stocked the slave auctions at Dēlos—page 303
21 Under Roman rule the interior of Turkey was studded with prosperous cities having a population greatly exceeding that of modern times
22 Copper from Cyprus was combined with tin from the Atlantic coast to make the bronze of antiquity. The word "copper" is a corruption of "Cyprus"
23 Cleopatra lived in Alexandria, center of the eastern Mediterranean
24 Roman ships brought gems and spices from Ceylon via the Red Sea-Nile canal—page 300
25 Silt of the Nile floods made Egypt Rome's richest grainland
26 Animals from the Sudan and the Sahara were imported for the wild-beast fights in the Colosseum of Rome
27 Torches used in Roman siegecraft were sometimes soaked in petroleum from the Near East—page 307
28 Caravans supplied Rome with rugs from Persia and silk from China. Silk was thought by the Romans to be produced by trees and was worth its weight in gold—page 300
FINLAND
Helsinki
Leningrad
Tallinn
ESTONIA
Riga
LATVIA
LITHUANIA
Kaunas
Warsaw
AND
Kiev
Kharkov
Stalingrad
Volga
Dnieper
Don
U. S. S. R.
Rostov
Dniester
Odessa
Dacia
ROMANIA
Crimea
Yalta
Caucasus Mountains
Caspian Sea
17 Bucharest
Danube
Black Sea
BULGARIA
Sofia
Tiflis
Baku
Istanbul
Armenia
Tabriz
cedonia
Dardanelles
Ankara
Cappadocia
TURKEY
REECE
Troy
Lesbos
Aegean Sea
Athens
Dēlos
Anatolia
[Asia Minor]
Tyana
Cilicia
Assyria
Tehran
IRAN
(PERSIA)
Corinth Canal
Antioch
SYRIA
Euphrates
Tigris
Baghdad
Rhodes
Candia
Crete
Cyprus
LEBANON
Beirut
Phoenicia
Damascus
Shahba
IRAQ
Babylonia
Abadan
Basra
KUWAIT
Amman
Caesarea
PALESTINE
Jerusalem
Judaea
TRANS-JORDAN
Sea
Alexandria
El 'Alamein
Suez Canal
Cairo
Neutral Territory
Neutral Territory
Persian Gulf
Nile
SAUDI ARABIA
EGYPT
Red Sea
Thebes
Riyadh
Medina
Aswan
(Syene)
Mecca
0 100 200 300 400
STATUTE MILES
European Boundaries as of January 1, 1938
Extent of Roman Empire
Drawn by H. E. Eastwood and Irvin E. Alleman

Erno Vadas

Barbarian Torches Transformed a Roman Emperor's Seaside Palace into a Town

In A. D. 305 Diocletian, wearied by imperial cares, retired to his magnificent seven-acre palace at Split (Spalato) on the Dalmatian coast (pages 325, 352). When invading Avars fired near-by Salona in the year 620, refugees built a town within its massive, fortlike walls. Parts of the ancient structure, which once housed some 3,000 people, still form the heart of this busy Yugoslav port.

which we have as black a picture as could well be painted. The historian Sallust tells of a foreign prince who came to Rome at the beginning of the first century to engineer a deal. He was rich and he succeeded, and as he left the town he said, "City in which everything is for sale."

A Man of Many Letters

During the strange and exciting days when the great Republic was coming to an end and the Empire was looming just ahead, there lived the most distinguished letter writer the world has ever known, one of Rome's very great men, Cicero the orator.

Hundreds of his letters have been preserved, along with many letters from his friends. They are of all sorts: letters of condolence, letters of affection, letters of apology, literary criticism, philosophical discussion, town gossip, business letters, and, outnumbering all the rest a hundred to one, political letters.

Such a ratio would be a matter of course to a Roman. The thing of paramount importance, away beyond everything else, was politics.*

Goodness apart from patriotism did not exist to the Roman.

Officials, party chiefs, "bosses" big and little, must face an ever-present possibility of having to die for their country. Ex-officials were allowed no more comfortable prospects.

Consulars, as they called them, men who had been consuls—Rome's ex-presidents—became oftenest commanders in the wars Rome was always waging in one or another part of the world.

Cicero, pre-eminently a man of peace, must yet put himself at the head of an army and live for months at a time as a fighting general. It was the price he paid for once having been placed at the head of the state.

And yet when Cicero was carrying on his Cilician campaign in strict accordance with Rome's great tradition, the Republic was dying and all but dead. That was in 51 B. C.

Nine years before, three powerful party leaders had come together; they agreed to pool their resources and take the government into their own hands. But it was all completely unofficial. The senate met; the consuls presided; the old respected political forms were strictly adhered to.

The fact that Caesar, Pompey, and Crassus held the reins did not seem to matter much, if they kept, as they did, in the background.

People got used to the idea of them and when four years later their powerful organization was completed and they began to act openly, honored and honorable patriots could find excellent reasons for acquiescing in their running the city.

Something had happened to Roman morale. The people were safe and at ease. Rome's enemies were outside Italy now (page 310), far away, shut off by mountains or sea, and although civilian commanders were the rule, fighting in other respects had become a matter for professionals.

Wealth was pouring into the city from conquered countries; easy money had become possible for a great many and the ideal for most.

Politics have become a money-making business; votes are bought and sold, so are judges. Everyone knows that there is one sure way to being elected or being acquitted, and nobody cares.

One day, Cicero writes, there was read out in the senate an agreement a candidate for the consulship had made with the two consuls to pay each of them a large sum of money in case he was elected, but failed to get for them the offices they wanted when their term was over. The compact called for false oaths not only from the principals but from two ex-consuls as well.

"It was regularly drawn up," Cicero continues, "with the sums promised, and drafts on the bank added, and so on. It does throw a lurid light on the consuls, but it was all the same to Appius Claudius [one of them]—he had nothing to lose by it."

Once the Claudii had been citizens Rome was proud of. The Appian Way was the achievement of an ancestor; so was the first water system, and the splendid aqueduct.

The present representatives, however, were not of the antique stamp. Appius, his brother Publius, and their three sisters, all noted for brilliancy and personal beauty, were talked of throughout the city for their reckless ways, their extravagance, dissipation, and worse.

Caesar's Wife Must Be Above Reproach

The celebrated case of that day and many a day to come centered in Publius, and Caesar's young wife, Pompeia, was corespondent.

As Cicero tells the story, it began at the festival of the Good Goddess, a highly important ceremony in which women alone took part. During the celebration no male could enter the house where it was held. Even pictures and statues of men were banished. Juvenal

* In Rome was born the custom that gave rise to our modern term, *mudslinging*. All candidates for office wore the white toga—*toga candida*. If they were unpopular, people threw mud at them till their white raiment became the *toga maculosa*, the toga defiled with mud. Cicero referred to senators thus disgraced as *senatores maculosi* (polluted senators).

© Orient Press by Z. Kluger

Named by a King to Honor an Emperor, Palestine's Caesarea Figured Prominently in Ancient, Medieval, and Church History

Built by King Herod, named for Caesar Augustus, this once-magnificent seaport was a Roman capital, Christian bishopric, and walled Crusader stronghold. St. Paul ... Traces of Roman city and fortified Christian town are still discernible.

Relang from Three Lions

A French Version of the Bullfight Has Replaced Gladiatorial Combats in the Roman Arena at Arles

© Donald McLeish

Soldiers of Civilization Kept Barbarism at Bay along the Roman Empire's Far-flung Borders

Hadrian's Wall, linking sea to sea across north England, marked the limits of the Roman world in this region and held back marauding Picts and Scots for 250 years

Staff Photographer Maynard Owen Williams

A Trademark of Roman Civilization Was the Aqueduct, Which Here Brought Water to Quench the Thirsty Anatolian Plain

An ancient way of travel rumbles beside ruins which once watered the Roman town of Tyana in southern Cappadocia, part of modern Turkey. Built on the Mound of Semiramis, legendary female founder of the Assyrian Empire, Tyana grew into a thriving city which became a Roman colony under the Emperor Caracalla.

Staff Photographer B. Anthony Stewart

Grim and Battle-scarred, a Veteran of 1,800 Years Broods over Men and Angels on the Banks of Father Tiber

Hadrian's Tomb (Castel Sant' Angelo) has been mausoleum, fort, castle, barracks, and museum. It was once magnificently marble-encrusted. The bridge is Ponte Sant' ... The angels were designed by Bernini and executed by his pupils in 1669-70.

says no male mouse dared to stay in the forbidden premises.

Caesar was pontifex maximus at the time and his house was chosen for the sacred rite. This suited Claudius exceedingly well.

His affair with Pompeia was not coming off, Plutarch thinks because of the strict chaperonage of her mother-in-law, "a very discreet woman," and here was an occasion when the most vigilant duenna might relax.

His smooth boyish beauty fitted well a woman's dress and he arranged with Pompeia to go to the house disguised as a singing girl and be met at the door by her own maid. The maid, bidding him wait, slipped away to find her mistress.

But she was long in coming back and Claudius started to find his lady for himself.

But something had gone wrong. Perhaps Pompeia's courage failed; more probably the very discreet woman had had her suspicions aroused, for as he went through the house her maid ran up to him and called out gaily that he must come and play with her, a custom, Plutarch says, at the festival—it would be pleasant to know what they played at—and upon his drawing back, asked him what was wrong.

Betrayed by His Voice

Claudius had the folly to speak to her in answer and his voice betrayed him.

She shrieked, "A man—a man!" and the fat was in the fire. Great was the to-do.

The "sacred things" were covered; the holy rites pronounced null and void; the house ransacked. To no purpose, however; Claudius had been smuggled out by Pompeia's maid.

All the same, he had been recognized and of course next morning the town buzzed with the delightfully horrific scandal.

A tribune was found to impeach the offender for profaning sacred ordinances.

Claudius contented himself with declaring that he was out of town at the time of the festival and had witnesses to prove it.

Caesar put the best face he could on the matter: swore he did not believe a word of it; Claudius had never been in the house; a lot of women's talk. It was true he divorced Pompeia, but then he was ready with a reason which commended itself to every masculine heart, voiced in the famous saying about Caesar's wife.

Claudius, we may well believe, enjoyed himself. A trial for sacrilege was certain, but he knew a way out from that.

Cicero was drawn into the affair. Rumor had it that he was extremely reluctant to move in the matter and that the reason was the lovely Claudia, the most beautiful and notorious of the three sisters.

It is certain that he often speaks of her in his letters, and his nickname for her, "our ox-eyed goddess"—elsewhere he mentions her great flashing eyes—would point to some intimacy.

At all events, Cicero's wife, a lady built on the lines of Plautus' Roman matrons, laid down an ultimatum and Cicero came forward as the chief witness for the prosecution. The enmity he aroused thereby followed him implacably through his life and even after.

Nothing happened. Well-meaning citizens would applaud, but when it came to doing anything that meant personal effort, not to say inconvenience and even possible danger, that was another matter. Not long after, Claudius was elected to high office.

To the modern reader of the record it seems incredible that anyone, let alone those shrewd, competent Romans, should have believed that such a state of things could go on and on and a republic in which no one trusted either the electorate or the courts could in the nature of things endure. But so it was.

Cicero writes his brother during a temporary lapse of his ruling passion: "Anything more corrupt than the men and times of today cannot be conceived. And so, since no pleasure can be got of politics, I don't see why I should fret myself. I find my pleasures in literature and my favorite pursuits and the leisure of my country houses and, most of all, in our boys."

Ten years after that letter was written the Republic was ended; Antony and Augustus were dividing between them the Roman world; Cicero's headless body was lying on the seashore. In one of his letters he says that it is easy to know how to pull the ropes in a bad cause, but hard in a good cause, and "it is a difficult art to rule a republic."

If only Cicero had not been such a keen politician! Only a sentence here and there, at the best a few stray passages, throw a little light on the way of the world as the smart society of Ciceronian Rome pursued it.

Interior of a Roman Mansion

What the house, with gymnasium and colonnade, must have been like can be seen in a letter about his brother's house: "All's right on your estate—nothing left to do but the baths and a promenade and the aviary. The paved colonnade gives dignity.

"In the bathroom I moved the stove to the corner of a dressing room because it was so placed that the steam pipe was directly under the bedrooms. Your landscape gardener has

London Electrotype Agency, Ltd.

Excavation Near Langport, England, Bared a Fine Roman Mosaic

It once was the floor of the cold room in a luxurious bath (page 334). The dashing rider in the foreground is clad in tight-fitting oriental costume, with Phrygian cap and cloak streaming in the wind. The octagonal panel (center) shows a lady disrobing between two cupids holding torches (page 269).

won my praise; he has enveloped everything in ivy—even the Greek statues seem advertising it. It's the coolest, greenest retreat. Statues, wrestling ground, fish pond, water system—all are fine. Really, an edifice worthy of Caesar—and there is no more fastidious connoisseur."

Sometimes we get a glimpse of the vast slave world which did all the work and provided all the amusements (page 303).

"Do send me two of your library slaves," Cicero writes Atticus, "to help glue pages, and tell them to bring bits of parchment for title pieces. I say, you *have* bought a fine troupe of gladiators. I hear they fight splendidly. If you had cared to hire them out you would have cleared expenses on those two shows. Enough of that—but, as you love me, remember the library slaves."

Gladiatorial contests Cicero rather inclined to—from moral considerations. People call them cruel, he says, and perhaps they are, as conducted today. But certainly the spectators receive an incomparable training in despising suffering and death.

Cicero Chose to Ignore Impropriety

The decorum of the letters is amazing in that day and in that city. There is hardly a suggestion of impropriety even. A sample of his scandal-mongering—there are not above half a dozen in all—is a story he tells Atticus about an unfortunate gentleman who had his baggage searched and among his goods "were found five diminutive busts of Roman ladies —married, all of them! One was Brutus' sister; another, Lepidus' wife. *He* won't fret."

This is as far as Cicero will go in the way of an off-color story, and yet he wrote at a time when Rome was full of the vilest vice and the foulest talk.

Through the letters great figures pass perpetually, great still to us today. Mark Antony, "a wretched, insignificant subordinate of Caesar's," Pompey from his height of aloof superiority calls him; "the toy captain," Cicero dubs him jeeringly to Atticus, "who carries round with him that actress Cytheris and in an open litter, too."

Pompey appears often, now the great statesman and superlatively great general, and then at the crisis of his life when he faced Caesar to see which would rule the world, suddenly showing himself neither a statesman nor a general.

"His way is to want one thing and say another," that engaging young scamp, Caelius Rufus, writes Cicero, "and yet he's not clever enough to hide what he wants. But," he adds gaily, "he's undergoing a reducing treatment at Bauli and is so extremely hungry, even I am sorry for him."

The great Augustus, first Emperor of Rome, the autocrat whose word was final throughout the civilized world, appears a very human young man before the splendid trappings of royalty covered him up.*

"A praiseworthy youth who had better be rewarded—and removed," is his (Cicero's) final pronouncement. That remark was repeated to Augustus; three months later he agreed to Cicero's assassination.

Caesar, the greatest man Rome produced, as we all believe with perhaps no very definite notion why, is seen less distinctly than any of the other notable personages Cicero discusses with his friends. That is our great loss, for Caesar was not given to explaining himself.

A book, no matter on what subject, could hardly be less personal than his *Gallic War*.† It is the one example in literature of an impersonal autobiography. Caesar figures on nearly every page, but in exactly the same way as all the other characters do.

Even the annihilation of a legion and the rescue of another just on the point of annihilation are recounted with no more feeling than if the narrator were a historian of deeds done centuries before him.

It is the greater pity that Cicero, who knew Caesar from boyhood and was the one man among his contemporaries with ability enough to understand him, should mention him only briefly and rarely.

And yet Cicero was a good friend.

Even on his arduous campaigns Caesar took the trouble to write often. "A most cordial letter from Caesar," Cicero writes Atticus. "The result of the war in Britain is looked forward to with anxiety. There is not a scrap of silver on the island, no booty either except slaves—and I don't fancy there will be any with literary or musical talent among *them*." That was in the year 54.

The last glimpse of Caesar is in a letter dated less than three months before the Ides of March. Cicero gives him a dinner party, a very splendid affair.

"It passed off perfectly delightfully," he

* See "Augustus—Emperor and Architect," by W. Coleman Nevils, NATIONAL GEOGRAPHIC MAGAZINE, October, 1938.

† Probably one explanation of this impersonal style is the fact that Caesar, being absent in the field most of the time, wrote reports of his deeds to be read in the Forum in support of his political candidacy. These reports, therefore, were written like news stories, and, like our modern publicity stories disguised as news, they were intended to win public favor for a political candidate.

tells Atticus. "A formidable guest, but he left no regret behind. Until one o'clock he admitted no one: at his accounts, I believe. Then he took a walk, and after two, his bath, and then, when he had been anointed sat down to dinner. He was undergoing a course of emetics, so he ate and drank as he pleased—a lordly dinner and well served."

Horace, a Wit Who Moralized

Horace was just turned 21 when Cicero died.

He took sides with Brutus and fought with him through the campaign that resulted in the final defeat of the republican cause and the establishment of Augustus and Antony as masters of the world.

He was a man of supreme good sense who saw that the Republic was gone irrevocably and the Empire had arrived to stay.

Who would not like to see Horace walk in through his door any day in the year? Immediately everything would seem more agreeable, the cocktails better flavored, the armchairs softer, even the comfort of the warm, sheltered room would take on the proportions of an active delight. And the talk would never center round himself. Every attempt to make it do so would be warded off deprecatingly with a touch of gay humor.

Sitting in your armchair he would be the most stimulating of listeners—but any balloon you launched would be in danger of a puncture from a sly dart of irony, which yet, with all its cutting edge, would fail to wound.

He is Benjamin Franklin turned poet, or rather, for he never borders upon the provincial, a poetical Montaigne (page 321). He is a poet whose distinguishing characteristic is common sense.*

Through thirty years he "played with words on paper," as he called his writing, and he never had any other pursuit. Yet the result is only one slender volume.

Horace had by nature, as no one more, the gift of brevity. The result of his freedom to write as he pleased was poetry which belongs to that rare order of verse which is distilled; only the essence left. He gave a good deal of advice, first and last, to would-be writers, and of it all "Be brief" comes first: "So that the thought does not stand in its own way, hindered by words that weigh down the tired ears." And remember always, "More ought to be scratched out than left."

Through the streets of the great city Horace strolled, cocking an amused eye at a fashionable lady's short dress, at a perfumed young elegant's latest thing in the way of togas, at the bearers of a great personage's litter—no carriages were allowed in the streets during the day—at his own slave on tiptoe to scan eagerly a poster of a gladiatorial show, at a grand funeral procession preceded by blaring brass horns and trumpets, and with especial delight at a fastidious poet's latest effusion hung outside the bookshop where it was being pawed over by the sweaty hands of the vulgar.

He stopped before a famous painter's work in a portico—there were miles of these roofed colonnades—had a look at a merchant's stock of "pearls from farthest Arabia and India, giver of wealth"; at other shops where could be bought "silver and antique marble and bronze and works of art, jewels, and Tyrian purple," rare and beautiful things from everywhere in the world.

Banquet Fare a Fearful Gorge

Cooking and serving and bills of fare occupy a great deal of Horace's attention. No less than the whole of two poems, and long ones at that, and the half of another are about nothing else: *Horace:* "How did you fare at the grand dinner party?" *Friend:* "Never better in my life." *Horace:* "Do tell me, if it won't bore you, what were the hors d'oeuvres?"

And a hundred lines follow which make fun of the menu, indeed, but give it nevertheless in greatest detail, together with a number of recipes for cooking the especially delicious dishes (page 319).

On that occasion those Roman gentlemen ate: cold wild boar with all sorts of pickled vegetables; oysters and shellfish with a marvelous sauce; two varieties of turbot; a wonderful dish where a great fish seemed to be swimming among shrimp, with a relish made of fish from Spain, wine from Greece, vinegar from Lesbos, and white pepper; then wild fowl served with corn; the liver of a white goose fattened on ripe figs; shoulder of hare ("so much more succulent than the lower part"); broiled blackbirds and wood pigeons.

Sweets are not mentioned and of fruit only bright red apples, but elsewhere Horace speaks of dainties for dessert as beneath the attention of a true epicure and advises a final course of black mulberries—but they must be gathered before the sun is high.

"We rise from table," he remarks, "pale from overeating," and the modern reader understands why the early Christians put gluttony among the seven deadly sins. The practice of using emetics to make more and more eating possible seems to have become the fashion only at a later date.

Along with the elegance and even magnifi-

* See "Horace—Classic Poet of the Countryside," by W. Coleman Nevils, NATIONAL GEOGRAPHIC MAGAZINE, December, 1935.

F. E. Williams

Farm Lands in England Still Yield Roman Treasure

In 1942 a laborer operating a tractor plow turned up from a field at West Row, Mildenhall, a rich cache of silver, of which these pieces were a part. Decorative motifs indicate that some of the vessels were made as late as the fourth century. Caesar's invasions of Britain occurred in 55 and 54 B. C., but actual conquest began with Claudius in A. D. 43. The country remained under Roman rule for nearly 400 years.

cence of Horace's dinner parties there might be on occasion a lack of ordinary decency.

Horace, aware of tablecloths because they were so often exceedingly dirty, sends an invitation to a friend with the promise that neither cloth nor napkins will make him wrinkle his nose in disgust.

Why should such things be, he laments, when cleanliness is so easy and so cheap. He ends the letter with the simple statement that his guest may count on plenty of room at table and not fear objectionable odors, as happens when people are seated too close.

And this is Rome of the stupendous baths!

The Glory That Was Rome

Unlimited the Romans were, in desires, in ambitions, in appetites, as well as in power and extent of empire. Always rude, primitive, physical appetites were well to the fore.

What constitutes Rome's greatness, in the last analysis, is that powerful as these were in her people there was something still more powerful; ingrained in them was the idea of discipline, the soldier's fundamental idea. However fierce the urge of their nature was, the feeling for law and order was deeper.

Their outbreaks were terrible—civil wars such as our world has not seen again; dealings with conquered enemies which are a fearful page in history. Nevertheless, the outstanding fact about Rome is her unwavering adherence to the idea of a controlled life, subject not to the individual but to a system embodying the principles of justice and fair dealing.

How savage the Roman nature was which the Roman law controlled is seen written large in Rome's favorite amusements: so-called wild beast hunts in the arena; naval battles for which the circus was flooded by hidden canals (page 350); and, most usual and best loved by the people, the gladiators, when the great amphitheater was packed close, all Rome there to see human beings by the tens and hundreds killing each other, to give the victor the signal for death and eagerly watch the upraised dagger plunge into the helpless body.*

* For additional articles on Rome, Italy, and Greece, see "Cumulative Index to the NATIONAL GEOGRAPHIC MAGAZINE, 1899–1950."

Lyre-playing Apollo Stands Before Sea Murals in the Roman Baths of Leptis Magna

Partial excavations at the Libian seacoast town, the modern Lebda, revealed North Africa's most imposing Roman ruins. The Emperor Septimius Severus lavished public works on this, his home town. Sand-covered mosaics and statuary were remarkably preserved. The scene on page 345 is laid in the basilica of Leptis Magna.

Ancient Rome Brought to Life

By Rhys Carpenter

With Thirty-two Paintings by H. M. Herget

HISTORICAL painters almost invariably start with the theme for their picture, usually some subject recorded by literature which has special appeal to them—Caesar's assassination, Virgil reciting the *Aeneid* to Augustus, Christians in the amphitheater. Having selected the subject, they sketch a background and supply appropriate accessories to their imaginary conception of the principal characters in action.

For our series of paintings for the National Geographic Magazine the procedure has been exactly reversed.

Mr. Herget's compositions are created in intimate collaboration with an archeologist who is a specialist in the civilization portrayed. This collaborator first assembles all available documentary material which can be grouped around some specific cultural aspect—for instance, the costumes and accessories used in official religious ceremonies, or the tableware, drinking vessels and eating utensils, serving trays and mixing bowls, couches and tables—all the furniture and furnishings of a banquet.

When these have been gathered, a conference between artist and archeologist decides how they can be put together into a picture.

Since all the elements are authentic ancient material, nothing that cannot be directly substantiated appears in the final painting.

A good illustration of the workings of this process is afforded by the painting of the Worship of Isis (page 339). The problem was to portray some feature from one of the highly popular mystery cults which existed in addition, and even in opposition, to the official Roman state religion.

No one alive today could reconstruct faithfully the appearance of the secret rites in the worship of the bull-slaying Mithras, because the visual documents do not exist. But for the comparable cult of Egyptian Isis,* when the material had been assembled, it was seen that enough was available for a complete composition.

There were the ruins of a small Isis shrine in Pompeii, a statue of an Isis priestess in the Capitoline Museum in Rome, a carved stone relief showing a cobra coiled upon a circular chest surmounted by the Latin inscription "Sacred to Isis," a column base with carvings of ritual celebrants, and, best of all, a faded fresco showing a ceremony being performed in honor of the goddess before a sanctuary with couchant sphinxes at the head of stairs which were flanked by shrubs and palm trees, with sacred ibises perched about.

Nothing had to be supplied from the imagination except the character studies of the lower-class votaries of this exotic religion. By exercise of ingenuity in adaptation and rearrangement, an effective painting was composed.

Even so fanciful a creation as the summer bathing resort on page 333 has been put together out of modern photographs of Campanian coastal scenery, amid which have been distributed various villas and summer houses taken from some much-damaged Pompeian wall paintings.

The fishermen's method of hauling their net is drawn from actual contemporary Mediterranean practice, which is not likely to have changed much through the ages. Even the sailing boat, the roped quay, and the lighthouse on the point have their ancient authority.

A few of the architectural features in the series are taken directly, or with little change, from surviving remains. The spectacular Alcántara bridge of page 305 still spans the River Tagus in a remote district of western Spain.

The triumphal Arch of Titus in Rome, constructed of Greek marble nearly 2,000 years ago and inadequately patched and rebuilt with Italian travertine early in the 19th century, reappears on page 309 in all its original sumptuous detail.

Other scenes have been resurrected more extensively from destruction. The austerely rich law court which serves as the setting for the trial on page 345 exists today only in a few shattered columns and pilasters among broken walls and floors rather recently freed from the drifting sands of North Africa.

The actual theater at Taormina has been stripped of almost everything seen on page 348 except the loveliness of Sicilian landscape; but it was not difficult to restore stage and gallery and create a play and spectators.

* See "Daily Life in Ancient Egypt," by William C. Hayes, with 32 Herget paintings, pages 71 to 167; from National Geographic, October, 1941.

Staff Photographer W. Robert Moore

Syrian Druses Tread Time-worn Steps to Get Water from a Walled Roman Well

This ancient well serves Shahba, the ancient Philippopolis, in Syria. Paved streets, ruins of large baths, aqueducts, colonnades, temples, and an amphitheater attest a third-century Roman emperor's rebuilding of his home town. Druses are both a race and a religious group, originally from the Lebanon. Modern water jars are made from gasoline tins.

The library of Timgad (page 346) is today a mournful ruin. But the founder's inscription still survives, the columns have been re-erected by the French Service of Antiquities, and the plasterless lower courses of the brick walls still frame the entrance to the semicircular room where the books were once shelved.

Our objective was a series of paintings in which all the range and varied greatness of Rome's cultural achievement should become apparent. Roman religious rites and ceremonies, spectacles and amusements, life in town and country, indoors and out, the trades and industries, the shipping and land communications by the great Roman roads and the marvelous Roman bridges, scenes of the army in the field—all should have their place.

A single plate has been assigned to the pre-Roman culture of Early Latium (page 292), and two others (pages 294 and 296) are devoted to the un-Roman culture of Etruria. In all the rest, though the scene may shift from the capital city and the homeland of Italy to North Africa or Spain, Dalmatia or Greece, the theme is always Roman, while the times are nearly always imperial.

Even so, and no matter how intrinsically Roman the theme, there will appear again and again reminiscences of the Greek past, on which Rome drew so liberally and so consciously. Greek columns and capitals and carven detail will be evident in the architecture, Greek echoes in the sculpture; even Greek garments are worn by the elegants in the Gardens of Lucullus (page 316) for the twilight party held during a period when it was fashionable to despise the native Roman toga.

But all these are largely incidental matters. A distinctively Roman modification of the Greek tradition is evident in the sumptuous

Drawn by Theodora Price and Irvin E. Alleman

Father Tiber Was the Main Artery of Roman Life

Working their way up the coast of Italy, Greek and Phoenician ships found good harbor at Ostia; and the river valley, giving access to the northern interior, made possible a phenomenal trade development. Valley roads such as the Appian and Latin Ways tapped the hill country to the south, supplementing the water routes. "Thus Rome waxed mighty and surrounded her seven hills with a wall" (map, pages 274-5).

interior decoration of the public baths (page 335), in the façade which forms the background to the stage in the scene At the Theater (page 348), and in the colorfully elaborate and archeologically exact painted walls of the houses which enclose the gossiping women in the Rich Man's House (page 322) and the banquet of late republican celebrities (page 318). In the latter, a practiced eye will be able to detect the faces of Cicero and Caesar among the guests at table and discover it to be almost a literal illustration of the dinner party described by Cicero on pages 285-6.

Above all, on the structural and engineering side, the unsurpassable use of the arch to build the bridges over the Tiber (page 298) and the Spanish Tagus and, on the decorative side, the gorgeous intricacies of the mosaic floors in the Emperor's audience chamber (page 313) and the Empress's boudoir (page 314) are achievements beyond the competence of earlier Greece.

Together with their running commentaries, the paintings make intelligible the enormous scope and variety of the Roman world.

It has been said often that the old frontier of the Roman Empire toward the east still pretty closely defines the line where the Western World ceases and the Orient begins.

However that may be, toward west and south the Empire has been overpassed, and in the Americas, Australia, and South Africa is emerging a yet greater world empire conscious of the undying Roman bequest of peace under law, with civic order based on individual rights and the freedom of universal tolerance.

Whether we succeed in achieving these or not, they were the ideals of Rome. In their promulgation and enforcement lay her true greatness. In accepting them, we truly lay claim to our Roman heritage.

© National Geographic Society

Painting by H. M. Herget

"Latium; Whence Came the Latin Race, the Lords of Alba, and the High Walls of Rome" —Virgil, *Aeneid*. "Such a Life the Old Sabines Once Lived; Such, Too, Remus and His Brother"—Virgil, *Georgics*

Before Rome Was Founded

WRITTEN descriptions of the lakeside communities which existed in central Italy in the centuries before the founding of Rome are lacking; yet archeological investigations have made possible the assembly of a picture of this early life.

The village here illustrated is set on the banks of the water-filled crater of a recently extinct volcano, similar to those which rise 1,000 to 3,000 feet in the Alban Hills and form the horizon to the gently rolling country of the Campagna southeast of the site of Rome. Since such a lake would abound in fish and eels and there would be game throughout the wooded slopes, most of the men are shown as fishers and hunters, but an armed warrior suggests that this seemingly idyllic life was not unvexed by quarrels with neighboring clans. The women, doing, as always in the times portrayed, much of the heavy work, are the water carriers.

The houses are of plastered mud, roofed with thatch on rudely cut timbers. Huts like these are still made by the fisherfolk inhabiting the lagoons at the head of the Adriatic; and by study of contemporary examples it is possible to give a realistic interpretation to the tiny clay models of huts which early inhabitants of Italy often put in graves.

During the so-called Early Iron Age, approximately a thousand years before Christ, it was the custom for relatives to preserve the ashes of their dead in a house-shaped receptacle made of baked clay, like a pot or urn. They buried this intended habitation for the dead person's soul in the earth along with weapons for war and for hunting and with painted jars for food and drink. Such burials uncovered in modern times have revealed how the early Latin people were armed in war, what tools they used in their struggle to fell the forest trees and make their clearings for villages, and how they used saplings and reeds for their dwellings.

Their boats must have been dugouts; and since they understood basket making, they had probably already devised weirs for catching fish.

At this period in Italy communities were small and widely scattered. There were as yet no proper roads, and nothing was manufactured on which commerce could prosper, though gold and silver were prized and worked with considerable skill and bronze had long been used for tools and weapons. Iron, because it was much more difficult to reduce from its ore and had to be worked on the anvil and tempered, was slower coming into use.

Where these people originated, how they reached Italy, whence they derived their knowledge of animal husbandry, agriculture, and metallurgy are all questions for disagreement among the experts. But a dominant element in this pre-Roman population of Italy must have come out of Europe—over the Brenner Pass from Bavaria or out of the Danube Basin by way of Trieste—since it imposed and transmitted a legacy of European speech over a considerable portion of the long, narrow Italian peninsula.

Oscan, Umbrian, Volscian, Faliscan, which survive only in brief fragmentary documents, were all a fundamentally identical tongue. Above this the stately Latin of the Romans was one day to tower as the ruling language of all the western world, the source of modern Italian, Spanish, French, and Romanian.

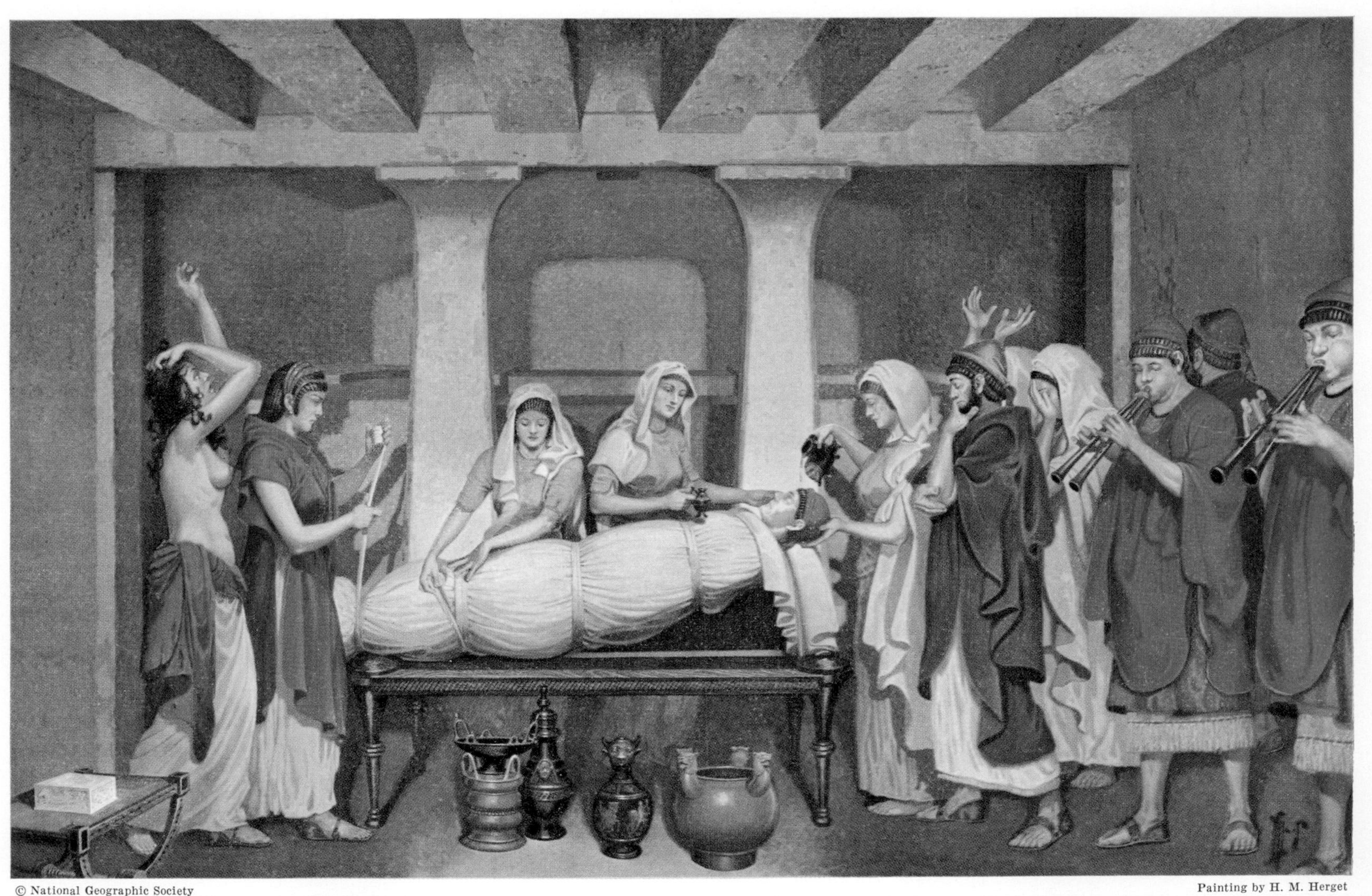

© National Geographic Society

Painting by H. M. Herget

"Lo, Gently in Her Arms She Holds the Aged Face and Bedews with Tears the Revered Gray Hair of Her Father"—Statius, *Silvae*

Etruscan Funeral

By the eighth century B.C. a mysterious ruling people, the Etruscans, had taken over many of the rude communities of central Italy.

Their earliest occupations were near the coast and they only later established themselves in the interior. Therefore, it seems likely that they came by sea from Asia Minor, from the west coast of the land nowadays called Turkey.

The full-blooded Etruscans, though evidently comparatively few in number, seem to have gained their hold by conquest of the native peoples. The center of their power lay to the north of Rome; but the little settlement beside the Tiber (founded, according to local belief, in 753 B. C., not far from the time when they came to Italy) fell easily under Etruscan domination.

The later Romans referred to their Etruscan overlords as the "Tarquin tyrants." When native Latin strength was great enough to expel them from the land, their fall was hailed as an epoch in liberation.

Etruscan occupation, however, had given Rome the basis of much of her civilization, alien and un-European though it might be. From the Tarquin tyrants Rome acquired a considerable part of her religious ritual, such as the pointed caps of her priests and the curved crooks of their augural staffs—probable precursors of the Christian bishop's crozier. She also took from them the axes and bundled rods of her lictors, which Mussolini's fascism was to revive and from which it was to take its name; her trumpets for battle; her lore of divination and auspices; her temple plans and life-size statues of baked clay—all these and much besides.

One strong indication that the Etruscan invasions of Italy came out of the Near East was their remarkable skill in working the native rock for chamber tombs and foundation platforms and in fitting quarried blocks to build walls for their cities. They were the first outstanding architects and engineers of Italy.

From them came the use of the arch, the main prop of Roman architectural mechanics. Its secret was known to the Greeks as to most of the Oriental people of the Mediterranean world, but its consistent exploitation for gateways, galleries, and drains came from the Etruscans.

Early in the seventh century B. C. the Etruscans learned to write, using the Greek letters taught to them apparently by Greek colonists on the Bay of Naples. Since these letters were never much altered from the archaic Greek forms, scholars of today have no difficulty in deciphering the characters in the thousands of surviving Etruscan inscriptions. Translation, however, remains a problem; for there is no obvious key to the weird vocabulary of the Etruscans.

The inner walls of many tombs are covered with brilliantly painted scenes, and the floors of some not touched by collectors are still laden with offerings in precious metals, cast bronze, and jet-black clay. Other tombs have rock-hewn imitations of timbered ceilings and paneled walls.

In these dark rooms the Etruscans laid out their dead on spindle-legged wooden couches, and, to the wailing of mourners and the sound of Asiatic flutes, gave the corpse its last anointing before laying it away in its sarcophagus on a rock-hewn shelf of the innermost recess.

Painting by H. M. Herget

"Thus Surely Etruria Waxed Strong. Thus Rome Became the Fairest of All Things and Enclosed Her Seven Hills with a Single Wall"

Etruscan Festival

ETRUSCAN enjoyment of festivals and physical pleasures in general shocked the Romans. To the severely simple early Roman mind Etruscan dancing seemed undisciplined and lewd, Etruscan music licentious, Etruscan singing immoderate, Etruscan processions beyond all bounds of decorum, and Etruscan feasting beyond all decency.

In later days under the Empire, the cosmopolitan and ultrasophisticated Roman probably left the Etruscan far behind in all such matters, but the old-fashioned Roman was a puritan.

People of today would readily understand the violent throwing about of limbs and bodies by a dancing couple depicted in a wall painting in a tomb at Tarquinia. The long processions in bright-colored garments, the trappings and accoutrements of the religious festivals, the spontaneity and vivacity, the wish to make the most of the fleeting moment—all this would seem nothing unusual to a modern spectator, though the flute music probably would be unintelligible even to the most modern ear and the words of the songs would be meaningless.

All through the 18th and 19th centuries of our era the Etruscan tombs of central Italy yielded a spectacular harvest of decorated vases, golden earrings and necklaces with soldered gold granules of unbelievable minuteness, carvings in ivory and amber, and vessels and furniture of bronze. Some of the finest Etruscan urns proved, to be sure, imported Greek, but others were of native manufacture.

In addition, the tombs fascinated modern eyes with their vividly colored paintings—colors doomed, unfortunately, to fade rapidly as the outside air and light touched once more the pigments which had been sealed away for more than 2,000 years. These paintings furnish our chief information about the banquets, games and processions, dancing, costumes, musical instruments, feast, and festival.

Impressive portions of some of the old Etruscan city walls are still standing, despite the wars of Roman antiquity, the Middle Ages, and modern times. With their arched gateways and superstructures intact, they must have been magnificently strong.

Inside the walls the houses seem to have differed radically from the native Italic and the imported Greek norm. The temples were roofed with wooden timbers which were protected from the weather by a sheathing of terra cotta carrying painted designs in strong colors. Unlike the Greek temples with broad, low steps running all around, they were distinguished by broad colonnaded porches in front and were lifted off the ground on tall platforms.

Rome, which took over so much else of Etruscan religious and cult detail, accepted the Etruscan temple and made it peculiarly her own. For centuries the temple of her three chief gods on the Capitoline Hill was unmistakably Etruscan.

The Etruscans and the Phoenician settlers of Carthage, seafarers all, controlled the western Mediterranean, shutting out the Greeks from the Spanish mines and the Atlantic trade until Rome destroyed Carthage and absorbed Etruria.

By the time of Cicero, Etruscan was becoming a dead language. The Emperor Claudius's treatise on Etruscan speech and institutions was a scholarly delving into the past.

Painting by H. M. Herget

"The Steersman's Cry, the Shouting of the Bargees, as over Sacred Tiber Skim the Gliding Keels"—Martial

Bridge over the Tiber

"TIBER, Father Tiber, to whom the Romans pray," started Rome toward greatness.

Until the seventh century B. C. little sea-borne commerce had reached Italy. What trade there was among the villages had been carried on by means of pack animals. Then the Phoenicians, and after them the Greeks, came coasting Italian shores, looking for hides and raw metals, and worked their way up the Tiber to Rome.

Open trails in the long river valley tapped resources of the interior communities all the way up to the rugged range of central mountains which shut off the eastern descent to the Adriatic. Thus the little city on the Tiber began to prosper, and under Etruscan rule trade and industry waxed mightily.

Rome grew from a group of hamlets into a walled town, from a small trade center into the ruling power of Latium, then Italy, and finally the entire Mediterranean. By imperial times grain ships from Egypt and other parts of North Africa, boats laden with olive oil and wine from Greece and Spain, were discharging their loads at the Tiber wharves and filling the warehouses at Ostia, seaport for the capital. Local transport by raft and barge and rowboat on the river vied with that by road and wagon.

Before reaching Rome, 20 miles from the sea, the Tiber, seldom fordable and often in heavy flood, has already run ten times that distance. The early settlement, ringed by the "Servian" Wall, lay wholly on the left bank; and all land communication with Etruria and the country to the north necessitated crossing the stream.

To the growth of the city, therefore, bridges were indispensable. The first spans, their timbers carried on piles, were easily swept away by floods, but after the Romans had learned from the Etruscans how to use stone blocks, the wooden structures were replaced by a bridge of stone on rock piers and arches. The modern visitor may still see in the stream close to the bend where the Forum communicates with the riverbank a few shattered remnants of such a bridge, built in 179 B. C.

A little farther upstream, pedestrians crossing to the island sacred to Aesculapius, god of medicine, move over the arches of another ancient bridge. This, bearing the clearly carved name of its builder, the Road Commissioner Lucius Fabricius, is only one of many structures still enduring to which the Romans set their hands 2,000 or more years ago.

Throughout the territory that was once the Roman Empire, arched viaducts may be seen today. These carried military roads or water channels over gullies and streams and even across great river valleys. The Pont du Gard, which brought water to Roman Nemausus on the site of present-day Nîmes, remains standing in southern France.

North African remnants of the old aqueducts testify that ancient Romans had a greater mastery over the encroaching desert than modern engineers have yet achieved.

Caesar's famous bridge across the Rhine was a temporary structure for military need. Trajan, however, bridged the Danube with a permanent crossing nearly three-quarters of a mile long. In Trajan's reign was erected the superb Alcántara in western Spain (page 305).

Market and Wharf at a Roman Port

The Near East today perpetuates the bazaar, where in a single street or under a single roof are grouped all the competing dealers in a commodity. From such bazaars, still to be seen in Athens, İstanbul, or Tunis, this Roman covered market differs little except for the architectural vastness of the brick-faced and plastered-concrete vaults thrown over the line of shops by the imperial builders.

Daylight from high overhead streams into the dark, cool niches where the lanternmakers, cutlers, coppersmiths, and other metalworkers display their wares. At the end of the broad central public way, the whole vault is left open to admit light and air.

Such a market can still be seen in Rome amid the excavated ruins of Trajan's Forum in the heart of the city. If it were built to take advantage of the proximity of the warehouses and landing stages of a seaport, instead of the tall buildings of metropolitan Rome, it might open on paved quays and jutting wharves against which the sailing cargo vessels would be moored stern first.

The bales and bundles are strewn about, waiting for the porters and carters, who are asleep or idle during the heavy heat of midday. In the sunlit open, a chance crowd of shoppers has gathered to watch a mountebank girl perform her juggling act.

Such quays, paved with slabs of marble, were common to the larger maritime cities in the Greek East and the Roman West of the Mediterranean. For Rome itself, Ostia was the port; and here a magnificent harbor town sprang up, with capacious storehouses for the grain on which the lower classes depended. There were market places, open and covered, baths and a theater, temples and shrines, and brick apartment houses many stories high, with overhanging balconies giving them an almost modernistic appearance.

In another mouth of the Tiber, close by, Trajan constructed a supplementary harbor. This was a great sheltered basin with wharves and docks protected by moles and breakwaters marked by a lighthouse toward the open sea.

The Mediterranean economy depended principally on grain, oil, and wine. Since wine had to be aged, a reserve could be stored to carry over bad vintage years; and the hardiness and long life of the olive trees ensured a supply of oil. Grain, more perishable and rapidly consumed, was the most precarious factor in Roman economic and, consequently, political life.

The Romans fell heir to a highly organized system of exchange of goods which they exploited and expanded through every corner of their inland sea. Under the Empire, caravans brought rugs out of Persia and even silk out of China. A fleet sailed annually to Ceylon and perhaps to India, bringing back gems and spices and other rarities up the Red Sea and thence by canal to the Nile and Alexandria.

The Suez Canal thus had a predecessor which had been opened first under the ancient Pharaohs. It had been kept open with extreme difficulty, however, and was hardly of any commercial importance except for a few centuries under Roman rule. It would be an exaggeration to say that it ever represented the "lifeline of empire" for the Romans of Italy; yet the parallel with British imperial trade is there.

Painting by H. M. Herget

"Think Not that Any Distinction Can Be Drawn Between Perfumery and Leather: the Smell of Gain Is Good from Any Source"—Juvenal

At the Slave Market

In classical civilization it was taken for granted that much of the labor of everyday life, including agriculture and the arts and crafts, should be performed by slaves. The Romans used the Greek island of Dēlos as one convenient center for a slave trade so big that some contemporary accounts, hardly credible, put the number of slaves sold under hammer there in a single day as high as 10,000.

The Dēlos auction platform pictured here is built of planks and timbers and sheltered by an awning suspended on two long poles. Roman purchasers, some of them professional dealers and others personal bidders, wander over the mottled marble pavement, examining the slaves still to be offered or bidding for those put up for sale.

Although the range of types and races represented here among the seated captives is probably more varied and comprehensive than would normally be assembled at any single auction, the composition is intended to suggest the geographic extent of slave traders' activities.

Asiatics were valued for their astuteness and submissiveness, blacks for their exotic appearance, Germans for their stature and strength. Most prized, however, seem always to have been the Greeks. The Roman, though he often rebelled against Danaan veneer on his native Latin traditions, thoroughly respected the Greeks' superior intelligence, language, and culture.

One slave might fetch considerably less than a hundred dollars in the open market, whereas another of superior quality might be sold for several thousand. High-grade dancing girls and mistresses for the wealthiest Roman houses brought excellent prices. At auction men and women alike, stripped and sold naked, were handled and examined like animals. Strict laws protected the purchaser's interests, with prescribed penalties for misrepresentation or fraud.

Basically, slavery was the outcome of war, for captives must either be set to work profitably or be put to death to get them out of the way. The number of captives taken while Rome was using her armies for conquest and territorial expansion was enormous, the subjection of Greece and Macedonia alone netting, it is estimated, a million slaves. When piracy was rampant in the Mediterranean, great numbers of slaves were acquired from this source also.

Both of these easy sources of supply dwindled, however, when Pompey suppressed the pirates, and the Emperor Augustus set limits to the rapid territorial expansion of the Roman dominions. Scenes such as that in the illustration became a thing of the past.

Since slaves could always be set free, and the practice of manumission was widespread, and since Roman policy consistently tended toward extending rather than restricting the right of citizenship, the proportion of slaves to free citizens began to fall. Rome consequently had ever less and less to fear from social rebellions from beneath, such as threatened her very existence in the earlier days.

Although Rome moved toward an ever-widening democracy of economic equality, slavery was never abolished. It merged ultimately in the serfdom of medieval feudalism, which is responsible for the profound class distinction which lingers in most of Europe to this day.

© National Geographic Society

Painting by H. M. Herget

"Doubtless This Slave Girl Is of Royal Parentage; Her Family Merely Suffers Cruel Fate. Think Not that One So True and Honorable Could Be the Daughter of a Mean Mother"—Horace, *Odes*

The Roman Army Crosses Alcántara in Spain

Rome held her empire together by magnificent roads over which she moved her administrative officials and her garrisons into the remotest of her provinces. To shift her armies with maximum speed, she relied on the broad, straight, all-weather highways, traces of which still exist along a 4,000-mile track from Scotland to the Persian Gulf and on the even longer stretch from Morocco through Egypt to Turkistan.

In constructing these highways, the engineers often selected a conspicuous landmark on the horizon and ran the road toward it with surprising disregard for topography. Cuts and fills, diked embankments, viaducts and bridges, and tunnels all contributed to preserving a straight direction and an even grade.

The roadbed was always excavated to hardpan or solid rock. Layers of rubble and coarse concrete packing carried a surface of closely fitted paving blocks. Curbs and shoulders and drainage ditches were added; and the result long outlasted the empire which created it.

The great bridges over the larger river valleys were the most spectacular feature of the military network of communication. Initial responsibility for their construction must have lain with the military commanders and provincial governors acting in the emperor's name; but local communities were not slow to copy these higher authorities.

In A. D. 105 the eleven communes inhabiting the hill country where the chief river of Spain, the Tagus, crosses the Portuguese frontier petitioned Trajan to be allowed to defray the cost of a bridge across the river. It was built entirely of granite blocks set without use of mortar. The six arches are opposed two and two, with the shortest under the approaches and the broadest pair with 90-foot spans carried on piers set in midstream. From the footing of the piers in the river bed to the roadway these arches carry, the height is nearly 200 feet.

An army could march across with eight men abreast, and 2,000 troops could be crowded on the bridge at one time. In marching order, however, a legion with its horsemen, artillery, and baggage trains would spread out for more than a mile, its van disappearing around the spur of the opposite hills before the rear guard reached the river. Three such legions were usually stationed in Spain.

The Roman bridgeways often carried arches at the end or, as on Alcántara, at the middle of the span. These could be fitted with tollgates or with heavy barriers to check unwelcome passers.

Alcántara was blown up by the British under Sir Arthur Wellesley (later the Duke of Wellington) in the Peninsular War, 1809, and by the Carlist insurgents in 1836. The arches were repaired, however, and the bridge stands in use today, one of the grandest of all Roman remains.

The *ballistae* and catapults being hauled across the bridge have been dismantled for transport. Neither, of course, ever carried an explosive charge, but relied on the sudden release of tightly twisted thongs made of hair or sinew. Even so, such crude artillery was sufficiently feared and effective in siegework to be worth transporting on oxcarts or mule-drawn wagons along with the marching legions.

Painting by H. M. Herget

"Remember Thou, O Roman, to Rule the Nations with Thy Sway. These Shall Be Thine Arts: to Crown Peace with Law, to Spare the Humbled, and to Take in War the Proud"—Virgil, *Aeneid*

Siege of a Walled City

EAST of the Mediterranean, where Greek architectural traditions had introduced a highly advanced type of fortification, the Roman armies encountered enemies quite different from the forest-inhabiting barbarians of Europe—enemies who stood siege behind high walls with powerful projecting towers sheltering metal-reinforced gates.

In the illustration the direct attack against the strongest part of the city defenses is largely a diversion; and the sapping at the left, under the "tortoise" of interlocked shields, is little more than a feint. Still, the defenders on the walls strive mightily with javelins, arrows, and boulders to break up the Roman assault before the diggers succeed in tunneling beneath the foundations to open a breach in the tower or the wielders of the metal-tipped, ram-headed timber shatter the bronze-studded panels of the portal.

Meanwhile, beyond the limits of the picture, at another sector of the encircling city wall, preparations are under way for a more prolonged siege in case this direct attack fails. The machinery which the Romans could bring against fortified strongholds attained truly formidable proportions. Engines of considerable variety and great mechanical ingenuity were employed.

Movable towers of wood, taller than the parapets of the walls, even walls 50 to 60 feet high, were erected of uprights and interlacing timbers on bases carried on huge, solid, wooden wheels. These ungainly structures were trundled close to the walls by the soldiers working under the protection of their interlocked shields. The towers carried platforms at several levels, firm enough to support artillery batteries of mechanical slings and still more powerful catapults.

From these points of vantage the attackers could clear the parapets until opportunity offered for lowering from one of the siege towers a wooden drawbridge across which a storming party could swarm to spread left and right along the wall top. More and more troops could be thrown in by this lofty bridgehead until the gate, if not battered in from without, could be opened from inside.

Alternatively, the walls could be undermined with tunnels and the resultant galleries shored up with timbers. The props of these galleries were then doused with pitch and set afire. With their collapse an entire sector of wall would fall in, leaving an open breach. The sapping trenches were protected by sloping roofs covered with earth, wickerwork, hides, or even wet blankets.

During the fifth century B. C. the superlative Greek technique of wall building gave a definite advantage to the defensive; but during the next century, in the time of Philip and Alexander of Macedon, the attack began to make good this handicap. Such engineers as Archimedes improved methods of assault in Hellenistic times; and finally the Romans made such remarkable advances in siegecraft that no adversary could build strongholds impregnable to their well-trained armies.

The decline of Roman civilization led to a lamentable lapse in siegecraft during the Middle Ages, so that the advantage shifted back to the defense. Hence the maze of petty strongholds, châteaux, and castles in which the feudal world shut itself up, until the advent of gunpowder gave attackers again the upper hand.

Painting by H. M. Herget

"Meanwhile, about Every Gate They Press to Slay the Foe . . . With Left Hands They Hold Up Protecting Shields. . . ."—Virgil, *Aeneid*

Triumphal Procession

IN REPUBLICAN times a Roman general who had conquered a foe on the field of battle and acquired new territory for his fatherland could petition the senate for a formal triumph. The senate would then assemble outside the city walls in the sanctuary of the war-goddess Bellona and, if favorable to the request, enact the legal fiction of extending the victorious commander authority within city limits.

Without such permission, the conqueror would lose all rank the instant he entered Rome. Fear of a military *coup d'état* by a victorious leader with his armed followers in the very seat of government was obviously behind this law, which in imperial times became so strict that only the emperor himself was ever permitted to celebrate a triumph.

The triumph having been voted by the senate, a long procession of horse-drawn floats, laden with booty and followed by captive princes and generals walking in chains, was assembled in the Field of Mars, in the bend of the Tiber opposite St. Peter's. This district, though densely settled in later times, lay beyond the old "Servian" Wall of republican Rome and thus technically outside the city.

Thence the senators and magistrates escorted the triumphal procession along an established route through the city streets and up the winding ascent to the Temple of Jupiter atop the Capitoline Hill. Sacrifices and thank offerings were made at the temple, then the prisoners were led away, traditionally to their death. A sumptuous feast followed, to which soldiery and populace were all invited.

In imperial times the emperor accorded a triumph rode on a gilded and laurel-wreathed car drawn by four horses, his military costume brilliant with gold breastplate and red-purple mantle. The procession swung past the huge Flavian Amphitheater, known since the Middle Ages as the "Colosseum," and followed the paved Sacred Way under the triumphal Arch of Titus. From there the road led to the Forum and the Capitoline Hill.

Domitian built the Arch of Titus in A. D. 81 to commemorate his predecessor's sack of Jerusalem and humiliation of the Jews. Later emperors added two more of these curious free-standing structures to adorn the processional way—one just southwest of the Colosseum in the name of the Christian Emperor Constantine, the other in honor of Septimius Severus, at a corner of the Forum where the Capitoline ascent began.

Such imperial arches were not confined to Rome. One of the finest stands at Benevento, and another at Ancona. Both were in honor of Trajan.

Except for a few that served as city gates, these arches had no utilitarian purpose whatever. One supposition is that they represented the yoke of submission under which captives were forced to march.

Representations of triumphal arches on coins and medallions always show them carrying a bronze chariot with four horses, similar to those in traditional use for the actual processions. The celebrated four bronze horses of St. Mark's in Venice are almost certainly from such a monument.

The Colosseum, largest of Roman amphitheaters, was completed by Titus in A. D. 80. Although two-thirds of the mammoth structure have disappeared, enough remains to remind us that "While stands the Coliseum, Rome shall stand; and with its fall, falls Rome and all the world."

Painting by H. M. Herget

"To Be Led Through the City, a Captive in Chains by the Conqueror's Chariot, Whereon the Victor Rides Resplendent with Purple and Gold"—Livy

Unconditional Surrender

THE WHOLE Roman Empire was held with only about 150,000 citizen soldiers, supplemented by a roughly equal number of non-Italian auxiliaries!

For efficiency in attacking, subduing, occupying, and administering enemy territory, the famed Roman legion has seldom or never been equaled by another military organization. The same legionaries who routed the enemy in the open could reduce a stronghold by siegecraft, and after the foe had capitulated they could handle disarmament control, police patrol, and general administrative supervision.

Julius Caesar, the best known and probably the most gifted of the Latin army leaders who not merely conquered but pacified, organized, and administered the hostile and rebellious nations which surrounded Italy, was not unique. Many of the emperors who came after him served for arduous months and even years in the field at the head of armed forces.

Trajan, a professional soldier born and bred, passed the greater part of his life with the troops. His exploits on the Danube frontier are vividly pictured on the relief carvings which wind around the marble shaft of a spectacular hundred-foot column, still standing above the ruins of his great hall of justice in Rome.

Besides battles in the deep forests and at the river crossed by the famous bridge, these reliefs show scenes in camp, the siege and capture of Dacian towns, surrender of prisoners, harangues to the soldiers, and distribution of rewards.

Some sixty years after Trajan's conquests the Danube once again beheld the embattled Roman legions under another great emperor, Marcus Aurelius. Two revolting German tribes in the lands which are today Czechoslovakia and Hungary fought stubbornly for several years and were as stubbornly pursued, defeated, and destroyed, with the Emperor himself in charge of the difficult campaign. The Piazza Colonna in Rome takes its modern name from the ancient hundred-foot Column of Marcus Aurelius, on which in rivalry with Trajan's Column the spiral band of carvings narrates the incidents of these Germanic wars.

The illustration is adapted from scenes on these two famous columns. A strategic pass in a densely wooded and mountainous region of central Europe, "across the Rhine and Danube," has been occupied by native tribes with a large log-built stockade set on an outcropping ledge of rock. Below it are the houses and stalls of a village, similarly built of logs hewn from the forests and set on foundations of roughly trimmed and fitted field stone.

The legionaries have had little difficulty in setting the stockade on fire by lobbing flaming timbers with their artillery and are now busy rounding up the few remaining warriors who still show fight. The women and unarmed males have already been captured and brought to the foot of the Roman commander-in-chief's podium, hastily put together from felled trees by the sappers.

Surrender is unconditional; but the subsequent treatment of the captives will not be merciless except where treachery and renewed rebellion prove to the occupying military authorities that the lesson of defeat has not been fully learned by these Germanic tribes.

Painting by H. M. Herget

"Germany Has Heard the Clash of Arms Through All Her Skies: the Alps Were Shaken with the Unaccustomed Sounds"—
Virgil, *Georgics*

An Embassy to Caligula

During the first two centuries of the Christian Era Rome was beyond all challenge the center of the world's civilization. Only China in the remote Orient deserved to be mentioned in the same breath.

The older cultural lands around the shores of the Mediterranean had long ago lost their importance. Egypt and Greece were minor Roman provinces; Assyria had vanished utterly; Phoenicia, Judaea, and part of Arabia had been absorbed in the Empire.

Babylonia and Persia had yielded to a hybrid culture in which Iranian, Scythian, and Greek were confused. Athens was a provincial university town.

Resurrected from utter destruction, Carthage was no longer Punic. Alexandria and Antioch were turbulent and dissolute, and, however rich and culture-loving, not the arbiters of the Empire's fashions. But Rome was a city of perennial splendor, the center of the world's interest.

To Rome came missions and embassies from all the earth. Augustus had received delegations from India, Claudius emissaries from Ceylon. In A. D. 99 Indian ambassadors sought audience with Trajan, but Trajan, a military man of plain speech and direct bearing, had no flair for pomp.

Not so had been Caligula, though the nickname *Caligula,* meaning "little boot," referred to the soldier footgear he had worn as the boy idol of Roman troops in the Rhineland. He loved to dress, not as a magistrate but as a triumphing field commander, and, enthroned godlike, to accept the adoration of his gorgeous visitors from beyond the eastern boundaries of his domain. In contrast, the sedate togas of his councilors bore witness that the strength of Rome still lay in simplicity and dignity.

The Roman toga was based on the draping of a single piece of cloth about the body, so wrapped as to leave the right arm free at need, but the left usually concealed. Although, when spread out, it was readily distinguishable in cut from the rectangular Greek *himation,* the dress of the two nations was essentially similar. The style survives in the robes of Arabs and North African Berbers.

The European sewn and fitted costume, with divided trousers and sleeved jacket, though not classical, was familiar to antiquity and common in northern Europe. Britons and Gauls wore sleeved coats and loose trousers; the Scythian horsemen of the Russian steppes, precursors of the Cossacks, wore tight breeches with straps under the instep; and the renowned Iranian highlanders wore trousers.

The mad Caligula had a dizzy bridge constructed to unite the Palatine and Capitoline hilltops. On this he might pass across to commune with his "other self," Jupiter.

Nero's insatiate ambition found even the Palatine too confined for him. When the great fire destroyed the lower district, he covered this with buildings and gardens utterly extravagant. As soon as he died, almost all of his fabulous House of Gold was demolished.

Some few decorated chambers in underground stories survived, to serve as inspiration for the arabesques with which Raphael and his pupils adorned the Pope's balcony apartment in the Vatican. The emperors returned to the Palatine, which they covered with ever more showy constructions.

© National Geographic Society

Painting by H. M. Herget

"Augustus Shall Be Recognized as a God on Earth by Britons Subject to His Rule and by the Dreadful Persians"—Horace, *Odes*

 Painting by H. M. Herget

"Terrified by Her Threats and Ill Temper, He (Nero) Determined to Destroy Her; and after He Had Three Times Tried to Poison Her and Each Time Discovered that She Possessed the Antidote, He Contrived a Mechanism by Which the Ceiling Should Fall on Her While She Slept. But She Learned of This in Time"—Suetonius, *Vita Neronis*

An Empress Makes Ready

TO THE HISTORIAN Gibbon's scathing catalogue of first-century emperors, "the dark, unrelenting Tiberius, the furious Caligula, the feeble Claudius, the profligate and cruel Nero, the beastly Vitellius, and the timid, inhuman Domitian" might well be added the list of their no less sinister womenfolk: the dissipated and shameless Julia, the intriguing and insatiate Agrippina, the profligate and reckless Messalina, the calculating and unscrupulous Poppaea Sabina.

Nor was it only the evil emperors who had evil wives and daughters. There was no more virtuous character in Roman imperial history than the benevolent Antoninus Pius or the grave Marcus Aurelius; but Faustina, who was at once daughter of the first and wife of the second, was an out-and-out wanton, whose violent intrigues were familiar to everyone except her unsuspecting and devoted husband.

Lucilla, the sister of the succeeding and thoroughly vicious Emperor Commodus, almost matched her brother in evil living. She was finally put to death along with a band of her wild lovers for attempting his assassination.

Although the younger Agrippina lived only 43 years, she had time to amass a reputation for infamy rarely attained by her sex. She was sister to the lunatic Caligula and mother to the worse than useless Nero. The latter repaid his filial debt to her by trying to have her drowned in a collapsible boat and, when she was fished alive out of the Bay of Naples, coolly had her murdered by other means ashore.

Perhaps he had a reason, for she was accused of poisoning her second husband. Not only that, but after beguiling her imperial uncle Claudius into marrying her, she fed him a mushroom from which he promptly died.

The Latin poet who satirized Claudius's mushroom eating pointed out that "there is nothing a woman won't do when she puts emeralds around her neck and fastens huge pearls in her distended ears."

Describing a boudoir scene like that in the illustration, the same poet wrote: "And another maid on her left will be combing her hair and twisting it into a braid while a family servant gives advice, and after her each in turn of age and dignity offers her opinion. So great is the business of attaining beauty!"

A peacock, perhaps imported from Ceylon especially for the Empress, perches on the edge of a great porphyry basin.

Not until the reign of Claudius was the wonderful purple-red volcanic stone known as porphyry brought from desert quarries beside the Red Sea to be cut and polished. Large quantities were imported later for imperial palaces and public buildings, particularly the baths.

So difficult is porphyry to work, however, that after the collapse of Rome artisans lost the secret. For this reason it ceased to be used in Europe until stonecutters of the late Italian Renaissance rediscovered how to handle it and helped themselves to the only supply then known, shattered fragments surviving from imperial days.

Plate glass was unknown to antiquity, but translucent glass lumps could be set in the brick-ribbed vaults and domes. These admitted a diffused daylight on the gaily painted plaster walls and the mosaic floors.

Painting by H. M. Herget

"This Most Noble, Most Handsome Youth of Patrician Family, Poor Wretch, to Be Sacrificed to Messalina's Eyes!"—Juvenal

In the Gardens of Lucullus

TWO THOUSAND years ago Lucullus, fabulously wealthy conqueror of Asiatic kings, patron of arts and letters, and lover of luxury and gracious living, converted the straggling slope of the Pincian Hill into a pleasure park with groves full of the Greek statuary he was one of the first Romans to appreciate. The Pincian Hill is still covered with terraced gardens overlooking the city.

A generation after Lucullus, Sallust, an unscrupulous civil servant who had amassed a fortune in North Africa, retired to write history. He laid out for himself even more sumptuous gardens on the slopes of the Quirinal.

Nearly a century passed. Then Messalina, predecessor of Agrippina in the series of wives of the dull-witted, scholarly Emperor Claudius, set covetous eyes on the Gardens of Lucullus. She schemed successfully to have Valerius Asiaticus, who had become the owner, charged with treason and condemned to death. Of course his property was confiscated to the imperial treasury, as were also eventually the estates of Sallust and others.

Amid the lovely surroundings conceived by Lucullus Messalina held her revels and debauched her lovers. It seems poetic justice that at the age of 26 she was secretly put to death here on advice of her husband's mentor, the freedman Narcissus.

Social wars under Marius and Sulla had brought on a rule of strong, unscrupulous men which culminated in dictatorship under Julius Caesar and monarchical control under dynasties beginning with Augustus.

The Roman satirists of the first century after the birth of Christ strongly disapproved of the emancipated women who now did so shockingly as they pleased.

Of a beauty Juvenal wrote: "She flits boldly about town, turning up wherever the men are gathered, and talking to the officers in their long military cloaks. She knows what is going on all over the world, what the Chinese and the Russians are up to, and all the disreputable gossip of the city."

Deploring overluxurious living, he warned: "We are suffering from the evils of protracted peace; more cruel than war, the hand of luxury has been laid upon us. No deed of lust or violence is lacking, now that poverty is dead in Rome. Soft wealth has corrupted the age with foul ease."

Yet the spoiled and idle rich young men of Rome could join the army as officer cadets and go to the wars to throw themselves wholeheartedly into a life of hardship and heroism. No modern critic of the open depravity of the early imperial court, headed and abused by such sinister figures as Tiberius, Caligula, and Nero, should forget how soon these conditions were to be followed by the efficient, sober, and manly rule of the vast Empire under the businesslike Trajan, the cultured Hadrian, the Humane Antoninus, and the sage Marcus Aurelius.

These were to make the Mediterranean and Europe so peaceful, prosperous, and politically stable that Gibbon wrote: "If a man were called to fix the period in the history of the world during which the condition of the human race was most happy and prosperous, he would without hesitation name that which elapsed from the death of Domitian [A. D. 96] to the accession of Commodus" [A. D. 180].

Painting by H. M. Herget

"I Like Dinner Parties! There I Can Discuss Whatever Is Afoot and Turn Grumbling into Guffaws"—Cicero, *Ad Familiares*

A Distinguished Dinner Party

For a lady to eat at table, reclining with the men and responding to their toasts as the young matron is doing at the wedding anniversary dinner illustrated, was an innovation in the days of Cicero and Caesar. Custom until then had decreed that even a wife, though she ate alone with her husband, should sit while he reclined on his couch.

Equally novel was the use of a round table, with mattresses arranged about it in a semicircle in place of the traditional three straight divans forming three sides of a square and accommodating exactly nine persons in strict order of social rank.

The circular arrangement permitted eight or ten to be disposed quite as comfortably and ceremonially as nine. Where the old arrangement was used, it was bad manners to put four on a couch, and a couch with only two drew attention to the empty space.

The silverware is of the finest at this party; and the food and wine are of the best—fowl and suckling pig, some sort of joint, an excellent mullet, fruit, and perhaps "a draught from the Alban Hills or a Setan wine whose vintage year the dust has obliterated."

To be sure, the menu lacks some of the items once sarcastically extolled by Juvenal—"a mullet from Corsica, a lamprey from the Sicilian Straits, a huge goose liver, a capon as big as a goose, and a steaming boar, with truffles in springtime, and apples for dessert."

First, there should be tasting of dainties, *gustatio,* and then the main courses, to be followed by dessert of pastry and fruit and a more leisurely sipping of some of the sweeter after-dinner wines. But wine was seldom drunk without a generous admixture of water.

These diners are not the epicures whose line runs from the great Lucullus and passes to the rich *parvenu* Trimalchio of Petronius's celebrated banquet. Probably no one at the table could "tell at the first taste whether an oyster is from the Circean beds or the Lucrine rocks and guess at a glance from what shore a sea urchin comes."

One can eat much more lying down, and a party like this might last for hours—without the disgusting Epicurean remedy for an overfull stomach satirized by Horace. It is still daylight, and though there are no windows in this room of false columns and plastered walls, on which the shutters are painted stripes and the panes are only panels in a bright pattern like watered silk, there is abundant light because the hither wall is open to a sunlit garden court.

The room, specifically a dining room, belongs to a wealthy house built on the slope of the Palatine, before the emperors pre-empted all the hill for their palaces. Just there, only a few years ago, overcurious moderns discovered the remains of precisely such a room with enough of the painted plaster to show the colors and the decorative scheme.

Dinners began in midafternoon and lasted until dark. There were those who ordered torches and lamp stands brought in and prolonged the eating and drinking till midnight; but the penalty was the home-going through the dark, noisy streets under the high, overhanging tenement houses whence "from the topmost roof some leaky, broken vessel may be pitched from a window down on your head!"

Painting by H. M. Herget

"That Corner of the Land Beyond All Others for Me Smiles, Where Heaven Sends Warm Mists and a Slow Spring"—Horace, *Odes*

Horace's Villa in the Sabine Hills

"WHO BUT the wealthy get any sleep in Rome?" complained the satirist Juvenal.

No wonder that the city-pent Roman dreamed of the countryside. No wonder that with the passing of winter Horace hied him to his beloved farm in the Sabine Hills.

Such retreats had been increasingly popular since late republican times. Cicero in his *Letters* admits owning no fewer than seven villas scattered between Rome and the Bay of Naples. So great an abundance of habitations was due partly to the need for resting places where he or his friends could put up on their journeys to the south. There were no hotels for the public in those times and the taverns offered only wretched accommodation.

Several of Cicero's villas were luxurious country houses, such as that at Tusculum in the hills overlooking the distant city, and included baths with warm-water pools, elaborate gardens, and rooms for reading, writing, and banqueting. All the comforts of the city were reproduced; yet no sooner was the typical Roman installed in the idyllic solitude of a country villa than he longed for the diversions and excitements of the city, to cry with Cicero, "The city! the city! That is the place to live, that is the light of life! Travel is mere concealment and misery for men whose activities can shed luster on Rome!"

The cosmopolitan town might be the perfect environment for those who practiced politics or lived off their fellows' wealth and favors; but there were professions which did not lend themselves so well to its endless interruptions. Horace, the court poet whose elegant verses were intended for cultivated city-bred ears, passed his days by preference in a solitary villa on a farm in the Sabine Hills. There, in the interval of talking to his rustic neighbors and overseeing the homely tasks of the eight slaves who worked his farm, he wrote the most carefully well-bred and cultured verse that Rome was ever to produce.

Through the winter he kept reasonably warm by returning to Rome; but the spring saw him back again to watch the anemones break on the hillside surrounding his little valley. He returned to the country long before his own carefully tended garden beds had bloomed behind their trellis grills below the long, raised portico where he used to wander up and down in sun or shade as the season changed.

Horace was neither wealthy nor nobly born. For him the simple actualities of peasant life were familiar and attractive. His country place was no transference of the magnificence of the Roman palaces to an ampler setting of fountain-cooled terraces and stately walks. His ancestors had lived off the land, not merely on it; and though the house was airy and comfortable, it smacked of rural simplicity and the devices of the farm.

There he enjoyed greater happiness than Rome or the emperor's court could give, a solitary but not a lonely bachelor. There, on occasion, his intimate friends from the town must have visited him. Among them the greatest of all Latin poets, his own unrivaled contemporary, Virgil, may well have sought him out in his retreat, bringing with him the young Propertius, a minor poet who wrote love verses such as neither Virgil nor Horace tried to equal.

Painting by H. M. Herget

"You're Pleasant and Unpleasant, Agreeable and Sour Alike: I Can't Live with You—and I Can't Live Without You!"—Martial

Interior of a Rich Man's House

THE TYPICAL Roman house, like Roman civilization in general, was a hybrid of native Italic, early Etruscan, and imported Greek. Actually, it was two houses in one.

The front half, to which the street door gave access through a side corridor, perpetuated ancient native construction by using an open rain-catch in the center of the ceiling of the large main room, or *atrium*. Above this, on the outside, the tiled roof sloped down from all four sides, throwing the rain through spouts into a marble-lined basin set in the floor.

There opened off this amply proportioned atrium several minor rooms, some useful as servants' quarters, and a master room, with wide doorway hung with curtains against the draft, the entertainment room of the large double house. In the atrium a rich and important proprietor received his following and adherents, his "clients" as they were called, at the early-morning reception with which he began his day.

Beyond the reception room with its flanking passageways for servants and familiars, the sunlight shines between the columns of a portico surrounding an open garden court, forerunner of the *patio* which Rome bequeathed to Spain and Spain transmitted to her American colonies. Here began the inner portion of the Roman double house, the part borrowed directly from Greece.

Sunroom, dining room, gaming room, and lounge were all likely to be located off this peristyle court. The main sleeping quarters were probably upstairs in a second story, the women's rooms almost invariably so. The ground floor turned blank walls to the outdoor world of streets and alleys, since it drew its light directly down into atrium and peristyle; but in the second story there were windows and balconies, equipped no doubt with shutters and grills.

Roman women were by no means confined to their quarters in Oriental seclusion. Even though chance visitors or business callers never reached the inner house, there was nothing to prevent the married women of the house from appearing in the atrium or frequenting the houses of their friends for news and gossip.

A wealthy Roman house was not so elaborately furnished as its American counterpart; but it was more carefully decorated, and color was used more freely. On the floors, where there would seldom be matting or rugs, the favorite tradition, as in Italy today, was for the coolness of tile, elaborated in the more important rooms to the geometric fantasies of intricate mosaic settings.

The most costly and spectacular way to decorate the walls was to cover them from top to bottom with a veneer of thin, sawn slabs of marble, white or colored, blank or veined, with contrasting materials such as alabaster, porphyry, and mother-of-pearl inserted in patterned shapes.

Painted imitations of the glories of veined and colored marble satisfied most requirements for private homes, however. More tasteful were decorative designs applied directly to the finished plaster.

Paintings in the grand manner, echoing famous Greek masters, were not put on canvas and hung, as in our homes, but were copied directly on the plaster walls themselves. Our most extensive information about the lost paintings of Greece has come to us from these copies, discovered in Pompeii under the ashes of Vesuvius.

© National Geographic Society

Painting by H. M. Herget

"There Was Nothing Lacking That the Poor Man's Table Requires, and Much There Was That Rich from Poor Might Borrow"—Virgil, *Moretum*

Vegetable Market

THE VEGETABLE market with its tented booths set up before the gate of a fortified town displays a surprising variety of foodstuffs bought and sold in Roman times. Although orange and lemon trees had not been introduced to the European West, nor had white and sweet potatoes and tomatoes migrated from the New World, the rich man's fare from garden and orchard was fabulously composed. Even the poor had a wide choice of things within their means, though leek and garlic were their favorites.

In late summer green-rinded watermelons, the much-prized honey melon, and large yellow Persian melons were available. Many kinds of grapes of excellent quality were abundant; and apples, though small and savory rather than showy in appearance, were much in demand.

All through Roman times there were pears and plums, the latter often dried as prunes; and quinces, which were better for preserves than for eating raw. Apricots were introduced rather late from Armenia, and peaches from Persia. Cherries had been mean and poor until a larger and more succulent kind, discovered on the shores of the Black Sea, was brought to the European West.

Occasionally pomegranates reached the Roman market, and figs, both purple and green, were almost overabundant. The figs, eaten soft and warm and ripe from the tree, were lusciously different from their brown desiccated remnants strung on a cord and hung up to dry for winter consumption.

Dates had all to be imported from Africa, because the date palm will not ripen its fruit in Italy or anywhere else on the northern shore of the Mediterranean, save for a few spots in southeastern Spain.

Whoever was fond of berries could choose from mulberries, blackberries, raspberries, and strawberries; and whoever liked nuts could purchase almonds, hazelnuts, walnuts, chestnuts, or even the subtle pistachio and the giant seeds of the stone pine which the Mediterranean world still loves to nibble.

The market pictured here is being patronized for its vegetables: unbleached celery, cucumbers of many shapes and sizes, gourds, yellow squash, cress, chicory, lettuce, and even endive. There are also green beans of several sorts, a change from the dried beans which, used for soups and porridges, shared with lentils and split peas the prime place on the peasant's winter table.

A rich man could grow his own asparagus in deep-dug, carefully planted beds; but if he wanted artichokes for his guests, the best would have to be sent him from Tunisia or from Spain. Cabbage and kohlrabi and Brussels sprouts were common in Roman markets.

If mushrooms were in season, some belonging to the ordinary genus *Agaricus* would be offered, as well as the *Boletus,* with its spongy mesh in place of gills. Truffles, too, which live underground till the pigs smell them and root them up, were dainties enjoyed in ancient Rome.

The countryman in the foreground, with his bird and rabbit slung from a stick over his shoulder, is bound elsewhere to dispose of his game, for this market has no stalls for sellers of meat.

Above and behind all towers the splendid fortified gate of Diocletian's palace in Dalmatian Spalato (p. 353).

Painting by H. M. Herget

O Happy Husbandmen, Too Happy if They but Realize Their Blessings—for Whom, Far from the Clash of Arms, Earth Most Just Pours Forth from Her Soil an Easy Living"—Virgil, *Georgics*

Tunisian Farm

Besides some sizable cities, among which recolonized Carthage was the leader, Roman Tunisia developed extensive and populous rural settlements, where landed gentry resided in luxurious houses on fertile farms.

Several of the Tunisian villas have been uncovered by the French Service of Antiquities, and the Bardo Museum in Tunis is stocked with their treasures. In surprising contrast, Carthage itself, however carefully its site has been explored, has yielded almost nothing to illustrate its thousand years of African supremacy.

Archeologists uncovered in one especially fine example of a villa a mosaic floor into which a rather incompetent but ambitious local artist had introduced little scenes from the country life of North Africa in his day. With remarkable vividness, but complete incoherence, he depicted a Tunisian cattle stead and its animals, a horse being watered, a farmer plowing with an ox team, a laden donkey being led to market, hunters on horseback with lances, and a man disguised under a goatskin driving quail into a decoy net. These scenes, assembled in proper perspective, afford a realistic picture of suburban life near ancient Carthage.

A dirt country road, dusty in dry weather, abominably muddy in wet, leads past an adobe wall of whitewashed plaster over sun-dried brick, carried on a hidden base of field stone and protected from disintegration by a cover of straw thatching held down by flat rocks. Within the wall stands a combination cattle shed and house, where the slaves in charge of this corner of the estate may eat and sleep.

An olive grove is growing in thin soil close to limestone cliffs across the road, and on a sunnier slope just outside the picture there will be grapevines. Every large estate produced its own oil and wine and at least enough grain to tide the livestock through the winter. On export of oil, wine, and grain the rich province primarily depended.

The owner's villa, the plan of which has been unearthed, was quite different from the little byre behind the thatched wall in the picture. Around a large interior garden court were grouped suites of rooms all laid with exquisite mosaic floors. The composition which adorns the principal room, showing cupids at work in grapevines, has passed into the handbooks as a specimen of Roman mosaic art at its most delicate and charming.

The typical *villa rustica* had ground-floor rooms equipped for pressing the oil from the olives and storing it in vats. There were rooms with wine presses, connected with cellars where the wine could be laid down in jars; cool airy rooms for drying and storing fruit; dry lofts for grain and straw; a threshing floor outside; and stables for the horses and cattle. In remote or unsafe districts there was sometimes a fortified compound, and slaves were kept armed.

With such an establishment under his orders, a landed proprietor could expect to be both busy and prosperous. Nor would he have entertained any qualms for his social position and privileges. The dyed-in-the-wool aristocratic Roman despised trade, business, manufacture, and all arts and crafts, no matter how lucrative or extensive. It was beneath his dignity to be anything except a warrior or a ruler, or a farmer with slaves to do all the work.

Painting by H. M. Herget

"A Cloud of Unusual Size and Shape Had Made Its Appearance . . . Rising from Vesuvius . . . in Form and Likeness Most Resembling a Pine Tree"—Pliny the Younger, *Letters*

Street Scene in Pompeii

POMPEII was not overwhelmed in an instant and buried under lava from Vesuvius, or even so covered with ashes that it was sealed away untouched and unrifled till its rediscovery just 200 years ago.

After the eruption of A. D. 79 had subsided, the townsfolk who had escaped—and these were probably ten times as numerous as those who had tarried too long and perished—returned to the scene.

Ashes and pumice, cinders and tiny stones lay so deep and had been so closely packed by the torrential rains which followed the disaster that only the charred tops of the houses emerged above what seemed to be solid ground.

All attempts to clear the site and rebuild the town were abandoned; but by means of shafts and tunnels through the debris, most of the valuable movable objects were recovered. Even the marble slabs veneering the public buildings were salvaged.

The town which the modern diggers uncovered not only had been collapsed and buried by a volcano, but had been ransacked and picked over by men. Even so, the ground plans of the buildings were clear. Most of the lower walls of the houses were standing erect, and enormous quantities of damaged furnishings and odds and ends had survived.

At first, modern investigators deemed thorough reconstruction of the houses impossible because of the loss of the roofs, upper stories, and ground-floor ceilings; but more practiced excavation revealed in the higher levels of the ashes traces of beams and joists. These discoveries betrayed the original construction. Today detailed archeological information makes reconstruction of the probable appearance of almost every important sector of the town comparatively easy.

Most of the streets ran straight, with the intersections at right angles. A curbing of upended blocks of volcanic stone framed a raised sidewalk, hardly wide enough for pedestrians to pass one another. The street itself was too narrow for more than a single cart at a time, and steppingstones set at crossings necessitated adroit maneuvering of wheels.

Although the paving blocks were of all shapes and sizes, they were expertly matched and fitted without broad crevices. The sidewalks were laid in similar fashion, but a thin coating of hard earth and pounded brick covered the joints.

During heavy rains water rushing from the lower slopes of Mount Vesuvius washed the long avenues clean. Cross streets, on the other hand, often accumulated dirt.

Blank stuccoed walls of private houses flanked the sidewalks, but there were windows and occasional balconies in the upper stories. At intervals along the street, open fronts of shops were built directly into the houses.

Much of the bread to supply the 20,000 inhabitants of Pompeii came from establishments which combined milling and baking. In mortarlike stone grinders, turned sometimes by donkeys or mules, sometimes by slaves, grain was crushed into coarse flour, which was made into flat loaves and baked in closed ovens or open hearths.

For 16 years after the earthquake of A. D. 63, Vesuvius poured out smoke and vapors; yet Pliny reports that many residents of Pompeii, scouting the idea of peril even after ashes began to fall in A. D. 79, stayed in their homes to perish.

Painting by H. M. Herget

"Now Is the Time to Drink and Beat the Ground Freely with Your Foot!"—Horace, *Odes*. "Out-Greek the Greeks, Be Drunk Both Day and Night"—Plautus, *Mostellaria*

In a Pompeian Tavern

Among the most frequent and frequented business establishments opening on the sidewalks of Pompeii were wineshops.

The counters held the wine jars erect in circular holes cut in the counter top, and customers could purchase wine directly at the "bar," even if they hardly lounged and sipped there in modern fashion.

To serve a client, the attendant lifted a jar out of its rack and tilted it over a pouring block. A Pompeian wall painting gives warrant for showing in the illustration a mule team bringing up a wagon loaded with skins full of wine. Doubtless jars of reserve stock were stored in an inner room or cellar.

Wineshops were patronized mainly by the lower classes and by people of doubtful occupation. Drinking and gaming and ready argument only too often led to open brawls. Two rude paintings preserved from Pompeii record such scenes.

In one, two men are seated with some sort of checkerboard balanced on their laps between them. Disagreement has already set in.

"I'm out!" shouts one.

"No," cries the other, "not three! It's a two!"

In the other picture two standing disputants are already pushing each other about and pulling hair, while the tavern keeper tries desperately to expel them from his premises, crying, "Out of doors with your brawling!"

The tavern keepers themselves were not in too good repute. Many must have acted as intermediaries for shady patrons, such as footpads off the highways and robbers from the hills. Pimps and panders, fences and stools, vagabonds and beggars made up a thoroughly dubious company.

Wine of many kinds was to be had at varying prices. The grapes thriving in the volcanic soil of Vesuvius yielded a good but fiery brand. The more northern regions of Campania produced the famous Falernian and the Caecuban which Horace praised as superior to all others.

If there was imported wine to be had here, it probably came by ship from Greece and had sea water or resin in it to preserve it on the journey. Travelers in the interior of Greece today have to acquire a taste for resined wine, often with no greater success than the Roman poet Martial, who thought very little of such *resinata vina*.

In Rome wine was to be had from all over the Empire—"Moselle" from the Rhineland; "sherry" from Spain; good Gallic wines from France, and Chian, Lesbian, and Rhodian from the Greek Aegean isles. There was even a brand from the Nile Delta.

Drinking cups were usually of baked clay, glazed to avoid porosity; whereas the exposed wine jars, like the water jugs, were unglazed, since evaporation kept them cool. When the last customer departed at night, wooden shutters were fitted into the slots on each side of the wide entrance and the light in the hanging lantern was extinguished.

From across the street the private dwelling turns a blank and probably disapproving stare on the wineshop with its noisy crew. Its street door is tightly shut, and all its windows, however small, are fitted with iron gratings as defense against tramps and burglars.

Seaside Villas

"NOTHING in the world can rival the lovely bay of Baiae!" exclaims a rich Roman in one of Horace's *Epistles*.

The visitor to this region today finds only remnants of brick and stucco hidden among the vineyards on the slopes, and breakers roll in on empty beaches above which Greek Cumae stood. Yet somewhere here Cicero had his Cumaean villa, and not far away his rival, Hortensius, fattened the lamprey eels on which he loved to dine.

Lucullus built here on a spectacular headland a country home wherein, a century later, the gloomy and degenerate Emperor Tiberius was to die, and Nero briefly was to live. In a villa near by, Nero had his mother Agrippina murdered.

Roman literature records that the gentry came here to summer villas when the capital city was oppressively hot. But neither historian nor archeologist has ever succeeded in putting together from the few and scattered fragments a visualization of the gaily dissolute life at the baths of Baiae and Bauli.

A series of pictures on the walls of the main room of a finely decorated house unearthed in Pompeii in 1900 seems the most credible source from which to assemble a picture of these long-lost Roman watering places. To be sure, what the Romans actually built and used cannot be determined exactly from the rather fanciful wall paintings, but as an experiment in recalling a civilization which has been virtually destroyed, our illustration merits attention.

Everything about these clustering villas is full of variety, movement, and life, and the effect is heightened by a liberal use of towers and pergolas and terraces and open colonnades. In the background are the hills, and in the foreground is the sea. Rowboats carrying folk on pleasure excursions move along stone quays which are lined with masonry posts spaced close along their edge.

All the bizarre and attractive materials which go to make up Mr. Herget's illustration have been taken out of the flatness of the ancient artist's conventional wall paintings and distributed over a realistic landscape. No details represented are without authority.

The structures depicted are not the splendid country houses of which Cicero and Horace make mention and which Pliny describes in detail. They are not permanent edifices containing many richly furnished rooms and nestling in complicated and ornate gardens full of covered ways and resting places.

Instead, they are inexpensive creations designed for the holiday use of a civilization in which great seaside hotels were completely unknown. They are the seaside cabins and bungalows of antiquity, in their architectural sprightliness much more imaginative and colorful than modern attempts at seashore colonies usually can claim to be.

Across the Gulf of Naples, above the sheer eastern cliffs of the isle of Capri, rose the pretentious palace of Tiberius. Outside of Rome, not far from the waterfalls of Tivoli, the Emperor Hadrian realized the most complex architectural dream this side of Kubla Khan's pleasure-dome in Xanadu. But such colossal enterprises give no proper idea of the simpler frivolities of a Roman seaside resort.

Painting by H. M. Herget

"The Curving Waters of a Tranquil Bay, a Spot of Nature's Bounty, 'Twixt Sea and Hill a Beach That Ends in Cliff"—Statius, *Silvae*

Roman Baths: Tepidarium

No other civilization has ever evolved the conception of a building for public recreation, exercise, and amusement even remotely comparable to the imperial Roman baths.

The Baths of Caracalla in Rome included an area of more than 20 acres, fitted with reading rooms, auditoria, running tracks, covered walks, and planted gardens, surrounding a single unified building which alone covered six acres.

In the central building were halls so vast that thousands could wander through them at one time, rooms with vaulted ceilings 70 feet above the floor, an enclosed swimming pool 200 feet long, and a steam room half as large as the Pantheon. Hundreds of bronze and marble statues, acres of mosaic flooring, and thousands of square yards of costly marble veneering were adornments.

Huge as this recreation center was, it was only one of seven in Rome. Others were the Baths of Diocletian, of Agrippa, of Nero, of Titus, of Trajan, and of Constantine. In every province of the Empire were similar, though somewhat smaller baths—in Germany at Badenweiler and Trier; in England, where the city of Bath still perpetuates them in its name; in Spain, France, Asia Minor, and North Africa.

The Roman bath of the illustration lay under drifting sand in Tripolitania until it was cleared and studied by Italian archeologists.

Framing and setting off the geometric mosaics of the floor, marble steps lead down into a marble-lined pool filled waist-high with lukewarm water from a pipe concealed in a statue base behind a bronze lion's-head spout and connected with the furnace boilers in the basement. An invisible overflow is located in one of the angles of the pool.

The room adjoining on the left is a disrobing room (*apodyterium*) and the niches in the wall are to be used as open lockers by the bathers. The elegantly carved marble basin partly visible at the extreme left foreground is fed with cold water for sponging.

For most of the wall surfaces, veined marble has been sawn into thin veneering slabs, and these have been spread out to take advantage of the pattern which their irregular markings can produce. Unfluted Corinthian columns add coherence to the whole composition and justify a continuous running cornice treatment for the wall top, as a transition to the intricate painted detail on the molded plaster designs which fill every inch of the lunettes and spandrels of the gorgeous ceiling.

Furnaces were concentrated in one part of the basement, and floors and basins situated nearest them had the greatest benefit from the hot air and the heated water (page 336). As the entering bather moved toward the sector underneath which the fires were kept, the temperature of walls and floors, of air and water, gradually increased to a maximum, and then as gradually dropped when he reversed his course. He took a final dip in the swimming pool in the *frigidarium* as precaution against chills when he went outside.

Often in auxiliary rooms, recitations, readings, lectures, and discussions invited attendance, and any citizen who had one cent to pay his admission to the bath could divert himself for an entire afternoon without quitting the premises.

Painting by H. M. Herget

"The Blue Translucent Flood in Its Snow-white Border, Whom Would It Not Tempt to Throw Off His Idle Garment and Plunge In?"—Statius, *Silvae*

Furnaces Beneath the Baths

THE GLORY that was Rome showed at times a battered and tarnished reverse to its medallion.

Upon the ground level of the resplendent baths all was magnificence and ease for unhurried patrons; but in brick and rubble-walled caverns under the mosaic floors public slaves sweated to keep the furnaces alight. They stoked the fires, carried in the fagots, supervised the flow of water, patrolled the intricately twisted passageways, and led a mole's life in stifling, overheated quarters.

Modern Trier on the Moselle River occupies, with its 88,000 inhabitants, only a portion of the ancient city which once stood there and which a late Latin poet called "Rome beyond the Alps," the second city of the Empire. In Trier, which was the favorite residence of the first Christian emperor, Constantine, may be seen the most extensive Roman remains in Europe north of the Alps.

Time-battered remnants of the vast public baths built in Trier in Constantine's reign have supplied extremely detailed information on the underground arrangement and workings of a great Roman thermal establishment. From this source is drawn most of the pictorial detail of Mr. Herget's illustration.

The squat, square shafts of brick and stone in the middle background support a solid concrete slab which serves as the underpinning of a warm pool in a large rectangular room similar to that illustrated in the preceding painting. Since the hot air from the open hearths of the furnaces, sucked through the labyrinth of underground passages, circulates under the floors and through the hollow tile inside the walls, not only the room containing the pool but adjoining apartments are kept warm. It is questionable whether a better way has ever been devised to heat a large building in a reasonably mild climate.

An aqueduct supplied the establishment with a steady flow of cold, clear water, which minor conduits of stuccoed masonry, terra-cotta pipes, and lead tubes and fittings distributed to the elaborate series of pools and basins. Hot water was conveyed through pliable lead pipes directly from the boilers to spigots of bronze in the sweating room and the tepid pool.

Since the soft lead could be easily cut, joined, and melted together, check and control valves were set in the pipes without any attempt to thread the metal. For the same reason there were no T joints or right-angled arms and bends. The pipes could be hung like modern telephone cables on hooks as they were carried under and through the floors and inside the walls.

Boilers of bronze or brass operated on the principle of huge kettles. Under the boilers wood (probably very seldom lignite or soft coal) was burned in open hearths, rather like domestic fireplaces of today. Long brick flues assured a steady draft and carried the soot and smoke well above the building.

Although much of the octopuslike plumbing looks crude to the modern eye, it must be judged by what it accomplished. The colossal scale of some of the thermal establishments proves that the heating system must have been little short of extraordinary. There was never any lack of hot water.

Painting by H. M. Herget

"Where Languid Creeps the Warmth Around the Building and a Thin Steam Spreads Upward from the Furnaces Below"—Statius, *Silvae*

Worship of Isis

FOUR TIMES within 10 years the Roman senate issued decrees forbidding the worship of the Egyptian goddess Isis and commanding her statues to be overthrown and her shrines razed. Apparently the effort was futile, for, half a century later, the Emperor Augustus and, after him, Tiberius issued orders to suppress the cult. It steadily gained adherents, especially among the lower classes.

At last, Caligula gave in to the inevitable. In A. D. 38 he decreed that an Isis temple should be built in the Field of Mars; and later in the century Domitian converted this into one of the most splendid buildings in all Rome. The cult of Isis was there to stay, as long as paganism should last in the world.

Whoever served the Greek Olympian deities or the State divinities of Rome was promised kindly protection during mortal life, but he was given nothing to look forward to after death but wandering bloodless in the cheerless underworld of departed shades. On the other hand, he who faithfully followed Isis was promised immortality and bodily resurrection like that of the Egyptian god Osiris.

Never to die, no longer to be wretched, oppressed, and unhappy! Against a religion that held forth such prospects to its adherents, senate and emperor alike were powerless.

The young woman standing on the topmost step in front of the shrine, with a fringed mantle about her shoulders and the sacred cobra on her forehead, is a priestess dressed as Isis. The bowl in her hands contains water from the sacred river, the Nile, and is so holy that even she may not touch it barehanded.

On either side of her there stands an attendant priestess shaking the sistrum rattle traditional to this service. At the foot of the stairway, the chief priest with the palm fronds of victory salutes the risen sun, while a woman fans the embers of yesterday's fire into fresh flame upon the altar, and a second priest with wands in his hands leads the singing of the morning hymn of adoration. This is the ceremony known as the Awakening of the God.

Isis, in the guise of her holy statue, has been sleeping as one dead all night within her closed sanctuary. Now, at the sound of singing and the tinkle of her sacred rattle, she has awakened and stepped forth, in the person of her priestess, to greet the sun and to witness the return of life to her faithful votaries.

In the fortunately surviving Latin tale *The Golden Ass,* more properly entitled *Metamorphoses,* Apuleius gives a vivid account of Isis worship. He describes a procession at Corinth in honor of the goddess on the annual occasion of the launching of her sacred ship to inaugurate the sailing season.

First came the mummers, then a group of maidens dressed in white and strewing flowers. Bands followed, leading white-clad initiates—men and women, old and young, high and lowly —all shaking sistrum rattles.

Next marched priests with upper bodies bare, heads shorn, and a sacred mark branded on their foreheads, and behind them elders carrying the tokens of the god—a lamp shaped like a golden boat, altars in miniature, etc. The gods themselves, disguised priests representing Anubis by a jackal's mask and leading a cow to signify Isis, brought up the rear where last of all was borne the Mystic Casket, containing what could not be shown.

Painting by H. M. Herget

"In Her Right Hand She Held a Curved Implement of Bronze, Crossed with Little Rods, Which When Shaken Gave Out a Sharp, Shrill Note"—Apuleius, *The Golden Ass*

Rehearsal for the Mysteries

THE CULT of Isis with its promise of immortality and bodily resurrection competed for a long time successfully against the rising faith of Christianity; but the most formidable competition came from Persia through Syria and centered in the mysterious figure of Mithras, the slayer of the bull.

Since this Mithras worship was strictly confined to men, women who sought a more emotional outlet than was offered by the rites of Isis turned to initiation in the secret revels held in honor of a god whom the Greeks called Dionysus, and Greeks and Romans alike recognized as Bacchus.

The effects of alcoholic intoxication are usually ascribed by primitive devotees to some sort of divine possession-taking. To partake of wine was, therefore, to commune directly with godhead and attain a more-than-earthly state.

Wherever the process of extracting and fermenting the juice from the ripe grape was introduced, the worship of a wine god accompanied it. From the interior of the Balkans the rites of this god reached Greece. The Greek emigrants who settled southern Italy brought them to the peninsula. Thence they spread among the Latin and other Italic people.

But in Italy there was already an indigenous worship of a pair of deities, Father Liber with his wife Libera; and, as often with pagan cults, the worship of the Greek Bacchus somehow fused and became identified with that of Liber and Libera.

Of the native pair, Libera was naturally the women's deity, as Liber was the men's; and since Libera seems to have been a protector of motherhood and childbearing, her worship added the notion of feminine fertility to the Bacchic rites which were conducted in her honor.

Such a combination of functions, abetted by nocturnal celebration, could easily give rise to misapprehensions among the noninitiated; and the staid Roman senate seems to have become thoroughly alarmed when it was informed, in 186 B. C., that Bacchanalian rites were being celebrated clandestinely within the city limits. Convinced that such practices were inimical to State religion and morality alike, they issued a national decree—still extant among our Latin inscriptions—on the strength of which they proceeded pitilessly to stamp out the offending cult.

By the time of Julius Caesar the cult had been reintroduced into Rome. A villa on the outskirts of Pompeii has preserved around the walls of a large room a series of paintings devoted to the celebrations in honor of Bacchus and Libera.

In these pictures, some of the characters seem to be contemporary Pompeian women, while others are even more obviously the imaginary creations of mythology. The chief theme appears to be a ceremony of initiation of young matrons, to whom is revealed the mystery of generation and upon whom is imposed a ritual flagellation to ensure fertility (a common superstition).

We have chosen to imagine that the mortal celebrants among the people of these wall paintings have assumed flesh and blood. Within this very room they are rehearsing their roles for the initiation ceremony which they intend to perform in honor of Bacchus and his consort, whom Greek mythology identified as Ariadne, but whom Italic piety had endowed with Libera's powers to induce fertility.

Painting by H. M. Herget

"Known unto All Are the Mysteries, Where, Roused by Music and Wine, the Women Shake Their Hair and Cry Aloud"—Juvenal

Sacrifice of the "Suovetaurilia"

The official State religion of Rome was a totally different matter from the popular mystery creeds. Perhaps it should not be termed a religion at all, but only a ritual, since it was largely impersonal, had no moral dogma, and evoked little emotional response.

It smacked of the practical Roman legal mind, regarding faith as a contractual relationship with deities, wherein man agreed to observe certain ceremonies and make certain offerings in return for divine protection. To avert calamity and ensure prosperity for the community through magical acts calculated to placate the unseen forces around them was the priests' business. If the proper magic was performed, the demons and spirits would be benign.

The calendar listed many such procedures, each set for its correct day or season and each scheduled to be performed in its due place and manner. Naturally some of these appointed days became general holidays, precursors of the numerous saints' days and fixed festivals of southern Europe today.

Among the common animals sacrificed to propitiate the gods, a pig was the least prized, a sheep of more moment, an ox or a bull of prime merit. A white steer was fitter for celestial gods, a black one for the underworld divinities, a red one for the fire god. Male animals were suited for male gods, and female for goddesses.

Once every five years, when the registry office of the two censors had completed its enumeration and property lists of the entire people, a specially elaborate sacrifice of lustration was performed on behalf of the populace. A pig, a sheep, and an ox, representing the three grades of living sacrifice, were solemnly led in procession as in the illustration and slaughtered at the altar.

The beasts must not be tugged or dragged, but must seem to come as if of their own accord. After incense and wine had been consumed on a living fire, the victims were sprinkled with wine and with coarsely ground salted meal and then slain according to a precise ritual. A strange superstition was that the favor of the gods and the fortune of men could be determined from the appearance of the victims' internal organs.

In the illustration the Roman temple on the distant hilltop is in the modified Etruscan tradition. That in the foreground adheres closely to Greek architectural forms, retaining from older usage only the high-platform base with the steps restricted to a single approach from the front.

As in Greek practice, the Roman altar stood out of doors and in line with the central doorway of the shrine which it served. It was sometimes, as in Greece, placed completely free on the paved area in front of the temple; at other times it was built into the stairway so as to be level with the temple floor, the steps descending around or past it.

The columns of the greatest temples rose 50 to 60 feet above their platforms, which in turn were raised considerably above the level of the heads of the human throng. Consequently, the victims and their attendant train might move to the altar where the high priest and his colleagues awaited them and yet be wholly unaware of the height to which the splendid temple towered above them.

Painting by H. M. Herget

"The White Flocks and the Bull, Chief Victim, Have Led Roman Triumphs to the Temples of the Gods"—Virgil, *Georgics*

In a Court of Law

OUR PAINTING shows a provincial governor newly arrived in Africa with the proud title of proconsul hearing a case in the basilica. Built originally as covered halls for public meetings of all sorts, basilicas came more and more to be used as courts of law.

The litigants here are represented by professional advocates, freeborn Roman citizens of rank and eminence. Besides the ordinary civil suits, the governor could adjudge criminal cases and, if he chose, impose the death sentence.

Only full Roman citizens had recourse to any higher authority than the provincial governor. "I appeal to Caesar!" could not be said by the ordinary provincial, until the late Empire abolished such distinctions.

In the early days of Rome's expanding power, when such men as Pompey and Cicero and Julius Caesar were alive, Roman governors undoubtedly plundered the provinces which were entrusted to their rule. When they returned to the capital city on the Tiber after a year or two of depredation under the guise of official administration, bringing with them inordinate wealth in precious metals and jewels, they were often impeached and tried before senatorial committees, but not often convicted and sentenced.

The theory of personal civil rights and universal impartial justice was so deeply rooted in the Roman mind, however, that sooner or later it won out. Little by little it led to the establishment of empire-wide government under codified law and firmly maintained order, with the pursuit of gainful enterprise guaranteed by a stable military and civil administration. Ancient Rome thus created and handed down to modern times its most cherishable contribution to the development of civilization.

Even as the organized tradition of the Roman law survived into medieval Europe, so the type of building in which legal assizes had been held influenced the architectural thought of the Middle Ages. The Christian church could not evolve from the pagan temple; for the temple was not a place of communal assembly but a god's private dwelling, open only to priests and temple servants.

After Christianity had emerged from the secrecy of subterranean chapels or private houses to become the State religion, it had need of buildings which could accommodate great throngs of worshipers.

Precisely such a type of building was the law court, or *basilica*. In its broad hall could gather the congregation; and on its raised dais in the semicircular apse could sit the bishop and his assistant clergy, even as in earlier times the judge and his ushers had taken their places for the pronouncement of earthly law.

In pursuance of this obvious inspiration, basilical churches were erected through the length and breadth of the Empire, with their rows of columns separating nave from aisles, their walls lined with marble veneer, their floors covered with inset patterns of stone. They reproduced all the splendor of Roman imperial architecture, even though not always on the same plane of craftsmanship.

Many of these churches have survived, and it is from them, rather than from the mournful ruins of imperial Rome, that we can gain the best impression of the lost basilicas.

Painting by H. M. Herget

"Wherefore You Ought to Maintain and Preserve That Public Inheritance of the Law, Derived from Your Ancestors, with No Less Care than You Do Your Own Personal Property and Possessions"—Cicero, *Pro Caecina*

Painting by H. M. Herget

"Now the Reader Has Had His Fill, and Even the Scribe Himself Says, 'Enough Now, Enough, Little Book!'"—Martial

The Library in Timgad

THE PUBLIC library with its reading room, where books from the stacks could be consulted, was to be found not only in long cultured Greek cities and in Rome but even in remote towns of North Africa and Gaul. Probably the shelves of a library such as that of Thamugadi (Timgad), in North Africa, held works in Greek as well as in Latin.

There is evidence, too, that the books could be borrowed and taken home. At some of the libraries in Rome borrowing of books is definitely known to have been permitted.

Philanthropists of ancient times sometimes presented libraries to their native towns. At Timgad a large block of marble, probably once set as the lintel above the main doorway, recorded in the elegant letters of the Latin monumental script the name of the donor by whose last will and testament the building was erected.

Written long before Europe knew mechanical printing and modern papermaking, the "books" were not bound volumes, but manuscripts on sheets of a material made by pressing and pounding together crisscross thin slices of the pith of a sedge called papyrus. The remarkable thing about papyrus, whence the word *paper,* was that it could last for 2,000 years in a desert climate.

Actually it was rare for both sides of a papyrus sheet to be used, the blank reverse being left comparatively rough and only the side intended for use being scraped and rubbed to a surface smooth enough to take the ink. The ancient ink, whether made from vegetable matter or the jet-black juices of the cuttlefish, must have been of extraordinary quality, for letters written with it remain legible to this day. Pens were made of reed and were trimmed with a penknife.

To make a "volume," or roll, sheets were glued end to end into a strip many feet long. Obviously there was no limit save that of reasonable bulk to the length that could be put together thus. Livy's *History* filled 142 rolls.

To peruse a book, a reader used both hands, unrolling with the right to expose a convenient portion of a vertical column of text, and rolling up with the left the portion read. When the entire roll had been perused, it would have to be completely rewound in reverse before another reading.

The rolls were thrust into cylindrical cases, "capsules," from which a written label or ticket hung with the title of the volume. The capsules were stored on shelves. Greek and Latin books were stored separately, but otherwise we have little notion of how they were arranged and catalogued.

Memoranda, notes, and letters not intended to be preserved could be written on wax slates with a pointed metal scratcher, or stylus. A pair of such slates, hinged face to face, tied with string, with a lump of wax or clay daubed over the knot and the imprint of a seal ring pressed upon it, would make a letter which could be sent by messenger. The recipient could scrape the wax smooth and reply on the same slate.

Books made of sheets of vellum bound together into tomes were known in antiquity, but did not really become popular enough to challenge the papyrus rolls until the very end of imperial times. Medieval preference was overwhelmingly in favor of such books ("codices") and almost abandoned the use of papyrus until contact with China brought in paper made from mulberry bark and other materials.

Painting by H. M. Herget

"You Would Never Guess It Was Only an Actor Talking, but Think It an Actual Woman—Thais the Courtesan, a Matron, a Dorian Girl"—Juvenal

At the Theater

THE ROMANS reconditioned the Greek theater into an organized structure. Undismayed by the weight of superimposed arcades, they solved the problem of throwing a sloping vault from "pit" to "gallery" to carry the tiers of seats for the auditorium.

Having erected the high, arcaded support underneath the spectators' section, the architects naturally evolved the idea of carrying up the remaining elements of central stage building and wings to an equal height and of tying them all together into a single, homogeneous unit. They thus produced a playhouse, complete although still uncovered except by awnings, whereas the Greeks had been content with an outdoor, hillside gathering place.

The portion of the circle of the dancing floor which projected beyond the mouth of the *cavea,* or tiers of seats, was sliced off, and a deep stage platform of wood was stretched all the way across. The stage was raised some five feet above the orchestra and backed by an elaborately ornate stone, or brick and stucco, façading to mask the actors' building. Over this broad, deep stage was suspended a sloping wooden ceiling to protect it from the weather and to serve as a sounding board for the actors' voices.

Heavy wings flanked the stage and maintained the effect of loftiness. For balance in the general design, a colonnaded, vaulted gallery was often carried above and behind the topmost tier of the auditorium, moving at the same level as the ceiling hung over the stage or the eaves of the heavy, towerlike wings. The painting shows better than words the interesting unified composition which resulted.

Famous Greek plays, both tragic and comic, were presented on the Roman stage in direct translation or modified adaptation for Latin-speaking audiences. In Sicily and southernmost Italy, where Greek continued to be spoken and many of the townsfolk were Greek by descent, the traditions of the Greek stage were faithfully observed.

Farther north, as in Rome itself, native Italic elements were introduced. Thus, until about Cicero's time, no masks were worn by Roman actors; and in the native type of play, such as the mime, ordinary costume was worn in place of the fantastic Athenian "mask and wig" and stilted shoe.

The Roman actor's art is said to have reached its zenith in the first century B. C. during the last years of the Republic. Under the Empire, the popular preference for stage spectacles led to a steadily mounting emphasis on elaborateness, expense, and purely quantitative display. Therefore the drama as a fine art rapidly deteriorated.

Interest in tragedy after the old Greek tradition and in the classic comedy of Plautus and Terence died out almost completely as the Roman adulation of pageants and contests invaded the theater from the circus and the amphitheater. Pantomime akin to modern musical comedy alone managed to preserve sufficient popularity to survive.

The painting shows a revival performance of a classic Latin comedy in a theater in Sicily, active Mount Etna in the distance. The building stands on the site of an older Greek theater, which has been remodeled in the Roman manner. So good were the acoustics that even the spectators in the curving gallery at the top could hear every word.

Painting by H. M. Herget

"If You Are a Spectator Lately Arrived from Afar, Let Not This Naval Warfare Deceive You with Its Fleet and Its Waters Like the Sea; Here Just a While Ago Was Dry Land"—Martial, *De Spectaculis*

Sea Battle in the Arena

THE COLOSSEUM was so called not because of its size but because of a colossal, gilded-bronze, "sun-god" statue of Nero which stood close beside it until long after the fall of Rome. Moved on rollers from Nero's House of Gold when that fantastically sumptuous palace was destroyed, the hundred-foot colossus probably was already in place for the inauguration of the gigantic stone and concrete amphitheater which Vespasian began and his successor Titus saw completed (page 309).

The ceremonies opening the amphitheater in A. D. 80 lasted for a hundred days of festivals, games, and displays to which flocked city dwellers, provincials, and foreigners.

"What race is so barbarous or so remote that a spectator has come not thence to thy city, O Caesar!" exclaimed Martial, the Spaniard with a genius for flattering the right people and lampooning the wrong ones.

"Sygambrians have come with their hair in knots and Ethiopians with different curl," he continued, and declared that some of the crowd hailed also from Bulgaria, Russia, Egypt, and Arabia. His verses on the games filled a large papyrus roll.

Since the huge structure stood on low ground previously covered by a pleasure pond in Nero's gardens, its central area could be flooded easily and converted into a miniature sea for sham naval battles. These spectacles, in which heads were broken, blood flowed freely, and sailors were drowned in the churning water, offered novel interludes among the gladiatorial combats, the displays of bloodthirstiness in the slaughter of thousands of wild beasts, and the pageants and processions which were the entertainment offered when the arena was left as dry ground.

The next emperor, Domitian, repeated the feat, but because of difficulties of installation presented the naval spectacles on artificial lakes dug especially for the purpose.

Julius Caesar seems to have been the first to devise and carry out such a project. During the games with which he celebrated his triumphs two years before he was assassinated, fleets of two-, three-, and four-banked vessels, manned by a couple of thousand rowers and bearing a thousand armed marines on their decks, fought and destroyed each other in the sight of the Roman holiday crowd.

The last such spectacle recorded was presented at the celebration of the thousandth year of Rome's existence, A. D. 248. It was staged in the flooded Colosseum arena.

Some fifty thousand onlookers could find sitting room in this greatest of ancient theaters. Since they surrounded the exhibition and looked down on it from all directions and angles, no coherent entertainment could be presented.

Particularly popular were dangerous struggles against wild beasts and dueling matches between trained fighters, one in full armor and the other equipped with only a casting net and a three-pronged fishing spear. Death instead of mere defeat was the usual outcome for the loser.

Mortal combats between different kinds of wild animals were loudly acclaimed. Among the human contestants more and more fanciful weapons and equipment were devised. Bassus perhaps outdid all rivals by strolling around the arena defending himself with a golden chamber pot.

Painting by H. M. Herget

"Could You Come Here and See the Vegetables That I Raise with My Own Hands, You Would No More Talk to Me of Empire"—Diocletian

Diocletian's Palace at Spalato

By the time of Septimius Severus, early in the third century of our era, the entire Palatine was covered with a maze of buildings for the Emperor's public and private use.

But at length there ruled an emperor who, after tasting its splendors, decided not to live on the Palatine or even in Rome.

Below the gray limestone mountains of his native Dalmatian coastland, Diocletian tried to forget the cares and fatigue of having been the ruler of the world for 20 years. A soldier of extremely humble origin, he was close to his fortieth birthday when his soldiers proclaimed him emperor and elevated him into the supreme power over the body of the commander of the Praetorian Guard he had killed with his own hands. That was in A. D. 284.

Soon Diocletian had reorganized the entire system of government for the vast Roman Empire by dividing it into four regions and putting each under its own ruler, installed in a separate capital city. The Emperor himself still kept the ultimate authority, which he strengthened, outwardly at least, by introducing the ceremonials of the Orient and enthroning himself like a god aloof from the eyes of the people.

Not since the mad Caligula had a Roman emperor insisted so strongly on his own divinity while still alive. This policy in Diocletian, however, was calculated, not dementia praecox. The senate met only to ratify his orders, and all semblance of democracy vanished from the State.

Fortunately, Diocletian was an able administrator with an extreme sense of responsibility. On the basis of his lifelong military experience he expanded the armed forces and reorganized the system of legionary occupation of the provinces. He changed the monetary basis for the coinage, suppressed trusts and monopolistic unions, contested graft and corruption, and in A. D. 301 fought a threat of inflation by proclaiming an elaborate schedule of ceiling prices on food and daily essentials as well as on wages.

Worn out with unremitting effort, he voluntarily retired before his sixtieth birthday to a quiet life in his native Dalmatian land, still possessed of sufficient wealth and authority to dwell in kingly fashion in a huge fortified palace which his Syrian architect built for him at the edge of the Adriatic. There he lived perhaps for eight, perhaps for eleven years, and there he died and was buried in the crypt of a temple within his palace.

His great scheme for combating inflation with ceiling prices had already collapsed, having proved a failure because, economists say, it cut too crudely across the workings of the normal forces of supply and demand. His wonderful palace on the Adriatic still stands.

Its plan, like that of a fortified Roman military encampment, was roughly a seven-acre square subdivided into four smaller squares by a pair of principal avenues running from the mid points of the four sides and intersecting at the exact center of the area. Of the four gates, named in Oriental manner after the four elements—gold, silver, copper, and iron—the modern visitor to Yugoslavia's Split may still see the remains of three and may enter the oldest part of town through the best preserved, the Golden Gate (page 325). The temple tomb of Diocletian is the cathedral church of Split.

Painting by H. M. Herget

"Funerals of Age and Youth Are Crowded Together; No One Escapes Relentless Proserpina"—Horace, *Odes*. "Death Should Even Be Looked Forward To if It Takes the Spirit Some Whither Where It Will Be Eternal"—Cicero, *De Senectute*

Dusk on the Street of Tombs

No heavy wagons or laden carts were allowed during daylight on the crowded, narrow streets of Rome. But after sundown the highways which led to the city gates from the surrounding country began to echo with the hoofs of mules and horses and the rumble of wheels as produce was brought in to feed the million inhabitants.

The living were fed with provisions brought in at night past the houses of the dead, which stretched on either side of the paved roads for many miles into the Campagna. The old Appian Way today still leads between the ruins and overgrown traces of almost innumerable ancient grave monuments.

Most ancient towns thus buried their dead at their gates, without setting aside hallowed ground comparable to our churchyard cemeteries, but merely invading the open fields to left and right of the roads. The natural desire to keep kinsmen and families together and to bar intruders led to the erection of walled enclosures.

Often, burial societies were organized with like intent, ensuring an undisturbed resting place to all subscribing members. Where cremation was in favor, a wall niche in an underground chamber would suffice for each; where entombment was demanded and the beneficiaries were numerous, their needs, expanding with time, ultimately produced the miles of subterranean passages and rooms called catacombs.

Above ground, whether for sarcophagus or urn, engraved tablets and carved markers would preserve the identity of the family or clan or corporation, or on occasion the individual deceased. The arts of architecture, sculpture, and painting were all employed to make important plots more memorable to mourning relative or casual passer-by.

A miniature colonnaded mausoleum might alternate with a tall shaft carrying a marble vase, to be followed by some elaborate storied structure, according to the ambitions of the family head and the competence of his architect. Even where the detail was coarse and the execution poor, the cumulative effect of such a succession of monuments could not fail to be impressive, especially when the slender, almost black spires of the cypresses and the greener, spreading umbrellas of the pines added their somber note of movement or repose.

At El Djem in Tunisia still stand the arcades of the fifth largest amphitheater ever built by the Romans. It once accommodated 30,000 spectators. Today the once-irrigated and highly productive countryside about its site is all but empty arid waste. The ruins, like the tombs along the Appian Way and the Latin Way on the approaches to Rome, bear witness to departed glory.

The Roman world of antiquity has passed away. But though outwardly it has disappeared or lies in ruins, many of its intangible glories survive. Its striving for a reasonable life ruled by law and order, its organized grouping of towns and cities into self-administered states, its basic belief in individual human dignity and in equality under secure government—all these have come down as a precious legacy to modern times.

Our letters are Roman; our speech is nearly a third Latin; the very fundamentals of our science and learning are those which Greece began and Rome preserved and transmitted.

NATIONAL GEOGRAPHIC Society

16th & M Streets N.W. *Washington 6, D. C.*

National Geographic Magazine

ORGANIZED IN 1888 "FOR THE INCREASE AND DIFFUSION OF GEOGRAPHIC KNOWLEDGE"

The National Geographic Society is chartered in Washington, D. C., in accordance with the laws of the United States, as a nonprofit scientific and educational organization for increasing and diffusing geographic knowledge and promoting research and exploration.

The Society has conducted more than 160 major expeditions and scientific projects. It disseminates knowledge to millions through its world-famous National Geographic Magazine, its 19 million color maps a year, its books, monographs, bulletins for schools, its information service for press, radio, and television.

INDEX

B

C